How To Build a Fortune

Investing In Your Spare Time

Stephen Littauer

Dearborn
Financial Publishing, Inc.

While a great deal of care has been taken to provide accurate and current information, the ideas, suggestions, general principles and conclusions presented in this text are subject to local, state and federal laws and regulations, court cases and any revisions of same. The reader is thus urged to consult legal counsel regarding any points of law—this publications should not be used as a substitute for competent legal advice.

Senior Associate Editor: Karen A. Christensen
Managing Editor: Jack Kiburz
Editorial Assistant: Stephanie C. Schmidt
Cover Design: S. Laird Jenkins Corporation
Interior Design: Lucy Jenkins

Printed in the United States of America

95 96 97 10 9 8 7 6 5 4 3 2 1

Library of Congress Cataloging-in-Publication Data

Littauer, Stephen L.
    How to build a fortune—investing in your spare time / Stephen
Littauer.
        p.   cm.
    Includes index.
    ISBN 0-7931-1343-1 (paper)
    1. Investments. 2. Finance, Personal. 3. Stocks. 4. Mutual
funds. I. Title.
HG4521.L735 1995   95-113
332.6—dc20   CIP

Contents

$ $

Preface

$ $

You probably don't invest full time. Most likely you're busy making a living and have little time to spend studying the financial markets and selecting the best investments. So how can you fit investing into your life and still build a fortune?

This book reveals an amazingly simple strategy you can use to build a fortune *in your spare time*. Not only does this approach take a minimal amount of time to execute, but it also makes the ups and down of the market work to your advantage. Instead of trying to time the market, buying at the lows and selling at the highs, this technique shows you how to ride out the ups and downs, while amassing impressive returns on your investments.

Divided into three parts, *How To Build a Fortune—Investing in Your Spare Time* will give you a lifetime investment strategy that requires only a few hours each month to execute. Part I, *Achieving Financial Independence*, shows you how to identify your personal financial objective and what steps you can take to realize it. You will become aware of the risk associated with different types of investments, and we'll give you simple techniques to blunt the tax blow by reducing your taxable capital gains and income distributions.

Part II, *Building Your Fortune in Common Stocks*, guides you in your quest to realize returns on your invested capital by developing a portfolio of individual stocks that performs above the market averages. As a prudent investor, you will learn to think of stocks as components of a portfolio, rather than as single entities. A diversified group of holdings reduces the overall risk of stocks. Long recognized by sophisticated investors as an important advantage, diversification is often ignored by many who think in terms of single stocks rather than a portfolio as a whole.

A growth approach to investing can help you find stocks with the potential of significant price appreciation. Chapters on investing in growth stocks, investing for growth and income, and investing in the worldwide arena, highlight specific securities that you can easily include in a diversified stock portfolio.

Because the cost of buying and selling securities can have an important impact on your long-term investment returns, you want to keep such costs as low as possible. You will learn how to minimize brokerage costs as well as what you can expect to get for your money.

You will also discover the opportunities and time-saving advantages of DRIPs (dividend reinvestment plans). Many companies now offer the means for you to automatically reinvest your dividends. This low-cost service is explained in detail, and a special appendix lists most of the companies that offer DRIPs.

Part III, *Building Your Fortune in Mutual Funds*, explains how mutual funds work, the importance of the funds' investment objectives and policies, how the funds get paid, how you can buy funds directly and avoid sales charges, the impact of expenses in determining a fund's performance and much more.

Fund shopping networks are among the newest services available to mutual fund investors. Through these "one-stop" sources, set up by discount brokers, you will be able to buy and sell a wide range of mutual funds, both no-load and load. The number of such sources is growing, and the practice seems destined to become a dominant way for mutual funds to be distributed.

The goal of this book is to help you build your fortune, so you will also find guides to investing in growth funds, small company funds, growth and income funds, international funds, income funds and a way to invest in the whole market at once—through *index funds*. Each general class of mutual funds gives you one recommended fund that is representative of those that are well managed and have a history of healthy investment returns.

Finally, to build your fortune, start *now*. The most important single factor in successful investing is *time*. The sooner you get started, the more time your assets will have to accumulate and the greater will be the likelihood of your building a substantial amount of wealth—all in your spare time!

1

$ $

How *You* Can
Build a Fortune

$ $

Why invest? According to the American Association of Individual Investors (AAII), if you had invested $1,000 in the Standard & Poor's 500 Composite Stock Price Index at the end of 1940, you would now have more than $400,000 (reinvesting dividends and excluding taxes). Interesting, but what does that have to do with you? Is it really possible for you to build a fortune?

You bet, and that's what this book is all about. My purpose is to give you the tools you need and show you how *you* can build a fortune and achieve financial independence. And surprisingly, success does not depend on having a lot of time, luck or financial skills. You need determination, persistence and patience.

Constant Dollar Investing

Few investment techniques have so well stood the test of time that one can confidently say "This works." But such a method exists. It is easy, it works and you can do it. Called *constant dollar investing* (also known as *dollar cost averaging*), this plan is simply the practice of buying securities at regular intervals in fixed dollar amounts, regardless of price levels.

Small investors have amassed fortunes by making systematic purchases of shares over long periods of time. By putting aside as little as

$50 each month, you can take advantage of constant dollar investing, one of the simplest and most effective ways of building an investment portfolio.

When you follow this procedure, you purchase more shares at relatively low prices than at high prices. As a result, the average *cost* of all shares bought turns out to be lower than the average of all the *prices* at which purchases were made. The combination of buying shares at a variety of price levels and acquiring more shares at low rather than high prices has proven to be an efficient and cost-effective method of accumulating securities.

Average Cost versus Average Price

The arithmetic that illustrates how constant dollar investing works is simple. You need remember only that by periodically purchasing shares with identical amounts of money, as long as share prices change at all during the investment period, the average cost of shares purchased will be less than the average of the prices paid. For example, say that you decide to invest $280 regularly. You make five purchases totaling $1,400 at prices between $10 and $5 a share. The number of shares bought for each $280 purchase in this example would be as follows (sales charges are not considered):

Price	Shares Purchased
$10	28
8	35
7	40
5	56
8	35

Total shares acquired for $1,400 investment: 194
Average cost of each share ($1,400 divided by 194): $7.22
Average price of shares purchased: $7.60

Why this program works: *Equal numbers of dollars buy more shares at low prices than at high prices*. It is essential that you make purchases at low prices when they are available. If you consider constant dollar investing, you must take into account your emotional and financial ability to continue making new investments through periods of low price levels.

Constant dollar investing does not guarantee that you will always have profits in your portfolio, or that you will never incur losses. Use an investment program like this only for long-term purposes. You should be pretty sure that you will not need these invested funds for several years.

Constant dollar investing can substantially reduce the risks inherent in securities investing. Shares are bound to be purchased over the years at a variety of price levels—high, low and in-between. That fact alone should provide a better income and capital gains than haphazard investing or buying only when the outlook appears bright.

Growth Is Not Essential

Fluctuating security prices are more important to successful constant dollar investing than long-term growth alone. This surprising fact arises because you get your best opportunity to acquire a large number of shares during periods of declining prices.

Continuing the previous example, assume that after you make the five purchases, the share price returns to $10, the level of the first purchase. The 194 shares you already own have a value of $1,940. Your profit is $560. Note: During the purchase period, we assume that the price has declined 50 percent.

Now, instead of a drop in price, let's see what happens if the share price had steadily advanced to an increase of 50 percent and the five equal purchases of $280 were made, again until the full $1,400 was invested. For this example, let's assume that you purchase fractional shares, as is the case with mutual funds.

Price	Shares Purchased
$10	28.00
11	25.45
12	23.33
14	20.00
15	18.67

Total shares acquired for $1,400 investment: 115.45
Average cost of each share ($1,400 divided by 115.45): $12.13
Average price of shares purchased: $12.40

In this example, the process of constant dollar investing also results in an average cost that is less than the average price. But notice that after a 50 percent increase from the initial price of $10 per share, the total value of the 115.45 shares at $15 is $1,731.75. Although still a profit, the result is about 10.7 percent less than the $1,940 that the 194 shares in the previous example were worth at $10.

Of course, investors have no control over the direction security prices will take once they start a constant dollar investing program. The plan's main advantage is that in the long run it will work to your benefit almost regardless of what the market does. This is particularly important if you are among those investors who fear starting an investment plan because you believe stock prices are too high. If you are correct and the market does decline, the timing may be just right to begin constant dollar investing.

Reinvesting Dividends

Many investors who invest in securities on a periodic basis can and do reinvest any dividends they receive. The effect in the beginning is minor, but as the program continues, the impact of compounding shares becomes more and more significant. The relative importance will vary, of course, depending on the emphasis that a particular company or fund places on paying income distributions on its shares.

To build a fortune by investing in securities is less a matter of investment skill or luck than of persistence and patience. The first decision to make is whether you truly are willing to forgo immediate gratification to achieve a long-term investment goal. Because the goal is to invest a fixed amount of money on a regular basis for many years, ask yourself the question: "Do I want a fine car today or a fortune tomorrow?"

Example of Constant Dollar Investing in a Mutual Fund

Many well-managed mutual funds are available. This book highlights some of the best, which you can buy directly (in most cases without sales charges). One such fund is *Mutual Shares Fund*, a portfolio of Mutual Series Fund, Inc. Begun in 1949, Mutual Shares Fund has produced substantial returns for its shareholders. The fund's shares declined in value during several years, but patient investors have enjoyed long-term growth in their capital.

If you had invested $5,000 in Mutual Shares Fund at the end of 1949 and then regularly added $3,000 each year for a total of $143,000, you would have amassed more than $10 million by the end of 1994! (See

Figure 1.1.) Assume that income and capital gains distributions were automatically reinvested. No provision has been made for income taxes.

FIGURE 1.1   Results of $5,000 Invested in Mutual Shares Fund on December 31, 1949, plus $3,000 Each Year to December 31, 1994

End Of Year	Total Return %	Amount Invested	Value of Shares	Accumulated Amount Invested
1949	-	$5,000	$5,000	$5,000
1950	28.25	3,000	9,413	8,000
1951	27.91	3,000	15,040	11,000
1952	16.45	3,000	20,514	14,000
1953	−3.89	3,000	22,715	17,000
1954	28.10	3,000	32,099	20,000
1955	11.49	3,000	38,787	23,000
1956	11.23	3,000	43,143	26,000
1957	−15.46	3,000	36,473	29,000
1958	34.50	3,000	52,056	32,000
1959	6.60	3,000	58,491	35,000
1960	6.22	3,000	65,130	38,000
1961	22.56	3,000	82,823	41,000
1962	−1.42	3,000	84,647	44,000
1963	20.61	3,000	102,092	47,000
1964	10.45	3,000	112,761	50,000
1965	20.93	3,000	139,362	53,000
1966	2.03	3,000	145,191	56,000
1967	32.22	3,000	194,971	59,000
1968	39.97	3,000	275,901	62,000
1969	−19.21	3,000	225,901	65,000
1970	−8.98	3,000	210,615	68,000
1971	22.28	3,000	258,094	71,000
1972	.53	3,000	262,462	74,000
1973	−8.11	3,000	244,177	77,000
1974	8.16	3,000	264,101	80,000
1975	34.12	3,000	357,213	83,000
1976	55.21	3,000	557,430	86,000
1977	15.61	3,000	644,445	89,000
1978	18.11	3,000	764,153	92,000
1979	42.69	3,000	1,090,371	95,000
1980	19.38	3,000	1,304,684	98,000
1981	8.93	3,000	1,424,193	101,000
1982	12.87	3,000	1,610,486	104,000
1983	36.64	3,000	2,203,568	107,000
1984	14.47	3,000	2,525,425	110,000
1985	26.73	3,000	3,205,470	113,000

FIGURE 1.1   Results of $5,000 Invested in Mutual Shares Fund on
December 31, 1949, plus $3,000 Each Year to December 31,
1994 *(continued)*

1986	16.99	3,000	3,750,740	117,000
1987	6.34	3,000	3,991,537	120,000
1988	30.69	3,000	5,219,540	123,000
1989	14.93	3,000	6,004,817	127,000
1990	−9.82	3,000	5,418,144	130,000
1991	20.99	3,000	6,558,412	133,000
1992	21.33	3,000	7,960,322	137,000
1993	20.99	3,000	9,634,193	140,000
1994	4.50	3,000	10,070,866	143,000

Beginning a Constant Dollar Investing Plan before a Downturn

If, however, you had started the plan in Figure 1.1 with a $5,000
investment on December 31, 1968 (after the fund had enjoyed two
very good years), the account would have shown a substantial loss at
the end of both 1969 and 1970. In 1969, the fund showed a net loss
per share of 19.21 percent and a net loss of 8.98 percent in 1970. At
the end of 1969, with $8,000 invested ($5,000 plus $3,000 at the end
of 1969), the account value would have been $7,040, and at the end of
1970, with $11,000 invested, the value would have been $9,407.

An investor who persevered, however, would have benefited by
buying more shares at the lower prices. In 1971, the fund rebounded
with a gain of 22.28 percent, then had mixed results for the next three
years. But in 1975, the fund gained 34.12 percent and then 55.21 percent in 1976. By the end of 1976, with $29,000 invested, the investor
would have had a value of $57,028.

During this erratic eight-year span, with substantial losses in three
years and one flat year, a persevering investor would have ended up
with a very nice profit. More important, by not losing heart during the
down years, the portfolio was set to take advantage of the next 17
years, during which only 1990 had a negative return. By the end of
December 1994, with $83,000 invested, the account would have had
a total value of $1,267,268.

Here is some brief data about Mutual Shares Fund. You can call for
a prospectus and complete information. Remember, however, that past
performance of any mutual fund does not necessarily indicate future
results.

Mutual Shares Fund
51 John F. Kennedy Parkway
Short Hills, NJ 07078
800-553-3014

Minimum initial investment: $5,000
Minimum subsequent investment: $100
Date of inception: July 1, 1949
Portfolio manager: Michael F. Price

Mutual Shares Fund's principal investment objective is capital appreciation; a secondary objective is income. The fund pursues these objectives primarily through investments in common stock and preferred stock as well as debt securities and securities convertible into common stock, which are judged to be available at prices less than their intrinsic value.

To start a mutual fund investment program, you must buy shares in the fund of your choice in an amount equal to at least the fund's minimum requirement. The minimum for Mutual Shares Fund is $5,000. The initial investment requirements for other funds can be more or less. Some mutual funds require as little as $100 to get started.

In Your Spare Time ...

Invest a fixed number of dollars each month, regardless of price levels. Many investors have built their fortunes by buying shares systematically over long periods and refusing to let temporary reversals shake them out.

2

$ $

Creating Your Own
Financial Plan

$ $

Achieving financial independence requires a disciplined, systematic approach to investing. You need to know whether you have the right mix of investments for your personal situation. Today investors can choose from more than 5,000 stocks and 4,500 mutual funds. This chapter will help you know how to form your own investment objectives, sort through the huge number of offerings and develop a well-designed plan for investing.

Long-Term Planning

The long-term focus of your financial plan considers commitments made for five years or more. For example, many investors set retirement and college funding as their high-priority objectives.

"Saving," where safety and conservatism are important, differs from "investing," which involves taking a certain degree of risk with your money in the pursuit of higher returns. Investment programs involving stocks, bonds, and mutual funds have delivered higher returns over time than FDIC-insured savings accounts and U.S. Treasury bills (T-bills), but they also decline in value from time to time, and are not FDIC-insured.

If you cannot tolerate fluctuating values in your assets, you probably should avoid the securities markets. This book is designed for investors who can patiently wait out short-term declines in the stock and bond markets as they pursue potentially higher long-term returns.

Short-Term Needs

Construct your long-term investment program on a savings foundation that holds sufficient funds for short-term needs. Short-term monies are those that you may need within five years. Goals may include a "rainy day" fund for emergencies or savings for a car, vacation, home or other purpose. Financial planners typically recommend an emergency fund of about six months' worth of living expenses. As much as a year's worth might be appropriate for someone who is self-employed or retired. You can add to that the total of other short-term goals you may have.

Your short-term savings should be accessible and safe. Popular choices for many investors include money-market funds, bank certificates of deposit, U.S. T-bills and short-term bond funds. Bank CDs (certificates of deposit) pay a fixed rate of interest and the principal is guaranteed by an agency of the U.S. government, but you may be subject to a penalty for early withdrawal. Money-market fund yields fluctuate and lack a government guarantee, but are quickly available and offer competitive market returns. Treasury bills pay a fixed rate of interest and are guaranteed by the U.S. government. Short-term bond funds may pay a little higher return and are an option for investors willing to take a small amount of risk.

Classes of Assets

To create a successful long-term investment plan, figure out how you want to allocate your assets. Strike a balance among the three common classes of investments.

1. **Cash reserve securities** provide stable investment value and current investment income. This group includes money market funds, T-bills, and bank CDs.
2. **Bonds** are interest-bearing obligations issued by corporations, the federal government and its agencies, and state and local

governments. The yields offered by these securities are generally higher than those of cash reserves, but their value fluctuates with bond market conditions.

3. **Common stocks** represent ownership rights in a corporation. They usually pay dividends and offer potential for capital growth. Stock market risk can be substantial, however.

Your future investment returns depend to a great extent on how you allocate your money among these three classes.

Risk and Return: Discovering the Tradeoff

Common stocks have historically delivered the highest average annual returns of the three investment classes. According to Ibbotson Associates, between 1926 and 1993, the average annual return on stocks was 10.3 percent. Bonds had an average return of 5.0 percent, and the average return on cash reserves was 3.7 percent. These percentages represent total return: income or yield plus any capital gain or loss.

Since 1963, the advantage of investing in stocks is even more dramatic. The following table illustrates the growth of $10,000 invested in each of the three classes of assets during the 30-year period ending in 1993.

Growth of $10,000 from 1963 to 1993

Cash Reserves	Bonds	Stocks
$69,000	$84,390	$197,700

SOURCE: *Stocks, Bonds, Bills, and Inflation 1994 Yearbook*™, ©Ibbotson Associates, Chicago (annually updates work by Roger G. Ibbotson and Rex A. Sinquefield). Used with permission. All rights reserved.

As these numbers show, during the last 30 years an investment in stocks would have grown to more than twice the value of the same money invested in cash reserves or bonds (not including income taxes and brokerage commissions).

Although stocks and bonds offer the potential for higher returns than cash reserves, they also expose you to more risk. This is a tradeoff: To pursue higher investment returns, you must be willing to assume higher risk.

Specific risk. Investors who own individual stocks are exposed to *specific* risk, the risk that problems with an individual company or bond issuer will reduce the value of your investment significantly. About 70 percent of the risk an investor faces is specific, or company, risk. You can reduce this risk substantially by investing in mutual funds, which spread investors' money among many stocks and bonds.

Market risk. Two other important risks remain, even if specific risk is eliminated. *Market* risk is the risk that the stock or bond markets will fall in value. The stock market is affected by Wall Street's changing expectations for individual companies and the economy. The bond market is influenced by expectations relating to interest rates and inflation. Emotional factors such as hope and fear play an important part in the direction the market takes.

Inflation risk. The third important risk is *inflation risk,* the risk that the general increase in the cost of living (inflation) will reduce the real value of your investment. If the total return on your investment is 10 percent, but inflation is 4 percent, your actual or "real" return is only 6 percent.

Allocating Your Assets—Striking the Right Balance for You

How you divide your savings among cash reserves, bonds and stocks depends on four factors: your financial situation, objectives, time horizon and ability to tolerate risk. Of these, perhaps the most important factor is time. The longer you have to invest, the greater the risk you can assume.

Investing for Retirement

For example, if you are investing for retirement, your objective during your working years is to accumulate assets. Your investment plan should emphasize growth. Retirement investing gives you the time to take measured risks. While you are in your 20s, 30s and even 40s, you have a time horizon extending for decades.

After you retire, your objectives include preserving the money that has built up and spending it to support your lifestyle. At that time your investments should emphasize income, with some growth of capital to offset inflation. With today's longer life expectancies, you could still be investing for 20 or 30 years. These long spans provide the time to ride out short-term market fluctuations.

With these objectives in mind, your asset allocation for retirement should emphasize stocks when you are young and bonds and cash reserves as you grow older. Of course, always keep separate savings reserved for emergencies and short-term objectives.

Investing for Your Children's Education

In some ways, investing for college education is similar to investing for retirement. When your child is young, your objective is to achieve maximum growth of your capital. Then when your child enters college, you need ready access to your money as various bills come due. At the same time, your education fund should continue earning a reasonable return.

Of course, an education plan has a different, shorter time frame than a retirement plan does. If your child begins college at age 18 for an undergraduate degree, the time is about 22 years. Once your child enters the teenage years, little time is left to recoup possible investment losses that may occur. The shorter the time left until college entry, the less risk you should take with your investments.

As in retirement planning, your asset allocation for college investments should emphasize stocks during the early years, when your child is young, then turn more conservative when your child enters the teen years. In the final span, your college investments should consist mainly of money market instruments and short-term bonds.

By diversifying your portfolio of securities, you can pretty easily strike a good investment balance to fulfill your objectives. Figure 2.1 suggests an asset allocation program to meet the needs of investors at different age levels.

If you are 20–50 years old, having a growth objective to build your retirement fortune is appropriate. When you near retirement, from age 51 to age 60, move to a balanced growth approach to reduce the risk of large losses. Then in early retirement, spread some assets into cash reserves to protect capital even more while maintaining conservative growth. During your later years, you will have more concern for current income than growth, so you can transfer more funds from stocks to bonds.

FIGURE 2.1   Allocating Assets at Different Age Levels

Objective	Your Age	Allocation	Historic Returns*
Growth	20–50	80% Stocks 20% Bonds	+9.6%
Balanced Growth	51–60	60% Stocks 40% Bonds	+8.6%
Conservative Growth	61–75	40% Stocks 40% Bonds 20% Cash Reserves	+7.4%
Income	76+	20% Stocks 60% Bonds 20% Cash Reserves	+6.2%

SOURCE: *Stocks, Bonds, Bills, and Inflation 1994 Yearbook*™, ©Ibbotson Associates, Chicago (annually updates work by Roger G. Ibbotson and Rex A. Sinquefield). Used with permission. All rights reserved.

Which Types of Investments Should You Choose?

Once you have decided how to allocate your assets to meet your long-term objectives, the next step is to select specific investments. Consider a number of important issues in planning your investment portfolio. Other chapters of this book cover each issue in some detail. Following are the main aspects you should consider.

Stocks

Stocks are generally divided into *growth stocks* and *value stocks*. You can purchase growth stocks when your objective is capital gains; buy value stocks generally when you want dividend income. Growth stocks are recommended for growth and balanced-growth style portfolios. Value stocks appeal more to older or more conservative investors whose portfolios are geared to conservative growth and income. Many stocks are further subdivided into such groups as aggressive growth, growth and income, income, and small company.

Bonds

Bonds vary according to risk and duration. In choosing a bond, consider several questions. How much risk are you willing to assume? In general, the higher the income yield a bond pays, the greater the risk. Should you investigate the benefits of tax-exempt versus taxable bonds? Top tax bracket investors can receive income that is exempt from both federal and state taxes.

Other Stocks and Bonds

* *International stocks and bonds* can provide additional diversification, but are subject to currency and other risks.
* *Small company stocks* have the potential for higher returns, but entail greater risk from stock market volatility.
* *Specific industry stocks* can offer possibly higher returns from high-growth areas such as health-care, energy or computers.
* *Junk bonds* produce higher yields, but at significantly greater risk because of the lower credit quality of their holdings.

Designing Your Investment Strategy

Timing Your Investments

Some investors pursue a strategy of attempting to "time" the market. This involves moving in and out of stocks and bonds, hoping to buy when prices are low and sell when prices are high, with a goal of avoiding market declines. Unfortunately, few investors (if any) can accurately foresee the direction of the stock or bond markets.

Constant Dollar Investing

Also known as "dollar cost averaging," this strategy avoids the pitfalls of market timing. Under a constant dollar investment plan, you invest a certain dollar amount on a regular schedule, regardless of market conditions. If you are investing in mutual funds, the plan can be implemented by using electronic transfers from your checking account to your fund, by automatic transfer from a money market fund, through payroll deduction in an employer-sponsored retirement plan, or by simply mailing a check each month to your fund.

As the previous chapter showed, constant dollar investing can be critical to your achieving long-term success in creating a fortune through investments.

Common Mistakes To Avoid

Try to avoid these common mistakes whether you are investing in mutual funds or individual securities.

1. *Buying the most recent best performer.* In any market environment some stocks and funds have produced phenomenal returns. Unfortunately, too often last year's best performers become this year's laggards. Special market conditions can make particular stocks act like shooting stars—but they can fade as suddenly as they appear. In the same way, aggressive or specialty techniques can rocket a fund to the top one year, then lead it to a dizzying decline the next. Stocks and mutual funds that consistently perform well, year in and year out, tend to end up in the top 10 percent over a decade or longer.

2. *Acting on intuition and hunches.* Few people are able to accurately forecast market trends. You will be better off developing a consistent, disciplined approach to investing and stick to it. Successful investors who endure practice discipline and consistency.

3. *Overdiversifying.* Diversification is a primary attribute of successful investing. But purchase and sale commissions make it costly for an investor of limited means to buy only a few shares of dozens of stocks. Often it makes more sense to buy a mutual fund and obtain instant cost-effective diversification. In the same way, investors who own dozens of mutual funds (which as a whole behave like the market) can save themselves a lot of trouble by buying a low-cost index fund.

4. *Selling too soon.* Investment styles tend to go in and out of favor. During some years the market will favor growth stocks, or small-cap stocks, or under-valued stocks. When a style goes out of favor for several years, stock performance in that group will suffer, but those stocks will also rebound when the style returns to favor. The danger you face as an investor is selling a stock or fund right before its performance improves in favor of a security whose performance is about to weaken.

Other Considerations

Always know the costs of investing in a potential security or mutual fund. Because costs necessarily reduce investment returns, lower costs inevitably mean higher returns.

Consider *taxes* in your investment planning. Investing in a tax-deferred individual retirement account (IRA) or company-sponsored retirement plan can have an important long-term effect on your investment return. Also consider the taxability of income and capital gain distributions, as well as the tax effect of going in and out of securities investments.

If you are evaluating a mutual fund, one factor to consider is its *past performance*. Remember, though, the caveat that applies to every mutual fund: Past performance is not necessarily an indication of future income or total return.

In Your Spare Time ...

Develop a long-term investment plan and apply your own individual objectives to guide you to suitable investments for your portfolio. Your investment success requires a disciplined, systematic approach to investing.

3

$ $

Developing a Tax-Efficient Investment Strategy

$ $

Taxation is a price you pay for successful investing. Investors typically concentrate on achieving maximum *pre-tax* returns. But, what matters most is what's left for you *after* taxes. Investing in stocks, bonds, and mutual funds has many advantages, but beware of a potential drawback: the turnover of securities within your own or a fund's portfolio often causes the realization of capital gains. *Capital gains* are the profits realized when the net cost of securities purchased is deducted from the net sales proceeds. For example, a fund must pass on these gains to all shareholders as taxable distributions, regardless of each investor's tax situation. For many investors, higher marginal federal income tax brackets as well as many states' taxes affect taxable dividends.

Let's look at an example of how both pre-tax returns from mutual funds and after-tax returns can work in two actual funds over ten years. The following chart shows the effects of a $10,000 investment made in each of two common stock funds in June 1984. Before considering taxes, the Vanguard Windsor Fund produced a significantly higher return than the Neuberger & Berman Manhattan Fund. But on an after-tax basis, assuming tax rates of 36 percent on ordinary income and 28 percent on capital gains, the net proceeds from the Neuberger & Berman fund were greater.

Value of Investment

	Before Taxes	After Taxes
Neuberger & Berman Manhattan Fund	$39,300	$29,300
Vanguard Windsor Fund	43,400	28,700

To help you develop a tax-efficient investment strategy, this chapter describes the impact of federal taxes on income and capital gains under the provisions of current tax law (the Revenue Reconciliation Act of 1993) and provides guidance on how you can minimize your portfolio's exposure to taxes.

Changes under the New Tax Law That May Affect You

The 1993 act includes several tax changes that can affect you as a securities investor. Let's take a quick look at some key changes.

Higher top rates.   Higher income individuals fall in two new tax brackets: 36 percent and 39.6 percent. Net capital gains (long-term gains in excess of short-term losses) are still subject to a top tax rate of 28 percent.

Higher alternative minimum tax (AMT).   The new law provides two AMT rates: 26 percent on AMT income up to $175,000 and 28 percent on AMT income greater than $175,000. Previously, the AMT rate was 24 percent.

You may be subject to the alternative minimum tax if you have deductions for accelerated depreciation and tax shelter losses or if you have tax-exempt interest from private activity bonds. The AMT may also apply if you have substantial itemized deductions that are not deductible for AMT purposes, such as state and local income taxes, certain interest expenses and miscellaneous deductions.

Capital gain rollover.   You may defer taxable gains on publicly traded securities you sell, if the proceeds are rolled over into common stock or a partnership interest in a *specialized small business investment company* (SSBIC). An SSBIC is a small business licensed as such by the Small Business Administration. A tax-free rollover must be completed within 60 days of the sale of securities and is limited to $50,000 of gain annually when filing a joint tax return.

Investment interest deduction.   In the past, capital gains realized from the sale of investment property were treated as investment income for purposes of figuring the *net investment income* ceiling for the investment interest deduction. Under the new law, if you claim the benefit of the 28 percent maximum rate for net capital gains, you can no longer treat those gains as investment income for purposes of the interest deduction.

Gains on market discount bonds.   All bonds acquired after April 30, 1993, are subject to the market discount rules that treat gain on the sale of a bond as ordinary income rather than capital gain to the extent of the market discount. A market discount arises when the price of a bond declines below its face amount because it carries an interest rate that is below the current rate of interest.

Stripped preferred stock.   Buyers of stripped preferred stock after April 30, 1993, are now subject to *original issue discount* (OID) reporting rules. OID is the difference between the stated redemption price and the purchase price, a portion of which must be reported as interest income each year. Stripped preferred stock results when the stock and its stripped dividend rights are sold separately.

Taxation of Interest and Dividend Income

Publicly held corporations will tell you whether their distributions are taxable. Taxable dividends paid to you are reported to the IRS by the paying company on Form 1099-DIV, a copy of which is sent to you. Taxable interest paid to you is reported to the IRS by the payer on Form 1099-INT. The IRS uses this information as a check on your reporting of dividends and interest.

Cash dividends.   Cash dividends you receive that are paid out of current or accumulated earnings of a corporation are subject to tax as ordinary income.

Dividends reinvested in company stock.   Some companies allow you to take dividends in cash or to reinvest the dividends in company stock. If you elect the stock plan and pay fair market value for the stock, the full cash dividend is taxable.

If the plan allows you to buy the stock at a discounted price, the amount of the taxable dividend is the fair market value of the stock on the dividend payment date, plus any service fee charged for the acquisition.

Stock dividends and stock splits.   If you own common stock and receive additional shares of the same company as a dividend, the dividend is generally not taxed. A stock dividend is taxed if you choose to receive cash instead of stock or if the stock is that of another corporation. Preferred shareholders are generally taxed on stock dividends.

Stock splits resemble the receipt of stock dividends, but they are not dividends. If you receive additional shares as part of a stock split, the new shares are not taxable. Even though you own more shares, your ownership percentage in the company has not changed.

Investment publications such as Moody's or Standard & Poor's annual dividend record books, available at many public libraries, provide details of dividend distributions and their tax treatment.

Real estate investment trust (REIT) dividends.   Ordinary dividends from an REIT are fully taxable. Dividends designated by the trust as capital gain distributions are reported as long-term capital gains regardless how long you have held your trust shares.

Return of capital distributions.   A distribution that is not paid out of earnings is a nontaxable return of capital. It is, in effect, a partial payback of your investment. The distribution will be reported by the company on Form 1099-DIV as a nontaxable distribution.

Nontaxable distributions result in a reduction of the cost basis of your investment. If a return of capital distributions reduces your basis to zero, any further distributions are taxable as capital gains.

Money market fund distributions.   Distributions paid to you by money market funds are reportable as dividends. Do not confuse these with bank money market accounts, which pay interest, not dividends.

Interest on corporate bonds.   Interest is taxable when you receive it or it is made available to you.

Interest on U.S. Treasury obligations.   Interest on securities issued by the federal government is fully taxable on your federal return. However, interest on federal obligations is not subject to state or local income taxes. Interest on bonds and notes is taxable in the year received.

On a T-bill held to maturity, you report as interest the difference between the discounted price you paid and the amount you receive on redeeming the bill at maturity. If you dispose of the bill prior to maturity, taxable interest is the difference between the discounted price you paid and the proceeds you received.

Market discount on bonds.   When the price of a bond declines because its interest rate is less than the current interest rate, a market discount occurs. Gain on a disposition of a bond bought after April 30, 1993, is taxable as ordinary income to the extent of the accrued market discount, unless you reported it annually as interest income.

Original issue discount (OID) on bonds.   OID occurs when a bond is issued for a price less than its face or principal amount and is the difference between the principal amount and the issue price. All obligations that pay no interest before maturity, such as zero-coupon bonds, are considered to be issued at a discount. Normally, a portion of the OID must be reported as interest income each year you hold the bond.

Interest on state and local government obligations.   Normally, you pay no federal tax on interest on bonds or notes of states, cities, counties, the District of Columbia, or a possession of the United States. However, interest on certain state and city obligations is taxable, such as federally guaranteed obligations and private activity bonds.

Most states tax the municipal bonds of other states, but not their own. A few states and the District of Columbia do not tax the interest on any municipal obligations.

Taxation of Capital Gains and Losses

Net capital gains (capital gains less capital losses) are added to your other income and subject to regular tax rates if your top rate is 15 percent or 28 percent. If your top rate exceeds 28 percent, net long-term gains in excess of short-term losses are subject to a top rate of 28 percent. Capital losses are deductible from capital gains, and are deductible from as much as $3,000 of ordinary income, with a carryover for the excess over $3,000.

The taxable gain or loss realized from the sale of a security is calculated by deducting your cost from your net sales proceeds. Purchase expenses, such as commissions, are included in your cost.

How it works. If your regular tax bracket for all income, including capital gains, is not more than 28 percent, net long-term capital gains are fully taxable at your regular rate. This is the same as for your short-term gains. If, however, your regular tax bracket exceeds 28 percent, your tax should be computed on net capital gains using the 28 percent maximum rate. The 28 percent rate applies to net capital gains, that is, net long-term gains less net short-term losses.

The period of time you own a security before its sale or exchange determines whether the gain is short term or long term. Gains or losses in 1993 and in later years are long term if the security was held more than one year.

Figuring the holding period. The holding period for stocks purchased on a public exchange starts on the day after your purchase order is executed. The day your sale order is executed is the last day of the holding period, even though delivery and payment may not be made until several days later (settlement date).

If you have purchased shares of the same security on different dates and cannot determine which shares you are selling, the shares purchased at the earliest time are considered the stock sold first. This is the *first-in, first-out* (FIFO) rule.

How Taxes Can Affect Your Net Investment Return

As noted earlier, individual investors and mutual funds typically concentrate on providing maximum *pre-tax* returns, which may ignore what matters most: what's left for you *after* taxes. Where possible, a tax-savvy investor seeks to reduce taxable capital gains and income distributions. Of primary importance to you are your net returns, *after* taxes. This is your real bottom line.

Your pre-tax and after-tax returns, can be substantially different, and the difference compounds over time. According to The Vanguard Group of Investment Companies, over the past five years, 28 percent of the average yearly return of the ten largest equity funds has been lost to taxes. The Vanguard Group reports that these ten funds provided an average annualized total return of 14.9 percent for the five years ending December 31, 1993. After taxes, the average annualized total return decreased to 10.8 percent—a 28 percent difference. The result assumes that all dividend income and capital gains distributions were reinvested after taxes were paid at the highest federal rates in effect during each year and that shares were sold and capital gains taxes were paid at the end of the period.

How To Minimize Your Exposure to Taxes

You can use several simple techniques to minimize the impact of taxes on your investment returns.

1. *Minimize portfolio turnover*. Frequent trading to *lock in* profits may also have the effect of *locking in* a continuous stream of tax liabilities. One effective way to minimize portfolio turnover is taking a market index approach to your equity investing. You can do this easily by investing in an index fund, such as an S&P 500 index fund that invests in substantially all of the stocks in the Standard & Poor's 500 Composite Stock Price Index. An index fund buys and holds stocks that track the performance of its designated index. This limits stock trading and, therefore, capital gains distributions.

2. *Use a disciplined sell selection method*. Use tax-minimizing techniques such as selling securities in your portfolio with the highest original cost. In addition, when sensible, realize capital losses to help offset any realized capital gains.

3. *Emphasize stocks with low dividend yields*. If current income is not an important objective for you, invest in a diversified group of stocks that pay little or no dividends. Companies that choose to reinvest their earnings back into the company to finance future growth typically enable you to realize growth of your invested capital, together with deferred taxation.

4. *Invest in tax-exempt securities*. You can avoid federal, state, and municipal income taxes (but not capital gains taxes) entirely by investing in tax-free bonds or bond funds. Tax-free bonds, issued by any state or municipality, are similar to bonds issued by a corporation or the U.S. government. They obligate the

issuer to pay bondholders a fixed amount of interest periodically and to repay the principal amount of the bond on a specific maturity date. Bonds issued by a particular state or its municipalities are also exempt from tax by that state or municipalities within that state.

5. *Open a retirement account.* Many mutual funds make available to their shareholders convenient vehicles for investing in different types of tax-favored retirement plans. Ask your mutual fund company about plans it makes available to shareholders.

Individual retirement accounts (IRAs) allow participants to make annual contributions and also roll over lump-sum distributions from corporate pension and profit-sharing plans.

If you own a corporation, consider establishing a pension or profit-sharing plan. *Prototype corporate retirement plans* can be adopted with minimal cost and red tape.

Keogh custodial accounts are available for self-employed individuals who want a tax-sheltered retirement plan. Such individuals may invest in mutual fund accounts and need only have an established plan and a bank custodial account.

Simplified employee pension plans (SEPs) were designed primarily for businesses that do not have employee retirement plans and also may be used by those companies that do have plans, but with some limitations.

Mutual Funds to the Rescue

Mutual fund companies are beginning to recognize the importance of minimizing the impact of taxes. The Vanguard Group offers the Vanguard Tax-Managed Fund to tax-conscious equity and balanced fund investors. Its three portfolios—the Growth and Income Portfolio, the Capital Appreciation Portfolio, and the Balanced Portfolio—seek to reduce the impact of taxes on investment returns in four ways:

- Minimizing portfolio turnover by using an index-oriented approach to equity management
- Selling securities with the highest original cost
- Emphasizing capital appreciation and de-emphasizing taxable income

- Encouraging long-term investors through the use of a redemption fee: 2 percent on shares redeemed after being held for less than one year and 1 percent on shares held for more than one year but less than five years.

In Your Spare Time ...

Develop a tax-efficient investment strategy to minimize your investment portfolio's exposure to taxes. What's important to you is your net return, after taxes.

4

$ $

Building Your Fortune
with a Tax-Favored
Retirement Plan

$ $

One of the best ways to build your fortune is to take advantage of one (or more) of the tax-favored retirement plans available to taxpayers in the Internal Revenue Code. The trend in America today is for individuals to take responsibility for funding their own retirement needs. Businesses in increasing numbers are turning away from the pension plans that millions of workers traditionally have counted on for retirement income. Many companies now ask workers to pay for and manage their own retirement plans.

What are the principal tax benefits? *Contributions made to the plans are tax-deductible, and earnings grow free of taxation until actual distribution of the proceeds.* In planning your own tax-favored retirement plan, many strategies recommended for any long-term investment program apply. Here are some key points to consider.

- *Begin early.* Start putting money aside as soon as possible. The earlier you start, the more *time* will work for you, and the more you will have for retirement.
- *Contribute generously.* Invest as much as you can afford, up to the limit permitted in the plan that you choose.
- *Invest for growth.* If you can accept moderate risk and retirement is many years away, invest primarily in common stocks, which have provided the best long-term returns.

- *Diversify.* Spread your investment program adequately among individual securities and other types of investments. Invest in stocks for growth, bonds for income, and money-market funds for safety. When you diversify, risk is dramatically reduced.
- *Stay with your program.* Consistency of purpose is a key factor in having a successful retirement plan. Continue your investment program throughout up and down cycles of the stock and bond markets. This book's dominant theme is *constant dollar investing*, the practice of buying securities at regular intervals in fixed dollar amounts, regardless of price levels.
- *Remember inflation.* Keep the potential for growth in your plan even after you retire to guard against inflation. A 4 percent inflation rate will reduce the purchasing power of your dollars by half in 20 years.

This chapter highlights the main plans that may be available to you and how you can use them. Many mutual fund companies, as well as the major discount brokers and full service brokers, have prototype plans and agreements (IRS-approved, as to form) that you can participate in, often at little cost. Your broker or fund can provide you with free information and everything you need.

Individual Retirement Account (IRA)

The government-sponsored IRA is one of the best tax-advantaged ways to supplement your retirement income. Section 408(a) of the Internal Revenue Code of 1986 describes the individual retirement account, which allows you to establish a long-term retirement program with two important tax advantages:

1. All your earnings accumulate tax-free in your IRA until you begin making withdrawals. Over time, this tax-deferred accumulation will have a major effect on your IRA, causing your assets to grow at a more rapid rate.
2. Because your IRA contributions may be tax-deductible, you may be able to reduce your federal income taxes now.

Under a voluntary IRA program, you may make investment contributions on a regular monthly, quarterly or annual basis and thereby take advantage of the powerful effect of constant dollar investing. With this investment strategy, you invest equal amounts of money at regular intervals regardless of whether securities markets are moving up or down. This practice reduces your average share costs because you acquire more shares in periods of lower securities prices and fewer shares in periods of higher prices.

For most people, an IRA is a long-term retirement program, and the investments you select should be made with that thought in mind. According to Ibbotson Associates, the stock market has historically provided investors with an average return of 10 percent per year. In recent years the returns have been higher. For example, in the 15 years ending June 30, 1994, Standard & Poor's 500 Composite Stock Price Index had an average annual total return of 14.7 percent.

Past performance is no guarantee of future results. But as an illustration, Figure 4.1 shows the potential results of investing $4,000 per year in an IRA investment program for two working spouses over different time frames with an average annual return of 10 percent.

FIGURE 4.1 $4,000 Invested Each Year at 10 Percent

Number of Years Invested	Accumulated Value of the Account
5	$26,862
10	70,125
15	139,799
20	252,010
25	432,727
30	723,774
35	1,192,507
40	1,947,407

Eligibility.   Generally, anyone younger than age 70½ who earns income from employment, including self-employment, may make annual contributions to an IRA.

Amount you may contribute.   A maximum of $2,000 or 100 percent of your compensation, whichever is less, may be contributed to your IRA each year.

Your spouse. Because each employed spouse may open a separate IRA and contribute 100 percent of compensation up to $2,000 a year, a working couple can make total contributions of as much as $4,000 annually to their IRAs.

Nonworking spouse. If your spouse earns no compensation (or earns less than $250) for the year, you may be eligible to increase your total IRA contribution by having an additional but separate *Spousal IRA* established for your spouse. With a spousal IRA, your maximum annual IRA contribution may be increased to $2,250, which may be split between the separate IRA accounts of you and your nonworking spouse in any manner you wish, so long as not more than $2,000 is contributed to either account for any one year.

Tax-deductibility. Your IRA contributions will be deductible for federal income tax purposes if neither you nor your spouse is an active participant in an employer-maintained retirement plan. If one of you is an active participant in an employer-maintained retirement plan, the deductibility of your IRA contributions will be determined by your adjusted gross income as follows:

- *Adjusted gross income of $40,000 or less* ($25,000 on single returns): Your IRA contributions will be fully deductible.
- *Adjusted gross income above $40,000* ($25,000 on single returns): The deduction for your IRA contributions will be reduced proportionately as your adjusted gross income increases above these limits. Deductibility will be phased out completely when your adjusted gross income reaches $50,000 ($35,000 on single returns).

You are generally considered an active participant for a tax year if you participate in any employer-maintained retirement plan (including pension, profit-sharing, 401(k), SEP or Keogh plan) during any part of the year. The Form W-2 you receive from your employer each year should indicate whether you are an active participant in the employer's retirement plan.

If neither you nor your spouse is an active participant in an employer-maintained retirement plan, your IRA contributions will be fully deductible regardless of your income level.

Nondeductible IRA contributions.   You are permitted to make non-deductible contributions to your IRA to the extent you are not eligible to make deductible IRA contributions. Earnings on such nondeductible contributions are not subject to federal income tax until you withdraw them. In the meantime, you will enjoy one of the most important benefits associated with IRAs: compounded, tax-deferred earnings.

When IRA contributions may be made.   For each tax year, you can make deductible or nondeductible contributions to your IRA at any time until the due date for filing your income tax return (not including extensions). For most taxpayers, the latest date for any year is April 15 of the following year. But remember, the sooner you contribute to your IRA, the sooner tax-sheltered earnings will accrue.

Contributions are voluntary.   You do not need to make contributions to your IRA every year, nor are you required to make the maximum contribution in any year. You may contribute any amount you wish, provided you don't exceed the limits. However, if you decide in any year not to make the maximum IRA contribution, you may not make up the missed contribution amount in later years.

Age limitation on continuing contributions.   You may make contributions to your IRA for each year you earn compensation until the year you attain age 70 $1/2$.

Withdrawals from your IRA.   Generally, you may start withdrawals from your IRA as early as age 59 $1/2$. Withdrawals must begin by April 1 following the year you attain age 70 $1/2$.

Taxation of withdrawals.   Withdrawals from your IRA will be taxed as ordinary income, with the exception that if you make any nondeductible contributions to your IRA, your IRA withdrawals will be treated partly as a nontaxable return of your nondeductible IRA contributions and partly as a taxable distribution of your IRA earnings and any deductible IRA contributions.

Withdrawals before age 59 $1/2$.   Because an IRA is intended to provide for your retirement, the law imposes an additional tax of 10 percent if you withdraw prior to age 59 1/2 for reasons other than your disability. This 10 percent tax is applied to the taxable amount of your withdrawal and is in addition to the ordinary income tax you pay on your withdrawal. The 10 percent additional tax will not apply to distributions made to your beneficiary in the event of your death. Also, the 10 percent tax will not apply to certain installment or annuity payments made for your life or life expectancy or for the joint lives or life expectancies of you and your beneficiary, regardless of when these payments begin.

Methods of distribution. Withdrawals from your IRA may be made in one or more lump-sum payments or in regular monthly, quarterly or annual installments. Installment payments may be paid over a period that does not exceed your life expectancy or the joint life expectancies of you and your beneficiary.

In event of your death. Any amount in your IRA at the time of your death will be distributed to your designated beneficiary(ies). If you do not designate a beneficiary or your designated beneficiary(ies) dies before you do, your estate will become your beneficiary.

Transfers and rollovers. A *transfer* occurs when IRA assets are transferred directly from one custodian to another. You are permitted to transfer your existing IRA assets from one custodian to another without paying taxes. Such a direct transfer may be made as often as you wish. A *rollover* occurs when you receive IRA assets from one custodian and then move the assets to another custodian, for example, from a bank to a brokerage firm. If you receive a distribution of assets from an existing IRA, you may make a tax-free rollover contribution of all or part of the assets you receive to another IRA. The rollover must be completed within 60 days after you receive the distribution from your existing IRA to avoid paying income or penalty taxes. You may make only one such taxfree rollover every 12 months.

Simplified Employee Pension (SEP) Plan

A *simplified employee pension* (SEP) allows you as an employer to contribute to an IRA more than you can under regular IRA rules. If you are self-employed, own a small company or business or have a professional practice, a SEP plan provides a retirement plan that offers considerable tax benefits and is easy to administer. It is the retirement plan of choice for many sole proprietors and other small-business owners.

Key features of a SEP.   Simplified Employee Pension plans have the following five features:

1. As an employer you can deduct, from current federally taxable income, contributions of as much as $30,000 per eligible employee per plan year (to a limit of 15 percent of employed compensation or 13.04 percent of self-employed income). In addition, employees may make their own deductible or nondeductible IRA contributions each year up to the lesser of $2,000 or 100 percent of compensation, resulting in total annual contributions to their IRAs of as much as $32,000.
2. Contributions are simply made to your IRA and to the IRA of each covered employee.
3. Annual contributions are discretionary, so you can skip some years if you wish.
4. All earnings on SEP contributions accumulate in your IRA (or in your employees' IRAs)) on a tax-deferred basis. *Earnings grow free of taxation until actual distribution.*
5. Compared to a qualified retirement plan, a SEP plan is virtually free of paperwork. And the plan's streamlined structure results in administrative costs that are among the lowest of any employer-sponsored plan.

Administration of a SEP.   Just two steps are needed to administer a SEP:

1. Furnish each covered employee with a copy of a completed SEP-IRA contribution agreement.
2. Give every employee a statement each year showing the SEP amount contributed to his or her IRA.

No IRS Form 5500, no Department of Labor filings and no complicated plan and trust documents are needed.

Additional benefits of a SEP. Investment flexibility and low cost are two important pluses. The SEP allows you (and your SEP participants) to self-direct your investment among the large number of different investments appropriate for retirement investing. Annual custodial fees usually range from $10 to $25, although some full-service brokers charge more.

Limitations of a SEP. A SEP has certain limitations that may make other types of retirement plans more appropriate, particularly for larger corporations.

- *Lack of employer control over employee retirement savings.* Employer contributions under a SEP are deposited directly in the IRAs established for covered employees. These contributions are vested immediately and may be withdrawn by employees at any time (subject to the IRA rules that generally impose a 10 percent penalty on distributions prior to age 59½). The lack of employer control may limit the SEP as a vehicle for binding employees to the sponsoring employer.
- *Strict coverage requirements.* A SEP must cover all employees older than age 21 who have performed any service for an employer during any three of the past five years (except for certain union employees and employees who have earned less than $300, as indexed, in a year). This means that contributions under a SEP may be required on behalf of part-time and temporary employees even if they work less than 1,000 hours a year. Stricter coverage and eligibility requirements are possible under a qualified pension, profit-sharing or 401(k) plan.
- *No favorable tax treatment for lump-sum distributions.* All SEP funds that are distributed from an employee's IRA will be taxed as ordinary income. Thus, SEP monies are not eligible for the special five-year forward-averaging taxation that applies to certain lump-sum distributions from qualified plans. Of course, this limitation does not affect people who elect to receive their retirement plan distributions in installments over their retirement rather than in a lump sum. To avoid withholding tax on a distribution, SEP assets must be transferred directly to an IRA or qualified plan of another employer.

401(k) Plans

You may be eligible for a 401(k) plan, now available to employees at an increasing number of large and medium-size companies. In many major corporations, pension plans are rapidly being overtaken by these plans, which require employees to put in their own money for retirement and make their own decisions on how the funds will be invested. According to Sanford C. Bernstein & Company, more than 40 million Americans now have a 401(k) plan, up from hardly any 15 years ago. The number of employees covered by pension plans has dropped from more than 40 million in 1984 to an estimated 36.5 million in 1994.

Named after a section of the Internal Revenue Code that authorizes it, 401(k) plans have been available since 1978. Under such plans, employees put a percentage of their pretax earnings into an investment account, where the money grows free of taxation until retirement. Most 401(k) plans offer a selection of investment options, mostly mutual funds. At retirement, the plan provides one lump sum, the size of which depends on how much the employee saved during the years and how effectively it was invested. Like other retirement plans, assets may be rolled over or transferred to an IRA

Yet many participants are not setting aside enough money in their plans and they are poorly investing what they do save. In addition, participating employees frequently turn to these retirement accounts for cash to cover everything from houses to cars to medical bills. A successful retirement plan requires a long-term commitment to savings.

Pension and Profit-Sharing Plans

If you own a business, a qualified pension and/or profit-sharing plan may be your best bet. Many mutual fund companies and brokerage firms now offer complete, flexible and carefully designed tax-qualified retirement programs. They provide multiple plan selection and offer an exceptionally diverse range of investment options.

You may obtain, in many cases without charge, qualified retirement plans that meet all current standards under federal tax law. You can expect high-quality service from the best of these sources at little or no cost. Use the fund or broker's 800 number to ask for a complete kit for setting up a qualified retirement plan, which will typically include the following:

- A qualified retirement plan booklet containing plan highlights, answers to frequently asked questions, plan documents and IRS opinion letters
- Booklets that contain the adoption agreements and other material you will need to adopt the plan
- If from a mutual fund, information on the specific fund(s) you are interested in and a brochure describing all the currently available funds in the company's family of funds.

Qualified Retirement Plans

You may generally select from three different plans to meet your particular needs:

1. *Profit-sharing plan.* Contributions may be made whether or not your business shows a profit, and the percentage you contribute is discretionary. The deduction for participants' contributions generally is limited to 15 percent of employed compensation (or 13.04 percent of self-employed income).
2. *Money purchase pension plan.* Contributions are required annually and must be equal to a fixed percentage of each participant's compensation, regardless of profits. The maximum deduction is effectively the lesser of 25 percent of the participant's compensation or $30,000 (or 20 percent of net earnings for self-employed people).
3. *Combination of the profit-sharing and money purchase pension plans.* This is the most flexible arrangement. You may arrange combined contributions of as much as the maximum deductible amount (i.e., the lesser of 25 percent of compensation or $30,000) while retaining the flexibility through the profit-sharing plan to contribute lesser amounts. (Deductible limits for self-employed individuals are limited to 20 percent of net earnings.)

When setting up a qualified retirement plan, you may appoint a trust company as trustee or any other corporate or individual trustee (such as yourself). The simplified adoption agreements provided with the prototype plan will fulfill most employers' needs. Alternative adoption agreements that include additional plan options, such as more restrictive coverage provisions, vesting schedules and Social Security integration, are also available.

Designing Your Retirement Plan

Employee eligibility. In determining who shall be eligible to participate in your qualified retirement plan, you may require all employees to have attained a minimum age (up to age 21) and/or have completed a minimum period of service (as much as two years). You are also permitted to limit coverage under your plan to certain groups or categories of employees, provided that the Internal Revenue Code's nondiscrimination requirements are satisfied. Of course, you may elect not to impose any eligibility requirements, in which case all employees will be immediately eligible.

Employee vesting. Participating employees will become vested in their plan accounts according to the vesting schedule you select. As an alternative to full (100 percent) and immediate vesting, you may provide any vesting schedule that meets the statutory requirements of the Internal Revenue Code.

Integration with Social Security. You may provide a formula for integrating the allocation of employer contributions with Social Security. This will allow you to combine the employer's Social Security contributions with its plan contributions to permit greater contributions (as a percentage of total compensation) to the plan for higher-paid employees.

Plan investments. You may permit plan participants to self-direct the investment of their separate accounts under the plan or you may provide that the plan administrator shall be responsible for directing the investment of all plan accounts. Investments may include a mix of stocks, bonds, money market instruments and mutual funds.

Setting Up Your Plan

To participate in a qualified retirement program, follow six basic steps:

1. *Consult your attorney or tax adviser.* Before adopting a prototype money purchase pension plan or profit-sharing plan (or both), first meet with your attorney or tax adviser to determine whether the specific plan or combination of plans you have selected is appropriate for your particular circumstances.

2. *Complete the adoption agreement.* Complete the appropriate money purchase pension plan or profit-sharing plan adoption agreement. Detailed instructions will be provided for you with the forms. If you have any questions, call the fund or brokerage firm. In most cases, a firm representative will be glad to assist you.

3. *Adopt the plan documents.* As employer, you should formally adopt the appropriate prototype plan, trust agreement and adoption agreement no later than the end of the first plan year. For corporations, the forms booklet provided to you will usually show sample boards of directors' resolutions authorizing the adoption of these documents.

4. *Notify employees and distribute participant elections forms.* Announce to all your employees the establishment of your plan with its important provisions. Distribute election forms that may be used to designate beneficiaries and direct investments. The forms booklet will normally include a sample participant election form.

5. *Complete the contribution investment form.* Using the information supplied by your employees on their election forms, complete the contribution investment form and send it to your mutual fund or broker along with the completed adoption agreement and a check for your initial plan contribution.

6. *Provide notice to interested parties and a summary plan description to all plan participants who are common-law employees.* (Plans of partnerships that cover only partners and their spouses as well as plans of sole proprietors that cover only the sole proprietor and his or her spouse are exempt from this requirement.)

7. *Obtain a fidelity bond.*

In Your Spare Time ...

Take advantage of one or more of the tax-favored retirement plans that are available to tax-payers in the Internal Revenue Code. The contributions you make to such plans generally are tax-deductible and earnings grow free of taxation until actual distribution of the proceeds.

5

$ $

Discovering
Stock Market
Opportunities

$ $

This chapter provides a guided tour through some of the investment opportunities offered by the New York Stock Exchange (NYSE), American Stock Exchange (AMEX) and Nasdaq National Market System.

Getting Started

Always make investment decisions in terms of your own particular financial position, risk comfort-level and goals. Remember, no one is as interested in your financial situation as you are. So listen, learn and consult with people you trust. But in the end you must make your own decisions. If you don't understand a finance or investment term, consult the glossary.

Before making any investment decision, you need to consider three basic factors:

1. What is your investment objective?
   Are you mainly interested in seeing your capital grow? Then seek investments that are expected to increase in value to produce capital gains. Along with appreciation of the asset's value, consider reinvesting dividends and interest.

Is your objective income? Then identify investments whose primary feature is to provide a regular income. Find out whether a particular security produces an income of fixed payments or whether you can expect it to produce an income stream of gradually increasing payments.

Do you want to protect your capital from inflation? An investment whose value can be expected to rise at the same rate or at a rate higher than the rate of inflation is *inflation-sensitive* and will help protect the buying power of your capital.

Can you borrow against your investment? This question involves the general value of an investment as collateral for a loan. Borrowing can help you raise cash when an investment cannot readily be sold or when it may not be the right time to sell. An investment can also be used in a margin account with a broker. This gives you leverage, the ability to control a greater value of securities than the amount of cash you have available.

2. How much risk can you tolerate?

The answer is subjective and varies widely among investors.

Principal risk. You want to know what assurance you have of getting your full investment back. This involves two types of risk: The first is *market risk* and involves fluctuations in value due to forces operating in the market system, such as the optimism or pessimism of investors, changes in the economy or unexpected events occurring in the national or international arena. The other type of risk is *financial* or *credit risk*, the risk that an issuer of a debt security will default on a contractual obligation or an equity investment will lose value because of the bankruptcy or financial difficulty of the issuer.

Income risk. If you have an investment that produces income, you want to know the probability that the issuer will be able to continue the flow of dividend or interest payments.

3. Are taxes a consideration?

Unless your investments are included in a tax-deferred retirement account, such as an IRA, dividend or interest payments generally are subject to income tax liability. Profits taken when a security appreciates in value may be subject to a lower capital gains tax. These factors can influence how long you hold an investment and whether you buy stock in a company that reinvests its earnings or pays out a substantial portion in dividends.

Stock Market Investment Alternatives

You can choose from a number of investment alternatives traded in the securities markets that are available to you through a broker. You can ask your broker to send you annual reports on the companies you are considering. Following are brief descriptions of the major categories.

Common stock. For *total return* (capital gains and dividend income), no publicly traded investment offers more potential over the long term than common stock. *Common stock* represents the basic equity ownership in a corporation. A shareholder is normally entitled to vote for directors and in other important matters and to share in the wealth created by the corporation's business activities. Shareholders participate in the appreciation of share values and in dividends declared out of earnings that remain after debt obligations and preferred stock dividends are met.

The market values of shares in publicly held corporations are based primarily on investor expectations of future earnings and dividends. These expectations and the resulting stock values are often influenced by forecasts of business activity in general and by so-called investor psychology, which reflects the current business and economic environment. The relationship of market price to a company's actual or expected earnings is called the *price-earnings (PE) ratio*, or multiple. For example, a stock selling at $60 per share with earnings of $5 per share is said to be selling at a PE ratio of 12 times earnings, or a multiple of 12.

Stocks of young, rapidly growing companies tend to be volatile, have a high PE ratios, and usually carry a high risk. Such companies seldom pay dividends. Instead, earnings are reinvested in the enterprise to finance growth. As opposed to these growth stocks, the stocks of older, established companies with histories of regular earnings and dividend payments tend to have more price stability and low PE multiples. Some of these stocks are called *blue chips;* stocks paying out substantial dividends are called *income stocks.* Some blue chips are also income stocks and vice versa.

Preferred stock. This equity security includes features of both common stock and bonds; however, it is riskier than bonds because it is not debt.

The dividends on preferred stock are usually a fixed percentage of par value or a fixed dollar amount. Thus, share prices are interest-rate sensitive. Like bonds, prices increase when interest rates decrease and vice versa. Preferred dividends are not a contractual expense of the issuer, however. Although payable before common stock dividends, preferred dividends can be skipped if earnings are low. If the issuer goes bankrupt, the claims of preferred shareholders come before common shareholders, but preferred shareholders do not share in assets until bondholders are paid in full.

Preferred issues are designed for insurance companies and other institutional investors which, as corporations, benefit from an 80 percent tax exclusion on dividends earned. For individuals, though, the fully taxable yields are not much better than that of comparable bonds, but lack the greater safety bonds afford. Also, trading is often inactive, which means less liquidity and higher transaction costs for the small investor.

You can choose from several varieties of preferred stock:

Cumulative preferred stock is the most common. Dividends, if missed (not paid by corporation), accrue, and common stock dividends cannot be paid until all missed dividends on the preferred stock have been paid.

Noncumulative preferred stock is rare today. Dividends, if skipped, do not accumulate.

Convertible preferred stock is convertible into common shares, so offers growth potential plus fixed income.

Participating preferred stock is issued by companies having difficulty raising capital. Shareholders participate in profits with common shareholders in extra dividends declared after regular dividends are paid.

Adjustable rate preferred stock has the dividend adjusted quarterly to reflect money market rates and is marketed mainly to corporate investors seeking higher after-tax yields (remember their 80 percent tax exclusion on dividends) together with market price stability. For the individual investor whose dividends are fully taxed, a money market fund is generally a better choice.

Invest in preferred stock *only* if your objective is income, although appreciation is possible if shares are bought at a discount from par or redemption value or prior to a decline in interest rates. Unless you are a corporation, you are probably better off with a comparable corporate bond, which is less risky in terms of both principal and income.

Corporate bonds.   A *bond* is a contract between a borrower (the *issuer*) and a lender (the *bondholder*). *Corporate bonds* are debt securities of a corporation that require the issuer to pay the bondholder the par value at a specified maturity date and to make scheduled interest payments. Corporate bonds are attractive because they pay a higher yield than government bonds do and are relatively safe. *Unsecured bonds*, called *debentures*, have a claim on the assets of the issuing corporation. *Secured bonds* are usually backed by mortgages against specific assets of the corporation. Major bond rating services closely monitor the creditworthiness of corporate bonds. Interest on these bonds is generally taxable. The face amount of a bond (par value) is normally $1,000, except for **baby bonds** which have par values of $500 or less.

Three factors can affect bond prices. Bonds can trade in the market at a *premium* or discount to their par values so that their yield is in line with current interest rates. Bond prices and interest rate movements have an inverse relationship. When interest rates rise, bond prices decline, and vice versa. Bond prices also vary with the time remaining to maturity. Generally, the longer the maturity period, the higher will be the yield and the lower the price of a bond because time means risk and more risk requires a higher yield.

Another factor that affects bond prices is safety. This relates to credit risk, the borrower's ability to pay interest and principal when due. The financial strength of the corporation is reflected in the ratings assigned to its bonds by the major credit services. These ratings affect yield, which is adjusted by changes in a bond's price.

Bonds are usually issued in 5 bond minimum amounts ($5,000) and traded by brokers in round lots of 10 or 100 bonds ($10,000 or $100,000). Odd lots are often available at higher commission rates or dealer *spreads* (the difference between what a dealer buys and sells a security for).

Consider buying bonds when your investment objective is income. However, capital appreciation is possible when you can buy bonds at a discount or when declining interest rates cause bond prices to rise.

Convertible securities.   Some bonds and preferred stocks are convertible into common stock, usually of the issuer. *Convertible securities* offer both fixed income and capital appreciation potential. They pay a fixed dividend or rate of interest and are convertible into common stock at a specified price or conversion ratio. The yield on convertibles is normally less than that of nonconvertible bonds or preferred stocks and the potential for capital gains is less than with a common stock investment.

Convertibles usually offer less credit risk and market risk than common stock while providing an opportunity for investors to participate in the future success of the corporation into whose common shares convertibles can be exchanged. Convertible bonds and convertible preferred stock have the same priority of claim on a corporation's earnings and assets as regular bonds and preferreds. Bonds take precedence over preferred stock, and both take precedence over common stock.

Convertibles have an investment value and a conversion value. *Investment value* is the market value the security would have if it were not convertible. *Conversion value* is the market price of the common stock times the number of shares into which the bond or preferred stock is convertible. This is called the *conversion rate* or *ratio.*

Consider buying a convertible security if your investment objective is capital appreciation and if you want the greater yield and safety of bonds and preferred stocks. Remember, though, because potential for growth is a key feature, yield is less than on a straight bond or preferred stock. Convertibles tend to rise in value with increasing common stock prices, so they also represent a hedge against inflation.

From a risk perspective, convertibles will not sink in value below the market value the same investment would have without the convertible feature. But, like any interest-rate-sensitive investment, the investment value of convertibles varies inversely with interest rates. Prices rise when interest rates decline, and prices decline when interest rates rise.

As with regular corporate bonds and preferred stock, convertible bonds have priority over convertible preferreds in claims against the corporation's earnings and assets, and convertible preferreds have priority over the common shares. Assuming the issuer is financially strong and has dependable earnings, you have little credit risk to be concerned about.

Foreign stocks. You can take advantage of opportunities occurring where overseas economies or industry sectors may be growing faster than those in the United States by investing in *foreign stocks,* which are securities of foreign issuers denominated in foreign currencies. Total returns can be increased through profits on currency movements, but remember, this also means additional risk.

American depositary receipts (ADRs) provide a convenient way to invest in foreign stocks. U.S. banks issue these negotiable receipts which represent actual shares held in their foreign branches. ADRs are actively traded on the major stock exchanges and in the over-the-counter (OTC) market. You still face currency risks and foreign withholding taxes, but the depositary pays dividends and capital gains in U.S. dollars and handles splits, stock dividends and rights offerings. ADRs eliminate trading inconveniences and custodial problems that exist with trading in foreign stocks.

You can also buy foreign stocks through your broker in foreign markets. Depending on the issue and the market, problems include inadequate financial information and regulation, high minimum purchase requirements, higher transaction costs, taxes, possible illiquidity, political risk and possible currency losses. Unless you can take big risks and are sophisticated in international interest rates and foreign exchange, this avenue of investment may not be a wise one for you to take. You can readily achieve international diversification with much lower risk by investing in closed-end or open-end mutual funds.

Most foreign stock shares traded through ADRs represent solid, established companies, and volatility has tended to be low. Thus, these foreign equities on average can normally be safer than many domestic issues. Adverse currency fluctuations, however, introduce an added element of risk.

If your investment objective is growth of capital, foreign stocks offer you the potential for both capital and currency appreciation. From an income perspective, however, foreign stocks generally have lower dividend yields than U.S. stocks, and exchange-rate fluctuations are a factor in expected returns.

Put and call option contracts. An *option contract* gives the owner the right—for a price, called a *premium*—to buy or sell an underlying stock or financial instrument at a specified price, called the *exercise* or *strike price*, before a specified expiration date.

A *put* is an option to sell; a *call* is an option to buy. Option sellers are called *writers*. If they own the underlying security, they are called *covered writers*; they are called *naked writers* if they don't.

Options are traded on national stock and commodity exchanges and also in the OTC market. Those listed on the exchanges have greater visibility and are less expensive than those traded over the counter, which are individually negotiated and less liquid. Listed options are available on stocks, stock indexes, debt instruments, foreign currencies and different types of futures.

Options enable an investor to control a large amount of value with a much smaller amount of money at risk. The leverage that options provide means that a small percentage change in the value of a financial instrument can result in a much larger percentage change in an option's value. Thus, large gains and losses are possible. Options are usually bought and sold, then allowed to expire without ever being exercised. They are financial instruments with a life of their own.

Option prices are mainly determined by the relationship between the exercise price and the market price of the underlying security, by the time remaining before the option expires and by the volatility of the underlying security.

Consider using options if you are interested in speculating. Because a small change in a stock price causes a higher percentage change in a related option price, options can give you substantial leverage. Profits can be great, but losses can mount quickly if the underlying stock doesn't move in the right direction. Income in the form of premiums you receive from the sale of covered options can add to your income return on the underlying investment. The risk to the covered writing (selling) of options is that you may be forced to sell or buy the underlying security if the price moves in the wrong direction.

Closed-end funds.   A closed-end fund is a mutual fund with a relatively fixed amount of capital and whose shares are traded on a securities exchange or in the OTC market. The value of a closed-end fund's shares rises and falls based on the value of the fund's portfolio as well as investor confidence and other market factors. Shares of closed-end funds usually sell at a premium to or discount from the value of their underlying portfolios.

The closed-end fund's universe includes U.S. and foreign equity funds, convertible bond and preferred stock funds, taxable bond funds, tax-free municipal bond funds and dual-purpose funds. If you are seeking an investment that will grow in value, select a fund with appreciation as its primary objective. Bond funds generally have an objective of providing income. Dual-purpose funds have two classes of stock, with common shareholders benefiting from all the capital gains and preferred shareholders receiving all the interest and dividend income.

In Your Spare Time ...

Consider your investment objectives, how much risk you are willing to tolerate, and your tax situation before you venture into the stock market. The securities markets provide a virtual smorgasbord of investment choices.

6

$ $ $ $ $ $ $ $ $ $ $ $ $ $ $ $ $ $ $ $

Minimizing
Brokerage Costs

$ $ $ $ $ $ $ $ $ $ $ $ $ $ $ $ $ $ $ $

Attorneys' ads are often followed by a caveat such as "The hiring of an attorney is an important decision that should not be based solely upon advertisements." This is sound advice and applies to many other choices we make—including the selection of a stockbroker. In choosing your broker, consider what services you need from a broker, which broker—or type of broker—can serve you best, and finally, which broker can provide the services you need at the least cost.

Stockbrokers generally provide a variety of services for their customers, enabling customers to buy and sell stocks, bonds, commodities, options, mutual funds, limited partnerships, certificates of deposits, annuities and other financial products. In addition, brokers may offer asset management accounts which combine a customer's holdings of stocks and bonds with a money-market fund. The customer can then write checks against the account, which may also have credit-card features. Brokers can send you annual reports on the companies you are considering. These reports contain financial statements reflecting a company's assets, liabilities and income reports. Many brokers also offer individualized financial planning services. With the wide choice of products and services they have made available to the public, brokers today have a wide-ranging clientele, from novice investors to wealthy and sophisticated individuals.

Full-Service versus Discount Brokers

Prior to 1975, all brokers charged the same fixed commission rates. On May 1, 1975, known as May Day in the brokerage industry, the era of fixed commissions ended. Since then, brokers have been free to charge whatever they like. The resulting greater competition within the industry introduced the public to a new type of broker: the *discounter*. These brokers specialize in executing orders to buy and sell stocks, bonds, options and mutual funds. Usually, they charge commissions that are far less than full-service brokers, but they offer fewer services.

The 80 or so discount brokers account for about 25 percent of all brokerage trades of stocks and earn roughly 15 percent of commission dollars. They come in three types: (1) The "Big Three" are Charles Schwab, Fidelity Brokerage, and Quick & Reilly. Together they earn about 70 percent of the discount brokerage revenue. (2) Banks, which mostly operate locally, account for 10 percent of the discount business. (3) The balance goes to the approximately 90 *deep-discount* brokers.

On average, the Big Three charge 58 percent less than the commissions charged by full-service brokers, such as Merrill Lynch, Pierce, Fenner & Smith (the largest broker in terms of number of account executives). According to Mercer, Inc., a New York research firm, the 30 deepest discounters charge 78 percent less than the rates typical of full-service brokers. The Big Three and banks usually charge by a transaction's dollar value, determined by multiplying the number of shares times the market price. Deep-discount brokers charge by the number of shares traded in the transaction. Some brokers offer both approaches. Nearly all brokers have a minimum transaction fee.

Full-service brokers offer investors far more guidance on what investments are appropriate for each client. Clients pay substantially higher charges for this guidance. Full-service brokers may also engage in investment banking, helping raise capital for federal, state and local governments and for corporations. This involves underwriting new issues of stocks and bonds for corporations, as well as debt issues for governments, and distributing them to both institutional and individual investors.

If you are doing business with a full-service broker, be particularly careful about which account executive deals with you. Brokerage firm employees are paid on the basis of the amount of commissions they develop from customers. As a result, they are under constant pressure to "produce." This pressure to produce commissions often leads to various abuses.

One abuse to watch for is the recommendation of an investment that is unsuitable for you, but may be appropriate for a speculator with a high tolerance for risk. So-called *penny stocks* or other very volatile securities might be recommended if the broker believes you are looking for something that will quickly increase in price. Or, if you are seeking income, a risky *junk bond* might be suggested. Another abuse employed by a hungry broker is *churning,* excessive trading of a client's account. Churning increases a broker's commissions but usually leaves you worse off, or no better off, than before the activity occurs. Churning is illegal under Securities and Exchange Commission (SEC) and stock exchange rules, but is difficult to prove. Clients who believe they are victims of churning or being sold inappropriate investments can sue or take their complaint to arbitration.

If you are going to deal with a full-service brokerage firm, ask for a mature person who has been in the business for at least five years. After you have been assigned a broker, sit down together to discuss your financial situation and investment objectives. Be sure your broker knows how much risk you are willing to take. Being comfortable with your broker is important.

If you require less "hand-holding," a discount broker may serve you just as well and at much less cost. In many cases discounters offer more services than you might expect. Their objective is to offer an investing climate that is easy, convenient and inexpensive, plus a certain amount of the help you need to make informed decisions. In dealing with a discount broker, expect to pay less in commissions and account fees. The Big Three firms, mentioned earlier, offer free investment guides and even seminars. Plus, you have a wide range of different investments to choose from, such as the following:

- *Stocks*: both listed and over the counter
- *Mutual funds*: both load and no-load
- *Government securities*: U.S. Treasury bills, notes and bonds
- *Fixed-income investments*: municipal bonds, corporate bonds, government agency securities and other fixed income investments

Comparing Commissions

You will find substantial differences in transaction charges made by full-service brokers, large discount brokers and deep-discount brokers. But pricing in the industry can be complex. In addition to minimum fees, some brokers charge for postage, stock transfers and inactive accounts. Certain brokers offer discounts for electronically placed orders and rebates for monthly trading that exceeds a stated minimum. Figure 6.1 lists the results of a survey we made of several brokers. It indicates the commissions you would be charged if you bought shares in various amounts and at different price levels. Remember, commissions and fees are always subject to change. Ask your broker for a current commission schedule.

Like those at full-service brokers, customers' securities accounts at discount brokers are insured for at least $500,000 by the Securities Investor Protection Corporation (SIPC), a nonprofit company established by Congress.

FIGURE 6.1   Sample Commissions for Buying or Selling Stocks*

	50 Shares at $65	100 Shares at $25	300 Shares at $30	600 Shares at $30
Fidelity	$54	$54	$106	$137
Kennedy, Cabot	20	30	30	30
Merrill Lynch	88	78	204	331
Quick & Reilly	49	49	82	104
Charles Schwab	55	55	107	137

*Based on standard rates quoted on July 1, 1994.

To give you an idea of what commissions you would expect to pay one of the Big Three discount brokers for stock transactions, Figure 6.2 represents Charles Schwab's commission schedule effective June 1, 1993.

Deep-discount brokers charge much less, but deliver less service. Figure 6.3 shows K. Aufhauser & Company's commission schedule.

Some discount brokers permit you to trade directly via a touchtone telephone or by using your personal computer. AccuTrade, for instance, allows you to enter orders 24 hours a day; view your positions, balances and open orders; and receive stock quotes 24 hours a day. They charge 3 cents per share traded, regardless of stock price, with a $48 minimum commission. But always be sure to ask what other charges may be applicable.

It is almost impossible to determine who is the cheapest broker. The answer depends on the size and type of trade involved. To select the best broker for you, first determine what your average transaction size will be. Then shop around.

Fortunately, some researchers have already done the shopping for you. For a nominal fee, the American Association of Individual Investors (AAII, 312-280-0170) annually produces a report that calculates the fees for three typical trades—100 shares at $50, 500 shares at $50 and 1,000 shares at $5—charged by about 70 nonbank discount brokers. For a little higher cost, Mercer, Inc., provides much more detailed information in their "Discount Broker Survey," which features fees most industry brokers charge for 22 different trades (800-582-9854).

A discount broker is likely located near you. The yellow page section of your phone book under "Stock & Bond Brokers" lists all the discount brokers, as well as full-service brokers, in your area.

Following is a partial list of discount brokers that operate nationally. You can contact them directly for complete information on their fees and services.

FIGURE 6.2   Charles Schwab Commission Schedule for Stocks

STOCKS

Overriding Minimum: $39 per trade.

Transaction Size	Commission Rate
$0 - 2,499	$30 + 1.7% of principal
$2,500 - 6,249	$56 + 0.66%
$6,250 - 19,999	$76 + 0.34%
$20,000 - 49,999	$100 + 0.22%
$50,000 - 499,999	$155 + 0.11%
$500,000+	$255 + 0.09%*

OR the following minimums and maximums:

Minimum Charge: The greater of the overriding minimum of $39 or $0.09 per share for the first 1,000 shares, plus $0.04 per share thereafter for stocks below $5 per share or $0.05 per share thereafter for stocks $5 per share or greater.

Maximum Charge: $55 for the first 100 shares, plus $0.55 per share thereafter.

Stocks Less Than $1 per Share: $39 plus 4% of principal amount. For purchases, we require cleared funds in the account. When selling, we require stocks in advance.

*Large Block Transactions: Contact your local Schwab office on orders of 10,000 shares or more or on orders over $500,000. These orders may be eligible for special handling and/or pricing.

Miscellaneous Fees: $15 for each security registered and shipped to individuals. Securities are held in street name at no cost. $39 for Voluntary and Post-Effective Reorganizations.

OPTIONS

Options with Premiums of $0.50 or Under:

Overriding Minimum: $39 per trade.

Contracts	Commission
0-49	$1.80 per contract + 1.5% of principal
50-149	$1.10 + 1.8%
150-499	$0.75 + 2.0%
500-1499	$0.60 + 2.0%
1500+	$0.60 + 1.5%

Options with Premiums Greater Than $0.50:

Overriding Minimum: $37.25 + $1.75 per contract.

Dollar Amount	Commission
$0 - 2,499	$29 + 1.6% of principal
$2,500 - 9,999	$49 + 0.8%
$10,000+	$99 + 0.3%

Maximum Charge: $40 per contract on the first two contracts, plus $4 per contract thereafter.

Options carry a relatively high level of risk and are not suitable for all investors. Certain requirements must be met to trade options through Schwab. Please read the Options Disclosure Document titled "Characteristics and Risks of Standardized Options" before considering any option transaction. Call or write Charles Schwab & Co., Inc. at 101 Montgomery Street, San Francisco, CA 94104 for a current copy. Cleared funds must be in your account before option orders are accepted.

MUTUAL FUNDS*

Overriding Minimum: $39 per trade.

Transaction Size	Transaction Fees
$0-14,999	0.7% of principal
$15,000-99,999	0.7% on first $15,000
	0.2% on amount over $15,000
$100,000+	0.7% on first $15,000
	0.2% on amount between
	$15,000 & $100,000
	0.08% on amount over $100,000

More than 250 mutual funds are available without the above transaction fees. Call 1(800)2 NO-LOAD for a list of these funds.

Minimum transaction amounts apply for initial and subsequent purchases.

When placing simultaneous orders to sell one fund and purchase a new fund with the proceeds, you'll pay the standard fee on the larger transaction and just $25 on the corresponding buy or sell (policy not applicable to SchwabFunds® or other funds on which Schwab charges no transaction fees). Some funds may also charge sales and/or redemption fees. Please read the prospectuses for details. You can buy shares directly from the fund itself or its principal underwriter or distributor without paying Schwab's transaction fees.

*Applies to open-end mutual funds only. For closed-end funds, refer to the stock schedule.

FIXED INCOME INVESTMENTS

Corporate Bonds & Corporate Zeros:

Overriding Minimum: $39 per trade.

Transaction Size	Commission
0 - 25 bonds	$5 per bond
25+ bonds	$5 per bond on first 25 bonds
	$3 per bond thereafter

OR

1% of principal, whichever is less.

Large Transactions: Please contact our Bond Specialists on orders of more than 250 bonds. These orders may be eligible for special handling and/or special pricing.

Municipal Bonds: Markup included in price. Schwab acts as principal.

Treasury Bills, Notes & Bonds: $49 fee per transaction. Schwab may act as principal.

Zero Coupon Treasury Bonds: Markup included in price. Schwab acts as principal.

Certificates of Deposit: No commission. Schwab receives a fee from the depository institution.

Unit Investment Trusts: Sales charge; prospectuses available.

Schwab will not act as principal and agent simultaneously in the same transaction.

SOURCE: Reprinted by permission of Charles Schwab & Co., Inc.

FIGURE 6.3   K. Aufhauser & Company, Inc., Commission Schedule

Aufhauser

Commission Schedule 1:   2 cents per share, Listed or OTC, $34 minimum.

Commission Schedule 2:   US, Canadian, ADR, $24.99 minimum.

Shares	Price per Share							
	$1.	$5.	$10.	$20.	$30.	$50.	$75.	$100. +
1-399	$24.99	$24.99	$24.99	$24.99	$24.99	$24.99	$24.99	$24.99
400-499	$34.99	$34.99	$34.99	$34.99	$34.99	$34.99	$34.99	$34.99
500-599	$40.99	$40.99	$40.99	$40.99	$41.99	$41.99	$41.99	$41.99
600-699	$41.99	$46.00	$49.00	$49.00	$49.00	$49.00	$49.00	$49.00
700-799	$41.99	$47.99	$49.99	$50.99	$50.99	$52.99	$52.99	$52.90
800-899	$41.99	$53.00	$59.00	$59.00	$59.00	$59.00	$59.00	$59.00
900-999	$42.00	$53.00	$59.00	$63.00	$63.00	$63.00	$63.00	$63.00
1000	$42.00	$53.00	$59.00	$68.00	$70.00	$70.00	$70.00	$70.00

Each share above 1000 shares : . . . .   **Add 2 cents / 3 cents per share OTC / Listed to 1000 share base.**
Orders above 5000 shares: . . . .   2 cents OTC; 3 cents Listed.
Securities under $1.00 per share: . . . .   OTC $25 + 3%; Listed $25 + 3 cents.

Indicate your choice of Schedule 1 or 2 when submitting your application. (Default is 1.) You may occasionally change Schedules. The following apply to 1 and 2.

Exchange and Mailing Fee	$2.50 per executed order.
Bonds:	$5 per $1000 (min. $39).
No-Load Mutual Funds:	See verso.
Options:	$25 + $2.50 per contract or $2 (10th or more).
Sending securities in certificate form:	$15 per item (allow four weeks).
Checkwriting, Master Card	**Free** if equity > $10,000. **ProCash Plus** Account.
Gold and Silver (metals account agreement required)	2% of principle. Minimum $75. Storage: 1/4 % p.a.
Account opening fee	$20 (one time only, waived if initial equity > $10,000).
Option exercise; Short Sales (if less than 500 shares)	$.025/share; (Currency option: $250)
Late payment charges or inter-: .ount money journals	$15 per event
Returned Checks (any reason)	$20
Inactive fee: if less than 3 trades/yr. and we're custodian	$25.00. Doesn't apply to **ProCash Plus** accounts.
Cxl/Replace limit if order < 500 shares or 10 Contracts	20% surcharge.
Return of Securities not in deliverable form.	$15
Outward money transfers (wire or express service)	$20. (**No charge for checks by regular mail.**)
IRA's set up or maintenance	$35 annually ($50 termination charge).
Bond Redemption / Call	$5 / $20
Outgoing Account transfer fee	$50
Reorganization, Voluntary / Mandatory	$49 / $20
Foreign Securities Settlement (Not ADR's or Canadians)	$90.00/trade; $5/quarter/item custody.
Duplicate sending of confirms & statements	**Free** if you notify us in advance, otherwise $5 per month.
Change in Certificate Name/Account	$25.00/item (Legal , Gifts, Estates, Corporations).

(Effective 01/28/94)

SOURCE: K. Aufhauser & Company, Inc. Reprinted with permission.

Discount Brokerage Firms

AccuTrade
A TransTerra Co.
4211 South 102nd Street
Omaha, NE 68103-2227
402-331-2526
800-882-4887

K. Aufhauser & Company, Inc.
112 West 56th Street
New York, NY 10019
212-246-9431
800-368-3668

Brown & Company
20 Winthrop Square
Boston, MA 02110-1236
617-742-2600
800-343-4300

Fidelity Brokerage Services, Inc.
161 Devonshire Street
Boston, MA 02110
617-570-7000
800-225-1799

The R. J. Forbes Group, Inc.
150 Broad Hollow Road
Melville, NY 11747
516-549-7000
800-488-0090

Kennedy, Cabot & Co.
9470 Wilshire Boulevard
Beverly Hills, CA 90212
310-550-0711
800-252-0090

Barry Murphy & Co., Inc.
270 Congress Street
Boston, MA 02210
617-426-1770
800-221-2111

Andrew Peck Associates, Inc.
32 Broadway
New York, NY 10004
212-363-3770
800-221-5873

Prestige Status, Inc.
271-603 Grand Central Parkway
Floral Park, NY 11005
718-229-4500
800-782-8871

Quick & Reilly, Inc.
120 Wall Street
New York, NY 10005
212-943-8686
800-533-8161

Charles Schwab & Co., Inc.
101 Montgomery Street
San Francisco, CA
415-398-1000
800-342-5472

Security Brokerage Services, Inc.
5757 Wilshire Boulevard
Los Angeles, CA 90036
800-262-2294

Muriel Siebert and Co.
444 Madison Avenue
New York, NY 10022
212-644-2400
800-872-0711

Waterhouse Securities, Inc.
100 Wall Street
New York, NY 10005
800-765-5185

Jack White & Company
9191 Towne Centre Drive
San Diego, CA 92122
619-587-2000
800-233-3411

In Your Spare Time ...

Minimize your brokerage costs. In choosing a broker, determine the services you need and how much you are willing to pay. Generally, the less you pay, the fewer services you should expect to receive.

7

$ $

Reinvesting Dividends Automatically—DRIPs

$ $

Long-term stock market investors who are in the accumulation phase of their investment plans have always faced the problem of how to handle income. Dividends received by most individual shareholders are insufficient to buy additional shares economically. And yet, for buy-and-hold investors to maximize long-term total return, it is important that investment income be continuously reinvested. Happily, in many cases there is a simple solution: More than 750 companies offer dividend reinvestment plans (DRIPs). You will find a list of most companies offering these plans in Appendix B.

DRIPs are ideal for buy-and-hold investors and serve as a bonus for shareholders of companies with favorable long-term growth prospects. The plans are simple: The company applies the cash dividends of participating investors to the purchase of additional shares of company stock, instead of sending the dividends out in cash.

Participants enjoy several advantages:

- Dividend payments are put to work.
- Transaction costs are eliminated or held to a minimum.
- The additional shares are purchased gradually over time, an easy-to-effect form of constant dollar investing (investing a set amount of money periodically).

Special Features of DRIPs

Some company plans offer one or more of the following special features that make them even more attractive:

1. You may make optional cash payments to purchase additional shares through the plan.
2. Participants are permitted to receive cash dividends on some of their shares while reinvesting dividends on the remaining shares.
3. The prices of shares purchased under the plan are available at discounts, ranging from as little as 1 percent to as high as 10 percent.
4. Brokerage costs and service fees for share purchases are paid for by the company rather than the participant.

Most DRIPs require that you own shares registered in your name, that is, that you are a shareholder *of record*. That means your name must appear on the corporate records as the owner of the shares, rather than having the shares held in *street name*, the name of the broker or bank that may have bought the shares for you and who may be holding them for you. If your shares are held in street name, just ask your broker to transfer the shares to your own name.

Usually, a company will send you a DRIP prospectus or description and an authorization card once you become a registered shareholder. You can also call the company's stockholder relations department or the DRIP agent to request these items. The prospectus or description will provide information relating to eligibility requirements, plan options, costs, how and when purchases are made, how and when certificates will be issued and how you may withdraw from the plan.

Many companies will sell their shares directly to investors who do not yet own any stock. No broker is necessary for such transactions. These companies include Arrow Financial Corporation; Atlantic Energy, Inc.; Barnett Banks, Inc.; Central Vermont Public Service; COMSAT Corporation; Dial Corporation; DQE Company; Exxon Corporation; First Alabama Bancshares, Inc.; Johnson Controls, Inc.; Kellwood Company; Kerr-McGee Corporation; Mobil Corporation; SCANA Corporation; Summit Bancorp (NJ); Texaco, Inc.; and U.S. West, Inc.

How the Plans Work

DRIPs are part of a corporation's overall shareholder relations effort and basically serve existing shareholders. Some companies, such as utilities, have large investor relations departments and administer their own DRIPs; however, most companies hire an outside agent to serve as the administrator for the plan.

The plan administrator maintains records, sends account statements to participants, provides certificates for shares upon request and liquidates participants' shares when they leave the plan. The agent also buys company shares for the plan. When you join a plan, you will sign a card that authorizes the agent to act on your behalf to purchase shares.

Shares purchased under a DRIP are held by the plan and registered in the nominee name of the agent or plan trustee on the participants' behalf. An account is maintained for each participant under the plan. Most participants hold the company's shares in two places; your original shares will be held by you or in the custody of a brokerage firm or bank, and the shares purchased through the DRIP will be held by the plan.

Some plans permit participants to deposit certificates of shares registered in their own names into their DRIP account for safekeeping at no cost or for a small fee. These shares are then treated in the same way as the other shares in the participant's account, which means you can consolidate all your shares in one safe location.

Certificates for shares purchased under a plan are normally issued only upon written request, but often at no charge. They are also issued when a participating shareholder wants to terminate participation.

When companies have different kinds of stock outstanding, they may allow shareholders of several types of stock to participate. Reinvestment may sometimes be in stock of the same type, for instance, preferred reinvests in preferred. Or, perhaps dividends from all types may be reinvested into one type, for instance, all reinvestment is in common stock. The prospectus will indicate where your dividends will be reinvested.

Available Options

Partial reinvestment option.   Full reinvestment on all shares of stock registered in the participant's name is standard under the basic DRIP. But under some plans, you don't have to reinvest all dividends.

Instead, you may reinvest dividends on a portion of your registered shares, while receiving cash dividends on the remaining shares.

Optional cash payment. Many plans permit participants to buy additional shares by making cash payments directly to the plan, sometimes in large allowable amounts. This is a low-cost way to build a sizable holding in a company. The payments are optional and you are not committed to making periodic cash payments. However, for each payment made, there are minimums and usually a maximum as well. Because interest is not paid on payments received in advance, you need to find out approximately when the plan invests cash payments it receives.

Cash payment only option. Some companies allow registered shareholders to make cash investments without requiring them to reinvest dividends on the shares they are holding, although shareholders may do so if they wish.

Under most, but not all, DRIPs, dividends paid on shares that are purchased and held under the plan are automatically reinvested.

Costs of DRIPs

In general, the cost of participating in a dividend reinvestment plan is low, especially when compared to buying shares through a broker. Service charges and prorated brokerage commissions are the two forms of costs that plan participants may encounter. Service charges cover administrative costs and are usually made on each transaction. You can hold down costs by combining a cash payment with a dividend reinvestment transaction because charges are usually capped at a maximum of $3.00 to $5.00. When buying shares on the open market, the plan pays brokerage costs at institutional rates—considerably lower than the rate an individual investor would pay.

Many companies cover all the costs for share purchases from both optional cash payments and reinvested dividends. Some companies assess service charges, others prorate brokerage costs, and still others charge participants for both. The plan prospectus or description spells out which variations apply in your case.

When you terminate your participation, some DRIPs will sell plan shares for you if you wish, instead of sending you certificates. Your cost is usually any prorated brokerage commissions, a lower-cost choice than selling through a broker. Some plans will sell some of your plan shares for you, even when you are not terminating. Check the prospectus or plan description.

Purchasing Shares

The plan prospectus or description spells out the source of share purchases under a DRIP. The most common source is the *secondary market*, a securities exchange in which the shares are traded in the over-the-counter (OTC) market, or through negotiated transactions. In some cases the source may be the company itself, using authorized but unissued shares of common stock or shares held in the company's treasury. An advantage to a participant when shares are purchased directly from the company is that there are no brokerage expenses to prorate.

For the company, DRIPs that purchase shares directly from the company provide an inexpensive source of financing. The proceeds are often used for general corporate purposes. From the point of view of investors, however, new issues dilute existing shares, which can depress share prices.

The plan prospectus or description specifies when the agent purchases shares. Normally, this coincides with the dividend payment date, but some companies that permit participants to make cash investments have additional investment dates.

When shares are purchased in the open markets, most plans give some discretion to the agent on his or her buying. This is because a large purchase made on a single date could affect the share price. Usually under the plan all monies must be invested within 30 days. The share price for any participant is an average price of all shares purchased for that investment period.

The prospectus or plan description describes how the share price is determined when shares are purchased directly from the company. Usually it is based on an average of the high and low or the closing price for the stock as reported by a specified source.

Discounts on the share price are sometimes offered to participants in company plans, but with wide variations. In most cases discounts are available only on shares purchased with reinvested dividends. But some companies permit discounts on shares purchased both with reinvested dividends and with cash payments. A few companies offer discounts only on newly issued corporate shares and not on shares that are bought in the securities markets.

Taxation and DRIPs

No special tax advantages are connected with reinvestment plans. A taxable event occurs whether you receive your dividends in cash or have them reinvested. If your dividends are reinvested, the IRS considers the taxable amount to be equal to the fair market value of the shares acquired with the reinvested dividends. That value is the price on the exchange or market where shares are traded, not any discounted price. In addition, any brokerage commissions paid by the company in open market purchases are considered as dividend income to the participant.

At the time shares are sold, the tax basis is the fair market value as of the date the shares were acquired, plus any brokerage commissions paid by the company and treated as income to the participant. If you are a DRIP member, you will receive a 1099-DIV form each year from the company detailing dividends to be treated as income as reported to the IRS.

In Your Spare Time ...

Check to see if your dividend payments can be put to work by automatically purchasing additional shares. More than 750 companies now offer dividend reinvestment plans.

8

$ $ $ $ $ $ $ $ $ $ $ $ $ $ $ $ $ $ $ $

Investing in
Growth Stocks

$ $ $ $ $ $ $ $ $ $ $ $ $ $ $ $ $ $ $ $

Over the long term, investors who assume greater risk in their investments will be rewarded with better returns. This is a basic assumption that investors rely on in constructing their portfolios. Common stocks have historically delivered an average total return (income plus change in value) of approximately 10 percent, bonds have averaged about 5 percent, and cash reserves (Treasury bills, money market funds, etc.) a little less than 4 percent. An investor intent on building a fortune in securities should therefore concentrate on developing a well-diversified portfolio of common stocks whose value is expected to grow over the years.

Earnings growth is one of the most important criteria in equity investment. This chapter focuses on companies that have recorded superior per-share earnings gains in recent years and should continue to do so in the future. All the profiled companies have grown their earnings at a minimum 12 percent compound rate in the last five years and are considered by analysts to have superior growth prospects.

Such strong profit expectations do not come cheaply. Most of these stock issues trade at hefty premiums to the market's average PE ratio and can take a substantial hit if company earnings fall short of expectations or if other negative corporate developments occur. These *company risks* show why you need a well-diversified portfolio of common stocks.

As we have discussed, to ensure success in building a fortune, you must maintain a consistent program of constant dollar investing. Decide on an amount of money you can invest periodically, then discipline yourself to buy shares regularly: every month, every quarter, or every year. You will be glad you did. As you are able, gradually increase the amount of your periodic investments.

The Wm. Wrigley Jr. Company may seem an unlikely choice as my recommended stock for accumulation in a growth-oriented portfolio. But Wrigley is a good example of a financially strong company that has performed very well and has a bright outlook.

 A Stock Recommended for Accumulation

Wm. Wrigley Jr. Company
410 N. Michigan Avenue
Chicago, IL 60611
312-644-2121

Chairman & CEO: **William Wrigley**
Stockholders: 15,500   *Where stock trades:* NYSE
Employees: 6,700   *Symbol:* WWY

What the company does. The Wm. Wrigley Jr. Company is the world's largest manufacturer and seller of chewing gum, specialty gums and gum base. Its principal chewing gum brands are Doublemint, Spearmint, Juicy Fruit, Big Red, Extra, Orbit, and Freedent. A subsidiary, Amurol Products, makes novelty gums, including Bubble Tape, Big League Chew, and Hubba Bubba bubble gum. Foreign sales account for nearly half of the total.

The Wrigley spear has been associated with the established brands of Wrigley's chewing gum since it was first used in 1893 and is recognized by consumers worldwide. Wrigley brands are produced in 12 factories around the world and sold in more than 100 countries.

Comments. Years ago, when asked his advertising philosophy, the Wrigley founder replied, "Tell 'em quick, and tell 'em often." He continued, "You must have a good product in the first place, something people want. Explain to folks plainly and sincerely what you have to sell, do it in as few words as possible—and keep everlastingly coming after them." Mr. Wrigley had an unshakable faith in the products' quality and the power of advertising.

The company's consistent combination of quality products, effective advertising and reasonable pricing has resulted in nine consecutive years of record sales and earnings. In the highly competitive U.S. market, Wrigley brands' growth continues unabated. The company believes that the ability to attract new consumers to its products is as important as market growth, so it has restrained price increases.

The company began building additional manufacturing capacity in 1994 to meet future demand. Three new plants were in the works and a major addition was scheduled for the company's facility in Bischheim, France. Asian sales have been forging ahead, a result of expanding distribution in China beyond Guangdong Province, where Wrigley has its new plant. India may be the next bright spot, with the startup of a new plant there scheduled for the end of 1995.

Wrigley continues to make steady bottom-line progress, with increased shipments worldwide and selective price increases. The company's predominant domestic market share maintains its growth, despite increased advertising and new product introductions by rival gum makers. One reason has been Wrigley's conscious decision to keep the price of a single five-stick pack of each of its major brands— Doublemint, Spearmint, Juicy Fruit, and Big Red—at 25 cents since 1988, while competitors were raising their prices.

Past investment results.   The Wm. Wrigley Jr. Company has enjoyed consistent success in its goal to keep sales and earnings moving upward. Investors have been rewarded by the market's positive response. Figure 8.1 shows the results of an investment of $10,000 in Wrigley common stock in 1984 (at the average share price during the year), plus $3,000 each year thereafter in additional shares, for a total amount invested of $40,000. Annual dividends have been reinvested in additional shares. This would result in a holding of 7,632 shares by July 31, 1994, with a total value of $351,072. Brokerage commissions have not been considered. All numbers have been adjusted for a three-for-one stock split in 1986, a two-for-one split in 1988 and a three-for-one split in 1992.

Per share financial results.   Earnings per share and book value per share have risen steadily every year since 1984. The company has followed a policy of paying out approximately one-half of its earnings in dividends each year. PE ratios have increased steadily as the investment community bid the share price up. Figure 8.2 shows selected per share data from 1984 to 1993.

FIGURE 8.1   Wrigley: Results of Investing $10,000 in 1984 Plus $3,000 Per Year Thereafter

Year	Average Share Price	Annual Dividend	Shares Bought During Year	Shares Owned	Total Value
1984	2 ⅞	$556	3,671	3,671	$10,554
1985	4 ¼	624	852	4,523	19,222
1986	6 ⅝	949	596	5,119	33,913
1987	9 ⅛	1,433	485	5,604	51,136
1988	12 ¼	2,017	409	6,013	73,659
1989	14 ⅞	2,706	383	6,396	95,140
1990	17 ¼	3,262	363	6,759	116,592
1991	21 ¾	3,717	308	7,067	153,707
1992	31	4,452	240	7,307	226,517
1993	37 ¾	5,480	224	7,531	284,295
1994*	46	1,656	101	7,632	351,072

*Through July.

FIGURE 8.2   Wrigley Per Share Financial Results: 1984–1993

Year	Earnings	Sales	Average PE Ratio	Net Profit Margin %	Average Share Price
1984	.31	4.67	9	6.7	2 ⅞
1985	.34	4.90	11	7.0	4 ¼
1986	.43	5.51	16	7.7	6 ⅝
1987	.56	6.47	16	9.0	9 ⅛
1988	.73	7.48	16	9.8	12 ¼
1989	.90	8.42	16	10.7	14 ⅞
1990	1.00	9.45	17	10.6	17 ¼
1991	1.09	9.78	18	11.2	21 ¾
1992	1.27	11.02	22	11.5	31
1993	1.50	12.27	24	12.2	37 ¾

After hovering in the mid-to-high teens for most of the period, the PE ratio for Wrigley jumped into the twenties in 1992 and 1993. A high PE ratio indicates investor bullishness about a stock. Excessive optimism can lead to a price correction, both in a particular security and in the market as a whole. In early 1994 the median of estimated PE ratios of all stocks with earnings was 17.1. This exceptionally high multiple left the market vulnerable to a sharp correction, which then occurred.

Creating a Portfolio of Growth Stocks

To avoid the *company risk* of having all your money in one stock, hold at least ten stocks in your investment portfolio. Seek out the stocks of financially strong companies that have solid records of earnings growth and that are expected to continue to increase their earnings at above-average rates. If your objective is capital growth, consider investing in companies whose share earnings have compounded at a minimum 12 percent annual rate in recent years and can be expected to continue that performance. For conservative investment portfolios, companies should also exhibit characteristics of safety and price stability.

Following are several good-quality companies that meet these criteria. Many stocks have had solid past performance and a bright potential for the future that are not included in this list. But this list provides a group of companies that fit the criteria many prudent investors would want for a small portfolio of growth stocks that can be held without undue risk.

Company	Ticker Symbol	Annual Earnings Per Share Growth Last Five Years %	Average PE Ratio	10/12/94 Price
Cabletron Systems, Inc.	CS	57	20	47 ⅛
Cintas Corporation	CTAS	19	25	33 ½
Cracker Barrel Old Country Store, Inc.	CBRL	37	25	22 ½
Dollar General Corporation	DOLR	37	20	26 ⅝

Mark IV Industries, Inc.	IV	17	16	22
Michaels Stores, Inc.	MIKE	22	22	40 ¼
RoTech Medical Corporation	ROTC	34	18	26 ¾
Thermo Instrument Systems, Inc.	THI	24	24	30 ⅝
United HealthCare Corporation	UNH	86	29	54 ⅝
U.S. Healthcare, Inc.	USHC	75	18	46 ¾

About the Companies

Cabletron Systems, Inc. (NYSE) develops, manufactures and markets products that interconnect local area networks (LANs) and provides design, consulting, installation and support for LAN systems. Its products include electronic network interconnection equipment, high-speed Ethernet adapter cards for personal computers, network management software and LAN transmission media. International sales contribute about 27 percent of the total. Ten percent of sales are invested in research and development. (Employees: 3,600)

Cabletron has enjoyed strong demand for its Multi Media Access Centers (MMACs), intelligent hubs that connect dissimilar local area networks. Numerous domestically installed personal computers (PCs) remain unlinked to a network, indicating that strong U.S. growth prospects still exist. The relatively untapped markets of South America and the Pacific Rim offer additional expansion possibilities.

Long-term prospects appear bright. With the continued proliferation of networks, earnings growth for the company's existing products should remain strong throughout the 1990s. The company's next generation hub, the MMAC-Plus, incorporates bridging and routing capabilities and offers "SecureFast Packet Switching." It can connect unlike technologies as a stand-along unit and should be a sizable source of income in the next few years.

Figure 8.3 illustrates the company's financial results from 1989 to 1993. No dividends have been paid.

FIGURE 8.3   Cabletron Systems Per Share Financial Results: 1989–1993

Year	Earnings	Sales	Average PE Ratio	Net Profit Margin %	Average Share Price
1989	.87	3.99	24	21.3	13
1990	1.35	6.48	22	19.9	18 ⅛
1991	2.08	10.35	21	20.0	45 ⅜
1992	2.97	14.80	21	20.0	63 ¾
1993	4.20	20.95	24	19.9	96 ¾

Cintas Corporation (Nasdaq) designs, manufactures and distributes uniforms through its rental and national account sales divisions. The company also rents dust mops, entrance mats and wiping cloths and offers service programs including cleaning, repair and replacement. Cintas has distribution centers in Cincinnati, Houston and Los Angeles and manufacturing facilities in Owingsville, Clay City, and Mt. Vernon, Kentucky. (Employees: 7,800)

Internal expansion has driven Cintas Corporation's earnings in the past and should continue to do so. Cintas is the second largest renter of uniforms in the United States and its growth prospects remain bright as the company seeks out new clients and new markets. The company estimates that only one in seven work uniforms is rented and has been successful in selling the cost and service benefits of its uniform programs to clients who have never used a uniform rental service. Roughly two-thirds of the company's new accounts have come this way. These new accounts have the added benefit of being less susceptible to price competition than established customers who may be subject to aggressive bidding from competitors.

Cintas actively seeks acquisition candidates. Roughly 700 small, independent garment-services operators account for half of the industry's $3.5 billion annual revenues. As a leader in the uniform rental industry, Cintas will continue to play an active role in further consolidating this business. Cintas will likely continue to acquire operations that have three to five million dollars in annual revenues, thereby strengthening its position in existing markets or offering quick access to new markets.

FIGURE 8.4 Cintas Corporation Per Share Financial Results: 1984–1994

Year	Earnings	Sales	Average PE Ratio	Net Profit Margin %	Average Share Price
1984	$.20	$ 2.13	18	8.8	3 ⅞
1985	.24	2.76	19	8.6	5 ⅞
1986	.29	3.16	24	9.1	8 ½
1987	.36	4.17	25	8.5	10 ½
1988	.43	5.14	24	8.4	10
1989	.53	5.74	21	9.1	12 ⅞
1990	.63	6.69	22	9.4	15 ⅛
1991	.74	7.43	23	9.7	20 ⅞
1992	.79	8.69	32	9.1	27 ⅞
1993	.97	9.72	28	9.9	29 ⅜
1994	1.14	11.20	26	10.1	33

Figure 8.4 illustrates the company's per share financial results from 1984 to 1994. It's fiscal year ends May 31. (IPO: August, 1983)

Cracker Barrel Old Country Store, Inc. (Nasdaq) operates 178 combination restaurants and gift shops in 20 southern and midwestern states. The restaurants feature an old country store motif and moderate prices. Adjoining gift shops sell a variety of early American reproductions and food items. Almost all sites are owned, and nearly all units are located along interstate highways. Restaurants account for about 80 percent of revenues, with the balance coming from the gift shops (which have lower gross profit margins). (Employees: 14,500)

Cracker Barrel per-share profits have increased by more than 20 percent each year since 1986. Fiscal 1994 results achieved this standard despite severe flooding in Georgia, where 11 locations were affected. Analysts believe the favorable trend can continue. Results should be positively impacted by the opening of 36 additional Cracker Barrel Old Country Store locations in fiscal 1995.

The company is sticking with its proven strategy, and expansion will likely be limited to southern and midwestern locales along interstate highways. Cost control should not be a problem because the company owns virtually all its sites. Results late in the decade may also be boosted by a new concept the company is already testing, Cracker Barrel Corner Market. The Corner Market combines the company's hot and chilled cuisine with carry-out service. If successful, it should provide added expansionary flexibility.

The PE ratio on the common stock has narrowed considerably from the peak levels in 1992 and 1993, possibly reflecting concerns that the company may run into trouble in the near future. Investors with a long-term view, however, may have the opportunity to realize above-average capital appreciation from recent price levels.

Cracker Barrel paid dividends of one cent per share each year until 1992, then increased to two cents per share in 1993 and 1994. Figure 8.5 illustrates the company's per share financial results from 1984 to 1994. (IPO: November, 1981)

Dollar General Corporation (Nasdaq) operates a chain of about 1,900 self-service discount stores, located primarily in rural areas in 24 states in the South, East and Midwest. All stores are leased and average 5,700 square feet. The company also wholesales to 14 franchised stores, which accounts for 2 percent of total sales. Soft goods amount to 39 percent of sales; housewares, 27 percent; health and beauty aids, 29 percent; and shoes, 5 percent. The company's merchandise primarily consists of basic nonfood necessities, mostly priced at $1 to $20. (Employees: 10,000)

Dollar General has developed a successful niche in discount retailing. Despite numerous competitive discount-store openings and a rather dull retail environment since 1990, the company has posted double-digit same-store sales gains in each of the last three years. Two key factors behind Dollar General's success are its relatively low prices for basic nonfood necessities, which closely match those of Walmart, the industry leader, and the convenient location of its stores to its low-income and fixed-income customer base. The company has recently accelerated the annual pace of store openings and also increased the average size of its new store to 6,500 square feet. Analysts expect sales to advance by more than 20 percent in each of the next few years.

Most of the company's new store expansion in the next few years will be concentrated within existing markets. Management studies indicate that Dollar General's current 24-state marketing territory is

FIGURE 8.5   Cracker Barrel Per Share Financial Results: 1984–1994

Year	Earnings	Sales	Average PE Ratio	Net Profit Margin %	Average Share Price
1984	$.09	$1.78	21	4.8	3
1985	.06	1.66	21	3.6	1 ¼
1986	.09	1.99	15	4.5	1 ⅝
1987	.11	2.43	16	4.7	2 ⅛
1988	.18	3.07	13	5.8	2 ⅞
1989	.25	3.59	15	6.4	4 ⅝
1990	.32	4.74	18	6.8	6 ¾
1991	.44	5.57	22	7.6	14 ⅜
1992	.61	7.31	31	8.5	24 ½
1993	.78	8.69	35	8.8	28 ⅜
1994	.94	10.60	28	8.9	23 ¼

far from saturated and that planned store additions will leverage fixed advertising and distribution costs.

Dollar General pays out about 16 percent of its net profits in dividends and has been increasing its dividend payout each year since 1991. Figure 8.6 illustrates the company's per share financial results from 1984 to 1993.

Mark IV Industries, Inc. (NYSE) is a diversified manufacturer that has several business segments. The Power Transfer and Fluid Handling division is involved with industrial hoses and automotive parts. Mass Transit and Traffic handles electrical controls and passenger information systems. Professional Audio makes sound systems and microphones. Part of the company's growth has come from the acquisition of companies that complement existing business components. Foreign sales account for about 35 percent of the total. (Employees: 12,500)

Mark IV's growth has been fueled primarily by domestic operations. Broad economic trends work in the company's favor, as both sales and earnings remain strong. Environmental concerns are resulting in an increase in legislation that should help continue strong demand for both the company's vapor recovery hoses and underground fuel storage systems. Foreign markets are expected to positively affect Mark IV's future

FIGURE 8.6 Dollar General Corporation Per Share Financial Results: 1984–1993

		Average			
		PE	Net Profit	Average	
Year	**Earnings**	**Sales**	**Ratio**	**Margin %**	**Share Price**
1984	$.41	$ 9.53	11	4.3	4 ⅞
1985	.35	11.58	23	3.1	8 ⅝
1986	.09	10.67	77	0.8	6 ¾
1987	.13	11.85	29	1.1	3 ⅝
1988	.20	12.52	14	1.6	3 ⅛
1989	.25	12.52	15	2.0	3 ⅞
1990	.30	13.27	11	2.2	3 ½
1991	.42	15.12	16	2.8	6 ⅜
1992	.67	18.00	17	3.9	12 ⅜
1993	.90	21.48	21	4.3	20 ⅝

sales and earnings. The company is committed to broadening its revenue base through product development and overseas expansion.

The company sees substantial opportunity in the transportation market. In addition to the tag and reader equipment being developed for the E-Z Pass system, Mark IV also provides various products, such as door and lighting systems, to manufacturers of public transportation systems. Growth prospects seem favorable as order backlogs have been hitting record levels.

Over the past ten years, investors have received above-average total returns on their shares. Analysts believe this will be repeated in the next several years, based on Mark IV's increasing presence in higher-growth foreign markets. The company's goal is to have a 50/50 sales mix (foreign/domestic) by the end of the 1990s.

Figure 8.7 illustrates per share financial results of Mark IV Industries, Inc. from 1984 to 1993. All numbers have been adjusted for three-for-two stock splits in 1984, 1985, 1986, 1987, 1989 and 1992.

Michaels Stores, Inc. (Nasdaq) owns and operates a chain of specialty retail stores that feature a wide selection of home decoration and arts and crafts items, including picture-framing materials and services; silk, dried flowers and related floral items; hobby and art supplies; needle-crafts; and seasonal and holiday merchandise. The company

FIGURE 8.7   Mark IV Industries Per Share Financial Results: 1984–1993

Year	Earnings	Sales	Average PE Ratio	Net Profit Margin %	Average Share Price
1984	$.15	$ 2.15	5	7.2	¼
1985	.24	3.39	9	5.7	2 ⅛
1986	.42	11.93	11	3.5	4 ½
1987	.55	12.98	9	3.9	4 ⅞
1988	.41	23.90	9	1.7	3 ⅞
1989	.82	30.90	6	3.3	6
1990	.82	37.75	7	2.7	5 ¾
1991	.84	27.37	10	2.7	7 ¾
1992	1.01	28.97	13	3.8	12 ¾
1993	1.09	29.14	16	4.1	19 ⅞

owns and operates stores in 32 primarily southern states, from California to the Carolinas. (Employees: 10,000)

Michaels Stores recently purchased its largest competitor, Leewards Creative Crafts, which gave Michaels access to the Northeast market, where about thirty Leewards' stores operate. Analysts believe Michaels can significantly improve the sales and profitability of the acquired units because a typical Michaels retail operation of similar size generates much higher sales per square foot, due to pricing and better merchandising, than that of Leewards. Further, Michaels' large buying power enables it to buy merchandise at better prices, leading to better profit margins.

The company's strategy has been to grow its store count by about 20 to 25 percent each year, but this is expected to slow to about 15 percent in 1995 so that the Leewards acquisition can be fully integrated. Subsequent to 1995, the rate should return to normal levels.

The company continues to show excellent operating results. Gross margins have been expanding due to higher discounts from suppliers based on volume increases. Comparable-store sales have increased at a rate in the high single-digits and analysts expect margins to remain high. Michaels' strong hold on its markets, and its efforts to build on this dominance, should propel sales and earnings at a double-digit pace for the next several years.

Figure 8.8 illustrates per share financial results of Michaels Stores, Inc. from 1984 to 1993. (IPO: March, 1984)

FIGURE 8.8 Michaels Stores Per Share Financial Results: 1984–1993

Year	Earnings	Sales	Average PE Ratio	Net Profit Margin %	Average Share Price
1984	$.02	$7.23	NMF	0.2	3 ⅝
1985	.19	8.24	30	1.9	5 ¼
1986	.35	12.21	16	2.9	5 ⅞
1987	.50	17.51	12	2.9	5 ⅝
1988	.50	25.75	12	2.1	5 ¾
1989	.25	29.50	28	0.9	7 ⅝
1990	.57	36.61	8	1.7	4 ¾
1991	.87	27.29	12	2.6	10 ⅜
1992	1.21	29.94	19	4.1	25
1993	1.52	37.11	20	4.2	32 ⅛

RoTech Medical Corporation (Nasdaq) provides home infusion therapy, home respiratory care, chemotherapy, parenteral nutrition therapy, enteral nutrition therapy, antibiotic therapy, pain management therapy, and other outpatient medical services and equipment to a patient base referred to the company by primary-care physicians in smaller cities and rural areas throughout the South. (Employees: 400)

After adding 63 offices in the past year, RoTech operates 134 offices in 21 states, focused in small cities and rural areas. The company is expected to continue its aggressive growth strategy. By concentrating on rural territories, the company capitalizes on markets overlooked by many of its larger competitors, who favor metropolitan centers because of their large customer bases. Companies targeted for acquisition by RoTech usually offer only one of the firm's lines of services. RoTech then adds its other service line to the product mix to increase the acquired firm's profitability. The company has also begun to buy practices from primary care physicians in areas where it already has a presence so that the company can set up integrated services networks to further boost its sales and earnings.

RoTech shares appear to be a timely selection for growth-minded investors. The company has completed four consecutive years of double-digit earnings growth and analysts expect this trend to continue for the next several years. Investors with long-term investment horizons will likely see above-average gains for the balance of the 1990s.

FIGURE 8.9   RoTech Medical Corporation Per Share Financial Results:
1986–1994

Year	Earnings	Sales	Average PE Ratio	Net Profit Margin %	Average Share Price
1986	.09	1.51	49	6.0	4 ⅜
1987	.14	2.05	39	6.6	4 ⅞
1988	.00	2.08	NMF	NMF	3 ⅝
1989	.17	2.97	13	5.9	2 ⅜
1990	.30	3.75	11	8.1	5 ½
1991	.43	4.09	16	8.9	11 ⅞
1992	.60	6.05	22	9.9	14 ¾
1993	.77	6.68	16	10.6	12 ½

NMF = Not meaningful

Figure 8.9 illustrates per share financial results of RoTech Medical
Corporation from 1986 (its first full year in public hands) to 1993.
(IPO: December, 1985)

Thermo Instrument Systems, Inc. (AMEX) manufactures and
markets instruments used for elemental analysis and the detection and
measurement of toxic substances, nuclear radioactivity and air pollu-
tion. Services include environmental studies, water resource management, nuclear contamination monitoring and analyzing soil, air and
water for hazardous wastes. (Employees: 4,000)

The company has formed a new subsidiary, ThermoSpectra, that
contains three businesses outside its mainstream analytical and process
control businesses. Under a separate management team, the operation
will work on building Thermo Instrument's nondestructive analysis
instruments and high-speed digital processing businesses. This will
allow Thermo Instrument's management to concentrate on its original
goals as analytical instrumentation business.

Near-term earnings of Thermo Instrument should be boosted as a
result of ongoing efforts to integrate and streamline several recent
acquisitions, including radiation safety measurement, process controls
and measurement and lab instrumentation businesses. In addition,
continued economic expansion ought to help demand for the company's product lines.

FIGURE 8.10   Thermo Instrument Systems Per Share Financial Results:
1986–1993

Year	Earnings	Sales	Average PE Ratio	Net Profit Margin %	Average Share Price
1986	$.20	$ 2.74	20	7.2	4
1987	.26	3.44	18	7.5	4 ½
1988	.35	4.21	15	8.3	6 ¼
1989	.44	4.67	18	8.9	10 ½
1990	.49	7.27	19	6.6	9 ¾
1991	.61	7.85	23	7.3	13 ¼
1992	.77	9.49	22	7.8	18 ¾
1993	.94	12.64	29	7.7	28 ⅞

Long-term prospects look promising as well. The company allocates a sizable budget for research and development, keeping the firm's prolific product pipeline flowing and sales rising. Additional acquisitions are likely and can be easily financed from the company's strong cash flow from operations and substantial cash balance. Earnings growth over the next several years should produce above-average appreciation for the common shares.

Figure 8.10 illustrates per share financial results of Thermo Instrument Systems, Inc. from 1986 to 1993. The company has not paid any cash dividends. (IPO: August 1986)

United HealthCare Corporation (NYSE) owns 11 health maintenance organizations (HMOs) and manages an additional 10. The company also provides specialty services, including prescription drug benefit programs, through wholly owned subsidiaries. In 1993, United Health-Care had 2.437 million members enrolled in HMOs and 33.6 members enrolled in special services. Medicare accounted for 5 percent of HMO membership and 5 percent of revenues in 1993. (Employees: 6,500)

United HealthCare's stated policy is to increase membership in existing and new markets through acquisitions. A deal to acquire GenCare Health Systems was expected to be approved by stockholders in 1995. GenCare is the largest health-care provider in St. Louis, with about 194,000 HMO members and another 98,000 preferred provider organization (PPO) members. This, combined with United Health-

FIGURE 8.11   United HealthCare Per Share Financial Results: 1984–1994

Year	Earnings	Sales	Average PE Ratio	Net Profit Margin %	Average Share Price
1984	$.05	$.49	21	9.0	1 ⅛
1985	.04	2.11	54	2.0	2
1986	.04	3.46	67	1.2	2 ⅞
1987	d.01	6.81	NMF	NMF	1 ½
1988	.04	6.71	24	0.7	1 ⅛
1989	.15	5.18	15	3.4	2 ⅛
1990	.30	5.45	12	5.7	4
1991	.60	6.55	19	9.1	12 ¼
1992	.83	10.10	27	8.2	23 ⅛
1993	1.24	16.02	24	7.9	29 ⅜

d = deficit; NMF = Not meaningful

Care's own 128,000-member health plan, will give the company more than a 50 percent share of the St. Louis market.

Earnings should to grow rapidly in the near-term. Enrollment in the company's HMOs and lives covered by the specialty operations have continued to build. In addition, the medical loss ratio (medical expenses as a percentage of revenues), already one of the best in the HMO industry, continues to improve. Long-term prospects are also promising. The company has a very large cash position, facilitating future acquisitions. Analysts see sales and earnings rising quickly over the next several years.

Figure 8.11 illustrates per share financial results of United Health-Care Corporation from 1984 to 1993. The numbers have been adjusted for two-for-one stock splits in 1992 and 1994. The company paid dividends of one cent per share in 1990 to 1992, two cents in 1993, and three cents in 1994. (IPO: October, 1984)

U.S. Healthcare, Inc. (Nasdaq) owns and operates health maintenance organizations (HMOs) in Pennsylvania, New Jersey, Delaware, New York, Connecticut, Massachusetts, Maryland and New Hampshire. The company had about 1.5 million members enrolled in the HMOs in December 1993 and also provides management services to other health organizations. (Employees: 3,400)

U.S. Healthcare's medical loss ratio improved by nearly five percentage points—to 69.9 percent—in 1994 over 1993, primarily due to a significant decline in average hospital use by patients.

Earnings should continue to grow rapidly as a result of new markets and expanded product lines. The company has already started to sell its products in Georgia, a market where HMO penetration is relatively low, and analysts look for quick penetration given U.S. Healthcare's powerful presence and underwriting expertise. Further membership gains are likely to come from a new point of system product (POS), which allows HMO members to receive treatment from outside the company's network of providers. The POS plan is now being offered in all of the company's markets except Connecticut.

U.S. Healthcare shares appear attractive for long-term investors. The company's earnings are rising rapidly and no slowdown is expected. A strong balance sheet and strong growth potential in new and existing markets lead analysts to look for earnings growth at an average annual rate of 20 percent for most of the 1990s.

Figure 8.12 illustrates per share financial results of U.S. Healthcare from 1984 to 1993. The numbers have been adjusted for three-for-two stock splits, twice in 1984 and 1985 and again in 1991, 1992 and 1994. The company has been paying dividends since 1985, and the dividend yield is currently about 2 percent.

FIGURE 8.12   U.S. Healthcare Per Share Results: 1984–1993

Year	Earnings	Sales	Average PE Ratio	Net Profit Margin %	Average Share Price
1984	$.07	$ 1.29	29	5.3	2
1985	.15	2.13	31	6.8	4 ⅜
1986	.21	3.14	24	6.8	5
1987	.01	4.14	NMF	0.2	2 ¾
1988	.04	4.80	53	0.7	1 ⅞
1989	.18	6.42	18	2.8	3 ⅛
1990	.48	8.39	10	5.8	5 ⅛
1991	.93	10.77	14	8.8	13 ¾
1992	1.23	13.57	23	9.1	25 ⅝
1993	1.84	16.33	17	11.3	32 ½

NMF = Not meaningful

In Your Spare Time ...

Concentrate on developing a well-diversified portfolio of growth stocks. Long-term investors who assume greater risk in their investments by buying common stocks can expect to be rewarded with better returns.

9

$ $ $ $ $ $ $ $ $ $ $ $ $ $ $ $ $ $ $ $

Investing in
Stocks Worldwide

$ $ $ $ $ $ $ $ $ $ $ $ $ $ $ $ $ $ $ $

The U.S. market now accounts for about only a third of the world's total stock market value. So if you restrict yourself to that market, you ignore the growth potential of the other two-thirds, mainly Europe and Asia. An individual investor easily can buy shares in many companies headquartered outside the United States without dealing directly with foreign exchanges.

Investors who want to participate in foreign-domiciled company investments can buy *American depositary receipts* (ADRs, also are called *American depositary shares*) in U.S. markets, instead of buying shares in overseas markets. ADRs are traded regularly on the NYSE, the AMEX and the Nasdaq. ADRs are receipts for shares of foreign-based corporations, and they are held in American bank vaults. Three American banks—the Bank of New York, Citibank and J.P. Morgan—are the major depository institutions for ADRs. They provide custody of the foreign shares, change dividends into dollars and help distribute company reports.

An ADR owner in the United States is entitled to the same dividends and capital gains accruing to a shareholder who purchases shares on an exchange in the home country of the company. Each ADR represents a specified number of common shares of the company it represents. Quoted prices reflect the latest currency exchange rates, for ADRs are denominated in U.S. dollars. You can find ADR prices in the stock listings of *The New York Times, The Wall Street Journal* and other newspapers, as well as in electronic databases.

Foreign corporations with ADRs normally are well-established and financially stable companies with international operations. In many cases you will be familiar with them because their products and services are offered in the United States. Altogether, some 1,000 ADRs are traded on U.S. exchanges, with 10 to 15 new ADRs added each month. More than 250 trade on the NYSE and the AMEX, with the largest number listed on the AMEX. For a complete list of ADRs and how they work, see *The McGraw-Hill Handbook of American Depository Receipts* (McGraw-Hill, Montery Ave., Blue Ridge Summit, PA 17294; 800-233-1128).

In selecting shares of foreign corporations, evaluate ADRs the same way you would shares of U.S. companies. Consider such issues as your personal investment objective, the relative safety of the company and whether the timing is right in terms of the particular industry and company. If you own mutual funds, a simple way to see what the pros are buying is to check your mutual fund report and see what its largest international holdings are.

Morningstar, an independent financial-information company, has developed *Morningstar ADRs*, a detailed, systematic approach to researching and reporting on international equities (225 W. Wacker Dr., Chicago, Il 60606; 800-876-5005). The bi-weekly reports cover 700 stocks representing 30 countries. A three-month trial subscription is available.

ADRs represent virtually every international industry group. One industry with good potential for long-term capital appreciation in the 1990s is telecommunications.

 An ADR Recommended for Accumulation

Reuters Holdings, PLC
85 Fleet Street
London EC4P 4AJ, England
U.S. Address:1700 Broadway
New York, NY 10019
212-603-3500

CEO: Peter Job
Shareholders: 16,600   *Where ADR trades:* Nasdaq
Employees: 11,300   *Symbol:* RTRSY

What the company does. This 142-year-old company is the world's largest electronic publisher. On more than 223,000 screens in 150 countries, Reuters provides business news, market prices and historical data on currencies, securities and futures through a global communications network. Using Reuters software, the company's customers can create their own displays and analyze market trends, increasingly on the computer of their choice. Media customers buy Reuters news, graphics, still pictures and news video for their publications or for their radio and television programs. Sales in Europe, the Middle East and Africa account for 58 percent of the total. Of the balance, 21 percent comes from Asia and the Pacific Rim and 21 percent from the Americas.

Comments. Growth in Reuters' revenues and earnings have continued their impressive momentum. The company's strong gains come from its underlying growth plus acquisitions. Recent costs have risen at a slightly faster pace than sales, primarily due to a larger number of employees and increased development spending. Nevertheless, earnings per ADR have swelled more than revenues due to a share buyback program in 1993.

Transaction products, which account for about 21 percent of sales, will continue to play an important role in Reuter's future. The company's Instinet electronic brokerage system has had superior growth—recently contributing 8 percent of total revenue, an increase from 5 percent in 1993. Also, the Dealing 2000 electronic foreign exchange system reached its target of 5,000 trades daily in early 1994 and has continued to improve. Reuters' Globex futures trading system, while having sharply higher sales in 1994 compared to 1993, is a problem, however. Despite the addition of the French future exchange to the system, the company does not have the volumes or the number of new partners it expected. Looking ahead, the transaction products unit, especially Instinet and Dealing 2000, will likely contribute significantly to revenue growth. Reuters ADRs look attractive for long-term investors as part of a diversified portfolio.

Past investment results. Reuters shares have been strong long-term performers, both in capital appreciation and dividend growth. Had you invested $10,000 in Reuters ADRs in 1984 (at the average price the shares traded at during the year), reinvested dividends and added $3,000 more each year to purchase additional shares, you would have owned 4,592 shares with a value of $200,335 by September, 1994. Your total out-of-pocket cost would have been $40,000 (not including brokerage commissions).

Figure 9.1 shows the results of such an investment in Reuters ADRs from 1984 to September 30, 1994. The numbers have been adjusted to reflect two-for-one ADR splits in 1988 and 1994.

Reuters has proved to be an outstanding holding for long-term investors and a good illustration of the first-class opportunities that are available overseas. (IPO: June, 1984)

Per share financial results. Since its IPO, Reuters has enjoyed steady growth in both revenues and earnings. Annual sales of $363 million in 1984 expanded to more than $3 billion in 1994. Earnings during this period grew from $48 million to nearly $500 million. The company pays out about 30 percent of its profits in dividends to shareholders. Because dividends were not reduced when earnings slowed in 1992 and 1993, the percentage in those years was about 50 percent. Figure 9.2 illustrates Reuters' annual per ADR financial results for fiscal years 1984–1993. The numbers have been adjusted for the stock splits in 1988 and 1994.

Other ADRs with Long-Term Growth Potential

Following are several companies that appear to have solid potential for growth in sales and earnings. The emphasis is on telecommunications companies. Markets for these firms are expanding more quickly than the global economy. Mobile telecommunications are expanding even faster. Several of the companies reviewed are competing globally for contracts to install wired and wireless systems. Their biggest target is China, the world's fastest-growing economy. China plans to spend nearly $100 billion through the end of the 1990s to expand and modernize its antiquated telecommunications system. Most communications

FIGURE 9.1   Reuters ADRs: Results of Investing $10,000 in 1984 Plus
$3,000 Per Year Thereafter

Year	Average Share Price	Annual Dividend	Shares Bought During Year	Total Shares Owned	Value of Shares Owned
1984	4 ¾	$126	2,131	2,131	$10,126
1985	6 ⅝	213	485	2,616	17,330
1986	10 ⅛	444	340	2,956	29,931
1987	16 ½	827	232	3,188	52,601
1988	13 ½	1,052	300	3,488	47,090
1989	20 ½	1,465	217	3,705	75,969
1990	25 ⅞	1,778	184	3,889	100,645
1991	23 ½	2,061	215	4,104	96,452
1992	30 ⅞	2,626	182	4,286	132,337
1993	35 ⅛	2,828	165	4,451	156,375
1994*	43 ⅝	3,160	141	4,592	200,335

*Through September

FIGURE 9.2   Reuters PLC Per ADR Financial Results: 1984–1994

Year	Earnings	Sales	Average PE Ratio	Net Profit Margin %	Average Price Per Share
1984	$.19	$1.38	25	13.2	4 ¾
1985	.27	2.29	24	11.8	6 ⅝
1986	.41	3.32	26	12.3	10 ⅛
1987	.63	5.85	27	10.7	16 ½
1988	.83	6.58	16	12.6	13 ½
1989	.98	6.65	20	14.2	20 ½
1990	1.37	9.14	19	14.4	25 ⅞
1991	1.42	9.44	16	14.5	23 ½
1992	1.29	8.12	24	15.3	30 ⅞
1993	1.40	9.76	24	13.8	35 ⅛

between China and the rest of the world pass through Hong Kong Telecommunication's transmission facilities. This company and its parent, Cable & Wireless, seem to have the edge to develop telecommunications systems for China.

Company	Ticker Symbol	PE Ratio	10/12/94 Price
Cable & Wireless PLC	CWP	19	20 ⅛
ENDESA	ELE	12	43 ¼
Ericsson (L.M.) Telephone AB	ERICY	13	57
Hong Kong Telecommunications Ltd.	HKT	21	21 ⅜
Novo-Nordisk	NVO	15	22 ⅜
Telephonos de Mexico, S.A.	TMX	10	63
Vodafone Group PLC	VOD	23	34

About the Companies

Cable & Wireless PLC (NYSE) is a global telecommunications company with interests in local telephone companies. The enterprise operates worldwide digital radio and fiber optic submarine cables and has major ownership interests in other companies. It owns 58 percent of Hong Kong Telecommunications Ltd. and 80 percent of Mercury Communications, the second biggest provider of telecommunications services in the United Kingdom. Approximately 45 percent of Cable & Wireless' revenues come from the Asia and Pacific regions, 32 percent from Europe, and 18 percent from the Western Hemisphere. The rest of the world contributes the remaining 5 percent. (Employees: 41,348)

Cable & Wireless is looking for global alliances. The company has had discussions with the regional Bell companies, which have been seeking partners to break into the U.S. long-distance market. C&W also is trying to line up consortia to compete with European national telecommunication monopolies. Despite weakness in the ADRs in 1994, analysts believe the shares offer attractive long-term capital appreciation potential.

Dividends amounting to 37 percent of net profits were paid to shareholders in 1993. Current yield on the ADRs is about 2 percent. Figure 9.3 shows the company's per ADR financial results 1984–1993. Numbers have been adjusted for two-for-one stock splits in 1986 and 1993.

FIGURE 9.3   Cable & Wireless PLC Per ADR Financial Results:
1984–1994

Year	Earnings	Sales	Dividend	Net Profit Margin %	Average PE Ratio	Average Price Per ADR
1984	$.29	$1.77	$.10	13.8	12	3 ½
1985	.43	1.97	.15	20.5	14	5 ⅝
1986	.46	2.85	.21	16.1	17	7 ¼
1987	.48	3.45	.25	13.7	20	10 ⅛
1988	.37	3.78	.27	9.6	28	9 ¾
1989	.53	5.37	.25	9.7	24	12
1990	.74	6.35	.31	11.6	18	13 ⅛
1991	.79	7.68	.35	10.3	18	14 ½
1992	.63	7.98	.34	7.9	24	16 ⅛
1993	.83	9.68	.37	8.6	24	20

ENDESA (NYSE) is the largest producer of electricity in Spain, accounting for about 35 percent of the total electric energy produced there. The ENDESA group was formed in 1983 with the consolidation of ENHER, GESA, UNELCO and other energy-related companies. In 1985, the company also purchased interests in three nuclear generating facilities. Fossil fuel is the source of 70 percent of the company's power. Of the balance, 27 percent is nuclear and 3 percent hydroelectric. Approximately 75 percent of the company's shares are held by the Instituto Nacional de Industria (INI). (Employees: 15,700)

Analysts believe this utility has many more years of above average expansion as a result of its strong position in an economy with good growth prospects and a favorable regulatory climate. The ADRs appear to be a good holding for long-term investors. Management has indicated that it will recommend dividend increases at a rate slightly less than gains in earnings, suggesting hikes in the high single digits.

Dividends amounting to 32 percent of net profits were paid to shareholders in 1993. The current yield on the ADRs is about 2.4 percent. Figure 9.4 illustrates the company's per ADR financial results 1988–1993. (IPO: June 1988)

L.M. Ericsson Telephone AB (Nasdaq) is a major manufacturer of public, private, mobile and defense telecommunications systems. The company has plants and investments in its base, Sweden, and 13 other

FIGURE 9.4   ENDESA Per ADR Financial Results: 1988–1993

Year	Earnings	Sales	Dividend	Average PE Ratio	Average Price Per ADR
1988	$2.27	$15.87	$.80	6	13 ⅜
1989	2.60	19.13	1.14	7	18 ¼
1990	3.38	22.82	.90	6	21 ⅝
1991	3.92	27.64	1.05	6	24 ¾
1992	3.66	24.06	1.05	9	31 ½
1993	3.40	20.23	1.05	11	40 ⅛

countries. Ericsson is part of a joint venture with General Electric Company in cellular equipment. About 10 percent of sales come from Sweden, 46 percent from other European countries, 12 percent from the U.S. and Canada, 11 percent from Latin America, 13 percent from Asia, and 8 percent from the rest of the world. (Employees: 70,000)

Ericsson continues to post significant earnings gains, which are driven by volume growth in mobile telephone equipment, well-managed expenses and strong order bookings. The company is well-positioned in digital cellular systems, holding more than a 50 percent share for wireless equipment. Equipment demand has been growing at 45 to 50 percent each year. With a global penetration rate of less than 1 percent, Ericsson's prospects in this area are strong. The U.S. and Japan are the company's most important mobile communications markets. Ericsson can produce cellular systems that conform to all the major global standards, as a result of its heavy investments in research and development, currently at about 16 percent of sales.

Dividends amounting to 27 percent of net profits were paid to shareholders in 1993. Current yield on the ADRs is about 2 percent. Figure 9.5 shows the company's per ADR financial results 1984–1993. Numbers have been adjusted for a five-for-one stock split in 1990.

Hong Kong Telecommunications Ltd. (NYSE) was formed in 1987 when Hong Kong Telephone Company and a subsidiary of Cable & Wireless PLC merged. In December 1988, a global offering of 877.5 million shares took place. As part of this offering, slightly more than 6 million ADRs were sold in the United States and then listed on the NYSE. With more than of $3.5 billion total revenues, Hong Kong

FIGURE 9.5   L.M. Ericsson Telephone AB Per ADR Financial Results:
1984–1993

Year	Earnings	Sales	Dividend	Net Profit Margin %	Average PE Ratio	Average Price Per ADR
1984	$.43	$17.73	$.20	2.4	19	7 ½
1985	.52	23.11	.24	2.3	11	5 ⅞
1986	.50	24.32	.26	2.1	14	7
1987	.59	29.08	.31	2.0	12	7 ¼
1988	1.05	26.66	.34	3.9	8	8 ⅝
1989	1.69	31.01	.45	5.3	11	20 ¼
1990	2.89	39.03	.62	7.5	12	36 ¾
1991	1.01	40.02	.63	2.5	29	27 ¾
1992	.89	32.30	.50	2.8	25	22 ⅝
1993	1.92	34.76	.54	5.5	22	41 ⅞

Telecom has exclusive franchises for local telecommunications services in Hong Kong until 1995 and international services to 2006. International calls represent about 63 percent of revenues; local calls and other telecommunications account for 27 percent; and equipment sales and other services, 10 percent. (Employees: 16,000)

China represents Hong Kong Telecom's biggest market. Approximately half of all calls in and out of Hong Kong are with China. Traffic between Hong Kong and the mainland grew 31 percent in 1993. However, profit margins on this business are not as high as on calls to the United States, the second biggest destination. The company's mobile phone services continue to grow very well. Although it faces competition from three rival services, its cellular unit is getting subscriber growth of more than 50 percent per year.

Dividends represent more than 70 percent of the company's growing profits. The current yield on the ADRs is about 3.5 percent. Figure 11.6 illustrates Hong Kong Telecom's per ADR financial results from 1988 to 1993. Numbers have been adjusted for a 15 percent ADR dividend in 1988 and a three-for-one split in 1994. (IPO: December 1988)

Novo-Nordisk (NYSE) is the result of a 1989 merger of Novo and Nordisk. Based in Denmark, the company is a major producer of enzymes and insulin. It controls about 44 percent of the world market for insulin and 48 percent of the world market for enzymes. Its health

FIGURE 9.6   Hong Kong Telecommunications Ltd. Per ADR Financial
Results: 1988–1993

Year	Earnings	Sales	Dividend	Net Profit Margin %	Average PE Ratio	Average Price Per ADR
1988	$.38	$1.36	$.29	28.0	18	7 ⅜
1989	.46	1.62	.36	28.1	14	6 ½
1990	.61	1.87	.42	32.5	13	7 ¾
1991	.62	2.11	.49	29.5	15	9 ¼
1992	.75	2.49	.56	30.3	16	11 ¼
1993	.83	2.79	.65	29.9	20	17 ¼

care group contributes 68 percent of sales; bioindustrial and other products account for the other 32 percent. The company invests about 14 percent of its revenues in research and development. (Employees: 11,600)

With total sales of more than $2 billion, Novo-Nordisk added five new factories worldwide in 1994. The plants will produce industrial enzymes, new ultra-thin needles for medical delivery systems, hormone replacement therapy products and antibiotics. The company should benefit substantially from these plants and cause share profits to accelerate. The fifth plant, an insulin-filling facility in North Carolina, is expected to receive approval in the United States toward the end of 1995.

Analysts believe Novo-Nordisk ADRs have good long-term appreciation potential. The company pays out about 10 percent of its earnings in dividends. Current yield on the ADRs is about 0.7 percent. Figure 9.7 illustrates the per ADR financial results from 1989 to 1993. Numbers have been adjusted for a four-for-one share split in 1994.

Telephonos de Mexico, S.A. (NYSE), known as Telmex, provides all domestic and international fixed-link and cellular mobile telephone services in Mexico. Telmex is the country's third largest company and the largest publicly traded company. It has 6.7 million phone lines in service, amounting to 8.1 per 100 inhabitants. Of its total lines, 52 percent are digital. Domestic long distance phone business accounts for about 40 percent of total revenues; local service brings in 36 percent; international service, 22 percent; and other services, 2%. (Employees: 49,000)

FIGURE 9.7 Novo-Nordisk Per ADR Financial Results: 1989–1993

Year	Earnings	Sales	Dividend	Net Profit Margin %	Average PE Ratio	Average Price Per ADR
1989	$.66	$ 8.33	$.13	7.9	16	10 ¾
1990	.99	10.48	.15	9.4	12	12 ⅞
1991	.86	10.60	.14	7.4	20	18 ½
1992	1.34	11.44	.14	11.6	17	22 ⅛
1993	1.92	11.97	.15	15.9	12	22 ¼

FIGURE 9.8 Telephonos de Mexico, S.A. Per ADR Financial Results: 1986–1993

Year	Earnings	Sales	Dividend	Net Profit Margin %	Average PE Ratio	Average Price Per ADR
1986	$.57	$4.20	$.08	13.6	1	¾
1987	.61	4.30	.04	15.0	3	3 ⅛
1988	.41	4.22	.04	10.0	5	2 ⅛
1989	.39	5.04	.05	7.7	11	4 ⅝
1990	1.76	7.24	.17	24.3	7	11 ⅜
1991	3.52	10.00	.17	35.1	8	30 ⅛
1992	4.65	12.56	.48	37.1	11	50 ¼
1993	4.85	14.98	.96	34.3	11	56 ⅛

Mexico's economic outlook got a boost from a recently announced agreement between the government, business and labor. Earnings for Telmex look good for the near term. Locally billed business, the company's biggest source of revenues, has been growing at nearly a 20 percent annual rate. International long distance service has been growing at about 12 percent recently. A fast growing economy, coupled with good long-term potential, should permit investors to see substantial appreciation in the ADRs. The shares tend to be subject to volatility, however, so *only* investors willing to stomach big swings in price should consider purchasing these shares.

The dividend payout ratio has been at 20 percent recently, giving the ADRs a yield of about 2.6 percent. Figure 9.8 illustrates the company's per ADR financial results from 1986 to 1993.

Vodafone Group PLC (NYSE) is the largest mobile telecommunications service in Britain. The company has 1,450,000 subscribers and a 52 percent market share. Vodafone provides services through its own operating company and 40 other firms, operates a data transmission and radio-paging network and has interests in other mobile telecommunications licensees in France, Sweden, Hong Kong, Australia, South Africa and six other countries. (Employees: 3,100)

Vodafone has a strongly expanding its customer base. Until recently it shared the United Kingdom market with Cellnet, which is 60 percent owned by British Telecom. In the past year, however, two new companies have introduced low-priced digital cellular services. The cheaper pricing has benefited Vodafone by opening the low end of the market. In its fiscal year ending March 31, 1944, Vodafone increased its subscriber base 40 percent and in the following six months accelerated the trend, with the number of users jumping another 24 percent. The company now is targeting the high end of the market through GSM technology, which permits subscribers to use their handsets anywhere in the world. Vodafone is also a member of the Globalstar consortium, which is working toward launching a satellite phone system.

Vodafone's prospects are bright, and the ADRs have attractive long-term capital appreciation potential. The dividend payout ratio is greater than 30 percent, giving the ADRs a yield of about 2 percent. Figure 9.9 illustrates the company's per ADR financial results from 1988 to 1993. The numbers are adjusted to reflect a three-for-one share split in 1994. (IPO: October 1988)

FIGURE 9.9   Vodaphone Group PLC Per ADR Financial Results: 1988–1993

Year	Earnings	Sales	Dividend	Net Profit Margin %	Average PE Ratio	Average Price Per ADR
1988	$.34	$1.35	$.05	22.4	38	10 ⅝
1989	.57	2.23	.18	25.3	36	19 ⅞
1990	.90	3.13	.18	28.7	21	18 ¼
1991	.94	3.38	.84	27.7	23	20 ⅜
1992	.99	3.33	.35	29.8	20	20
1993	1.15	4.14	.52	27.6	23	24 ¼

In Your Spare Time ...

Consider investing worldwide. By buying ADRs, traded on U.S. exchanges, you can participate in the growth potential of hundreds of companies headquartered abroad.

10

$ $

Understanding How
Mutual Funds Work

$ $

What is a *mutual fund?* It is an investment company that raises money from shareholders and invests it in stocks, bonds, options, commodities or money market securities. The fund pools the money of many people who share common financial objectives. Professional money managers then use the pool to invest in a variety of securities that are expected to help the fund's shareholders achieve their financial objectives.

When a mutual fund earns money, it distributes the earnings to its shareholders. If the fund receives the money as dividends from stock or as interest from debt instruments, the proceeds are distributed to shareholders as dividends. If the fund sells securities for a profit, the capital gains are distributed to shareholders as capital gains distributions. The shareholder may take the dividends and capital gains distributions in cash or reinvest them in the fund. Because all distributions to shareholders are paid out in exact proportion to the number of shares owned, shareholders who have only a few hundred dollars invested receive the same rate of return as those who invest hundreds of thousands of dollars.

Investment Objectives and Policies

Each mutual fund has a stated investment objective. Both the objective and specific investment policies on how the fund's manager attempts to achieve this objective are clearly described in the fund's prospectus. Investment objectives are generally stated in terms of one or more main goals, which may include the following:

- growth: increasing the value of invested principal
- income: generating a flow of current income through dividends
- stability: protecting the invested principal from loss

Investment *objectives* are important to both the fund manager and investors. The fund manager uses the objective as a guide when selecting investments for the fund's portfolio. Potential investors use it to determine which funds are suitable for their own particular needs. Mutual funds' investment objectives cover a wide range. Some funds follow aggressive investment policies to achieve the greatest return possible but at a higher degree of risk. Other funds seek more modest returns, attempting to maintain a minimal amount of risk.

An investment *policy* describes the means by which a fund will proceed to meet its objective(s). Discussed at some length in the fund's prospectus, it states the types of securities that the fund will hold and often the credit quality of those securities. For instance, some equity funds, in the quest for long-term capital growth, will invest only in the common stocks of large, well-established industrial companies. Other funds, seeking current income and some growth, will invest in the common and preferred stocks of utility companies. Still other funds will invest only in securities issued or guaranteed by the U.S. government, seeking current income with a high degree of safety. Funds seeking maximum capital appreciation might invest in the common stocks of small companies that seem to have the potential for rapid growth.

How the Funds Get Paid

All mutual fund companies are in business to make a profit. Many started out as investment managers for clients such as pension funds, college endowments, charitable trusts and wealthy individuals. The constant drive to increase the cost-effectiveness of high-priced investment management talent has resulted in a proliferation of new mutual funds as a way to bring large sums of money under management. In fact, from 1983 to 1994, according the Investment Company Institute, the number of mutual funds nearly quintupled, from 1,026 to almost 5,000.

The fund manager has, in effect, one client with one investment objective and a single set of investment policies. The larger the fund, the more cost-effective it may become. Although big funds often require more personnel to run them than small funds do, the number of people needed becomes proportionately much smaller as the fund size grows. The Fidelity Asset Manager fund, for example, with more than $11.2 billion in assets on June 30, 1994, charges a management fee of 0.52 percent of average net assets. With other expenses of 0.53 percent, total fund operating expenses run to 1.05 percent of assets. This one fund provides annual revenues of more than $117 million to Fidelity Investments (America's largest mutual fund manager). Although providing a large source of income for Fidelity, the 1.05 percent cost to the investor is quite modest.

Other funds charge more or less, depending largely on the efficiency of their operations. Small funds, or those just getting started, will of necessity run higher total operating costs than their larger peers. For example, the Rea Graham Balanced Fund, with just over $18 million in assets in mid-1994, had total operating costs that were 2.37 percent of assets. At the low end is the Vanguard Index Trust 500 Portfolio. Its total operating expenses have been running at 0.19 percent of the more than $8 billion it manages.

Every mutual fund must report its expense charges annually in its prospectus so investors can easily compare charges from one fund to another. Expense charges are just one factor to consider in selecting a fund. Other things being equal (management ability, past performance, investment objectives and policies), a fund with low expenses tends to produce a better return than one with charges that are out of line with the competition.

The management fee is usually the largest part of total expenses. The fee covers the salaries of fund officers and other employees as well as expenses relating to office space and facilities and the payment for investment management and advice. Other operating expenses borne by the fund include charges of the fund's *custodian* (the bank or other financial institution that keeps custody of stock certificates and other assets of the fund); accountants and attorneys; the cost of issuing share certificates and disbursing dividends; and expenses for printing, postage and mailing.

Many funds have also put into effect a distribution services agreement (Rule 12b-1) adopted by the Securities and Exchange Commission (SEC) under the Investment Company Act of 1940. This permits mutual funds to directly or indirectly pay expenses connected with the distribution and marketing of its shares. These 12b-1 fees range anywhere from 0.05 percent in some funds to as much as 1.25 percent in other funds. Such fees can adversely affect a fund's performance, especially when compared with similar funds that do not charge 12b-1 fees. The mutual fund listings in major daily newspapers indicate which funds charge these fees.

Expenses are paid by a fund primarily out of investment income, which is more than sufficient in most cases. One exception would be funds that invest substantially in growth companies that pay little or nothing in dividends. When investment income is not sufficient to cover expenses, the balance is paid out of invested capital.

Sales Charges: Load Funds

Many mutual funds, generally called *load funds*, are sold through stockbrokers and other salespeople who work on commission. The offering price of these funds includes a sales commission or load that can range from a high of 8.5 percent (the maximum permitted by law) to as low as 3 percent. With the increasing dominance of the mutual fund industry by such no-load companies as Fidelity Investments (which also markets some funds that carry a sales charge) and The Vanguard Group, load funds have been forced to reduce their commissions, many of which are now in the 4 to 5 percent range.

The only reason for a mutual fund to levy a sales charge is to cover costs of distribution. Most of the charge (about 85 percent) goes to the broker-dealer who handles the sale. Of that amount, about one-third goes to the salesperson (registered representative) who handles the transaction for the customer. The other 15 percent of the sales charge stays with the mutual fund company's own sales arm.

Sales charges can be paid at the time of purchase (a *front-end load*) or when the shares are redeemed (a *back-end load*). In some cases there may be a small charge at the time of purchase (*low-load*) and another charge at redemption.

Front-end loads. Mutual fund shares with front-end loads are offered for sale at a price marked up from the *net asset value* or NAV (the value of all assets held in a fund divided by the total number of shares outstanding) by the amount of the sales charge. The result is called the *offering price.*

The sales charge on a front-end load fund is usually tiered, with break-points at different dollar purchase amounts. Figure 10.1 is an example of a typical schedule of sales charges for purchasing shares of a front-end load fund. These schedules appear in the fund's prospectus. Front-end load funds with as much as a 3 percent maximum sales charge are generally considered low-load.

Back-end loads.   A fairly recent development in the marketing of mutual funds has been the *back-end load.* Under this arrangement, shares are purchased at the NAV. The investor pays no sales charge at the time of purchase. The sales person must be paid, however, so the investor will pay a deferred sales charge if the shares are redeemed prior to the end of a stipulated holding period. The charge amount declines over time until it eventually disappears. There are usually no break-points for large purchases in back-end load funds.

In typical back-end load funds, an investor is subject to a sales charge if the shares are redeemed within the first six years after purchase. For instance, early withdrawal charges might be assessed as follows:

Year after Purchase	*Withdrawal Charge %*
First year	5
Second year	4
Third year	3
Fourth year	2
Fifth year	2
Sixth year	1
After six years	0

It may seem that an investor who holds on to a back-end load funds for more than the stipulated holding period avoids any sales cost, but this is not true. The money to pay sales commissions and other costs of distribution is charged against the fund's income in accordance with Rule 12b-1.

Rule 12b-1 fees are assessed by many mutual funds, both load and no-load, but they are especially high for back-end load funds because such funds must recoup the commission paid to salespeople. The fee charged by back-end load funds is typically 1.25 percent each year.

FIGURE 10.1   Sample Schedule of Sales Charges

Amount of Purchase	Sales Charge as a Percentage of	
	Offering Price %	NAV %
Up to $10,000	4.50	4.71
$10,001 to $25,000	3.50	3.61
$25,001 to $50,000	2.60	2.67
$50,001 to $100,000	2.00	2.04
$100,001 to $300,000	1.00	1.01
$300,001 to $500,000	0.50	0.50
$500,001 and over	0.25	0.25

This directly reduces the fund's total annual return each year by the charge amount.

For example, consider two funds that are each invested in a portfolio of corporate bonds with an average income yield of 8 percent. Both funds have an expense ratio of 1 percent, resulting in a net income of 7 percent. One fund, however, pays out the full net income to its shareholders, providing them with a dividend distribution rate (yield) of 7 percent. The other fund, a back-end load fund with the same 1 percent expense ratio but charging an additional 1.25 percent annual 12b-1 fee, is able to provide its shareholders with a dividend distribution rate of only 5.75 percent. Thus the yield received by an investor in the back-end load fund in this illustration is 17.8 percent less than that of the fund charging no 12b-1 fee.

No-Load Funds: You Can Buy Direct and Save Broker Commissions

The first mutual funds to be offered without commission were brought out in the early 1920s. Now many of the largest and most successful funds are no-load or low load, including five of the ten largest funds in America (Vanguard Windsor Fund, Vanguard Index 500 Fund, Fidelity Puritan Fund, Janus Fund and Twentieth Century Ultra Fund). More and more investors are buying mutual funds directly from fund companies to avoid paying any sales fees or commissions (and sales pressure from brokers).

Unlike opening a bank account, mutual fund investors can open an account and make investments without ever setting foot into their fund's offices or even knowing where the offices are located! This is done by dealing directly by telephone and mail with no-load mutual fund companies. No-load funds are exactly like load funds in every respect except that shares of no-load funds are purchased directly and without the addition of a sales commission.

Comparing Loads and No-Loads

Today, the distinction between load and no-load funds has become somewhat blurred. Some funds considered to be no-load do, in fact, levy certain charges that are not related to the investment management cost. These charges may include 12b-1 sales distribution fees, low-loads, back-end loads, contingent deferred sales charges and fixed redemption charges or exit fees. A recent study by Morningstar, Inc., found that 28 percent of all mutual funds are pure no-loads, 8 percent are no-loads with 12b-1 fees, 10 percent have back-end loads, and 20 percent are front-end load only.

If you might invest in mutual funds, consider whether to purchase fund shares through a securities broker or to deal directly with a mutual fund company. According to *The Individual Investor's Guide to Low-Load Mutual Funds* (AAII), 826 mutual funds are no-loads or low-loads. This number includes funds that charge no front or back-end loads, as well as funds with as much as a 3 percent load, but no 12b-1 fees.

Differences in performance of load and no-load funds have been studied and debated for decades. Until recently, most studies have shown little or no difference in performance. Some recent analyses have indicated a slight performance advantage for load funds, perhaps because many load funds are larger (as a result of heavy selling efforts) and therefore have lower expenses. Whatever slight advantage there might be is of little consequence, however, because any added value is usually more than offset when sales charges are deducted.

So what does a sales load buy for an investor? In most cases a load pays for advice from a financial planner or broker on such matters as which funds to own, when to buy, when to sell, and how to plan for taxes. If you need information on these matters, you may want to pay a sales load or a fee to a competent professional. If not, you can contact the fund company of your choice directly by phone and save yourself a lot of money.

Example. The difference in growth of an investment of $10,000 in two comparable funds—one with an 8.5 percent load, the other no-load—can be dramatic. Over ten years, with an assumed 10 percent rate of return, the no-load fund earns $2,204 more. The following table illustrates how this works.

$10,000 Invested at an Assumed Rate of 10 Percent

	Value of Investment	
	Initial after fee	*End of 10 years*
Load Fund	$9,150	$23,735
No-Load Fund	$10,000	$25,939

The load fund investor is $850 behind at the beginning (8.5 percent of $10,000) and forever loses the 10 percent growth on that portion of the investment. Over an investing lifetime, the difference becomes greatly magnified.

In the end, able management is the best key to investment success. But given comparable managers, an investor is unquestionably better off investing in a fund with low costs and without sales commissions or fees.

Studies show that generally there is an inverse relationship between expenses and performance. Mutual funds with no 12b-1 fees have higher performance than funds that charge such fees. Further, the higher the 12b-1 fee levied, the worse the performance. On average, you can't buy better performance by paying higher fees of any kind. There are certainly exceptions, but the burden of proof lies with the salesperson or organization asking you to pay a load or higher expenses.

In Your Spare Time ...

Consider mutual funds. Each fund has a stated investment objective. The combination of professional management, diversification and low operating costs combine to give you the potential for high returns with relatively low risk.

11

$ $ $ $ $ $ $ $ $ $ $ $ $ $ $ $ $ $ $ $

One-Stop
Mutual Fund
Shopping

$ $ $ $ $ $ $ $ $ $ $ $ $ $ $ $ $ $ $ $

Fund shopping networks are among the newest services available to mutual fund investors through discount brokers. These networks enable you to buy and sell a wide range of no-load, low-load, and load mutual funds through one source. When you invest through one of these one-stop sources, you can choose from more than 2,400 mutual funds sponsored by more than 125 leading companies. And the number continues to grow. According to Don Phillips, vice president of Morningstar, Inc., the networks will become the dominant way to distribute mutual funds.

The basic idea is simple: You can buy and sell shares in numerous no-load funds without paying a transaction fee. That means you're putting the full value of your dollars to work for your investments. Transaction fees *are* charged on certain no-load funds, generally those that have chosen not to participate in the program. Load funds can also be purchased in some programs, in which case you will be charged the sales load as described in the prospectus. Business can be transacted with one telephone call, and everything is clearly summarized on one statement.

The two biggest programs in terms of assets are Charles Schwab's *Mutual Fund OneSource*, with more than $10 billion under management, and Fidelity Investment's *FundsNetwork*, with $5 billion. Other companies offering similar plans include Jack White & Company, Muriel Siebert & Company, and Waterhouse Securities.

How One-Stop Shopping Plans Work for You

You pay no loads or transaction fees to invest in a wide range of no-load funds available from different fund companies. The price you pay is exactly the same as investing directly with the fund itself.

Whatever your investment objective, from capital preservation to aggressive growth, a one-source mutual fund service gives you a nearly complete range of funds to choose from to help you reach your objective. You can move easily between funds, even if they're from different fund companies. This way you can adjust your mutual fund portfolio to reflect changing investment goals or market conditions.

Once you have established an account, you can invest in hundreds of mutual funds with a single phone call. Some firms offer limited commission-free trading and will buy funds on margin or sell short, two highly speculative trading techniques.

Because fund companies pay to participate, organizations that offer no-transaction-fee mutual fund network services are compensated by fees received directly from the fund companies. These fees range from 0.20 percent to 0.35 percent of the assets managed by the program. As long as these costs are not passed along to shareholders and fund expense ratios stay at reasonable levels, this should not be a problem to investors.

Although the general approaches for companies providing one-stop shopping plans are straightforward and pretty much the same, there are some differences. To get started, you must first open a discount brokerage account with the firm of your choice. This gives you access to the mutual fund network plus the opportunity to trade in stocks, bonds and other securities. Then, to purchase shares, instruct your representative the name of the fund, the dollar amount you want to invest and whether you want fund dividends and capital gains paid in cash or automatically reinvested in more fund shares. To sell, you need only to name the fund, the number of shares you wish to sell, and whether you want to receive the proceeds or have them credited to your account.

The fund consolidators maintain single, multimillion-dollar accounts at the mutual fund families, so they have some flexibility on minimum investment requirements. Schwab's OneSource program, for instance, has minimums that range from $250 to $2,000, which in some cases is below what you would have to invest when dealing directly with a fund.

One problem with the one-stop shopping system is that several excellent fund families, including T. Rowe Price, Scudder, USAA, and Vanguard, don't participate in any of the "free" programs. However, they *are* available if a transaction fee is paid. Generally, firms offering the program will let you transfer most outside funds into your consolidated account, at no extra cost. This way you can easily keep track of, your holdings.

The Major Players

To give you a general means of comparison, following are the major players in the game and a summary of their current rules for their one-stop mutual fund shopping programs. Prices and rules can change, so contact the broker.

Fidelity Investments
161 Devonshire Street
Boston, MA 02110
800-544-9697

Service: FundsNetwork

Buying or selling.   Fidelity equity fund purchases, both load and no-load, in FundsNetwork must be paid for within five business days of purchase. Fidelity *bond* funds must be paid for the following business day. Most other no-load funds purchased through FundsNetwork must be paid for the next business day. Other load funds must be paid for within five business days.

No transaction fees apply to purchases, sales, or exchanges of the participating no-load funds offered through FundsNetwork. Fidelity provides a directory of participating funds. Fees for nonparticipating no-load funds are determined by transaction amount and apply to both purchases and redemptions. A minimum fee of $28 applies to all transactions other than Fidelity funds. Fees start at $17.50 plus 0.8 percent of the principal amount for transactions of $5,000 or less, and decline to $157.50 plus 0.08 percent for transactions in excess of $95,000. If you purchase a no-load fund and pay a transaction fee, you must pay a transaction fee upon its sale. For load funds, you are charged the sales load as described in the prospectus.

Moving money between funds. You pay no charge for moving money between participating funds in *FundsNetwork*. With other funds you'll pay the standard fee to buy or sell, with a $28 minimum.

Pricing cut-off times. Buy and sell orders for Fidelity funds (except for Fidelity Select funds, where hourly pricing applies) placed by 4 PM Eastern time (1 PM Pacific time) are executed at that day's price. Orders placed after the cut-off time are executed at the next day's price. Orders for other no-load funds, including participating funds, have a cut-off time of 1 PM Eastern time. The cut-off time for load funds is 4 PM Eastern time. Exchanges within the same fund family have a cut-off time of 2:30 PM Eastern Time.

Trading frequency.   Fidelity reserves the right to charge transaction fees if you make five or more short-term redemptions (shares held less than six months) on funds available without transaction fees through *FundsNetwork* in a 12 month period.

Charles Schwab & Co., Inc.
101 Montgomery Street
San Francisco, CA 94104
800-526-8600

Service: Mutual Fund OneSource

Buying or selling.   When buying, you must have sufficient cash in your Schwab account to cover your purchase, plus any applicable transaction fees. You pay no fee to buy or sell *Mutual Fund One-Source* funds (funds that participate in Schwab's program) or *Schwab-Funds* (the registered name for Schwab's own mutual funds). To buy or sell other funds, you will pay a transaction fee (minimum $29 per trade) according to Schwab's fee schedule. The fees decline from 0.6 percent of principal on transactions of $15,000 or less to 0.08 percent on transactions in excess of $100,000.

Moving money between funds.   You pay no charge for moving money between *Mutual Fund OneSource* funds or *SchwabFunds*. With other funds you will pay the standard fee on the sell order ($29 per trade minimum) and a $15 fee on the buy order.

Pricing cut-off times. Buy and sell orders for most equity mutual funds (except for SchwabFunds) placed by 2 PM Eastern time (11 AM Pacific time) are executed at that day's price. Orders placed after 2 PM are executed at the next day's price. Orders for SchwabFunds have a cut-off time of 4 PM. Buy orders for most bond funds have a cut-off time at 9 PM Eastern time and are priced at the next day's close. Orders cannot be changed or canceled after the cut-off time.

Trading frequency. If you make five or more short-term redemptions of *Mutual Fund OneSource* funds over any 12-month period, Schwab will start charging you transaction fees on all your mutual fund trades. A short-term redemption refers to the sale of mutual fund shares held for six months or less. Redemptions in Schwab's own funds and funds that charge a load of 4 percent or more with which Schwab has formal distribution agreements are not included.

Muriel Siebert & Co., Inc.
885 Third Avenue
New York, NY 10022-4834
800-872-0666

Service: FundExchange

Buying or selling. You pay no fee to buy or sell *FundExchange* funds (funds that participate in the Muriel Siebert & Co. program). To buy or sell other funds, you pay a transaction fee (minimum $39.50 per trade) according to Siebert's fee schedule. The fees decline from $17.50 plus 0.8 percent of principal on transactions of $5,000 or less to $157.50 plus 0.08 percent on transactions in excess of $100,000.

Redemptions. No transaction fee will be charged on any redemption of shares originally purchased through Muriel Siebert's No Transaction Fee Program *and* held beyond the short-term holding period. The duration of the short-term holding period varies with the amount invested per fund as follows: $2,000 to $9,999 = 9 months; $10,000 to $19,999 = 6 months; $20,000 to $49,999 = 3 months; and $50,000 and over = 1 month. If shares are redeemed before the short-term holding period has elapsed, the firm's standard commission schedule for no-load mutual funds will apply to the sale only.

Waterhouse Securities, Inc.
100 Wall Street
New York, NY 10005
800-934-4443

Service: Mutual FundConnection

Buying or selling.   When buying, you must have sufficient cash in your account for settlement before a transaction can be executed. Credit balances in your account can be invested in one of three money market funds available at Waterhouse.

No transaction fees apply to purchases, sales or exchanges of the participating no-load funds offered through *FundConnection*. Waterhouse provides a directory of participating funds. Fees for other no-load funds are determined by transaction amount and apply to both purchases and redemptions. A minimum fee of $29 applies to all transactions. Fees start at 0.6 percent of the principal amount for transactions of $15,000 or less and decline to 0.08 percent for transactions in excess of $100,000. When buying load funds, you are charged the sales load as described in the prospectus. Sell orders for load funds will be executed for a flat $35 transaction fee.

Moving money between funds.   If you simultaneously switch from one mutual fund to another, Waterhouse will charge a transaction fee on the sale, but execute the buy order for only $15. These charges do not apply to those no-load funds that do not have a transaction fee.

Pricing cut-off times.   Buy and sell orders must be entered by 2 PM Eastern time to be executed at the closing price for your fund on the day you place your order. However, most bond funds will be executed the following day.

Trading frequency.   Waterhouse will reinstate transaction fees on an account if five or more short-term redemptions (shares held less than six months) are executed within a 12-month period.

Jack White & Company
9191 Towne Centre Drive
San Diego, CA 92122
800-323-3263

Service: Mutual Fund Network

Buying or selling.   No transaction fees apply to purchases, sales or exchanges of the mutual funds participating in Jack White & Company's No Transaction Fee Mutual Fund program. The minimum initial transaction and any subsequent transactions must total at least $5,000, otherwise, a fee of $27 is charged. Transactions in a participating fund require a 60-day holding period to avoid any transaction charges. Any positions liquidated within 60 days of purchase will be charged scheduled fees for the sale. More than 350 funds participate in the program; additional funds are added regularly.

The firm also offers more than 2,400 mutual funds, including more than 900 no-load and low-load mutual funds at low transaction fees in its Mutual Fund Network. Fees start at $27 for transactions in an amount up to $5,000. For transactions of $5,001 to $25,000, the fee is $35, and for transactions in excess of $25,000, the fee is $50. For load funds, you are charged the sales load as described in the prospectus.

Shorting of mutual funds.   Subject to availability, you can sell short shares of selected mutual funds. Because the firm maintains an extensive inventory of some of the most popularly held funds, it can take your orders to sell short, just as you would a stock. Transaction fees are the same as stated above.

Pricing cut-off times.   All cut-off times are Pacific time. Phone or letter redemptions will be executed the same day if received by 12:00 PM (except for certain funds, as specified in company instructions).

In Your Spare Time ...

Consider mutual fund shopping networks, one of the newest services available to investors through discount brokers. You can choose form a wide range of mutual funds through one source, often without paying any fee or commission.

12

$ $ $ $ $ $ $ $ $ $ $ $ $ $ $ $ $ $ $ $

Using the
Prospectus—
A Wealth of
Information

$ $ $ $ $ $ $ $ $ $ $ $ $ $ $ $ $ $ $ $

Mutual fund advertisements urge you to call for free information and a prospectus, then caution you to "read the prospectus carefully before investing."

The prospectus is the most important source of information afforded mutual fund investors. The law stipulates that a prospectus must accompany or precede the offering of any mutual fund for sale to the public. You can get one without charge from the fund or, in the case of a load-fund, from a broker.

A prospectus sets forth concisely the information that a prospective investor should know about a particular mutual fund before investing. A more detailed *statement of additional information* also may be obtained without charge by writing or calling the mutual fund company. The statement, which is incorporated by reference into the prospectus, has been filed with the Securities and Exchange Commission (SEC). Each prospectus also is required to display prominently the following statement: "These securities have not been approved or disapproved by the Securities and Exchange Commission or any state securities commission, nor has the Securities and Exchange Commission or any state securities commission passed upon the accuracy or adequacy of this prospectus. Any representation to the contrary is a criminal offense."

Before permitting a mutual fund company to offer a fund for sale to the public, the SEC examines the statement to be sure that it contains all the information that is required by law. When that requirement has been met, the fund company is notified that it may offer its fund for sale to the public.

What the Prospectus Contains: The Vanguard Wellesley Income Fund

To see what you can expect in a prospectus, let's look at certain information in the April 13, 1994, prospectus of the Vanguard Wellesley Income Fund, distributed by The Vanguard Group of Investment Companies. You will find the same type of data in most mutual fund prospectuses. The Wellesley Fund is an open-end diversified investment company and is one of 78 such funds managed by the Vanguard Group. Established on July 1, 1970, the fund held assets of nearly $6 billion in June 1994.

Investment Objectives and Policies

On the first page of the June 1994 prospectus of the Vanguard Wellesley Income Fund, management sets forth briefly the information you want to know about what the fund seeks to achieve and how it will go about doing it. The *investment objective* of the Wellesley Fund is "to provide as much current income as is consistent with reasonable risk." A secondary objective of the fund is to "offer the potential for moderate growth of capital."

A mutual fund's *investment policy* describes how management intends to accomplish its objectives. The Wellesley Fund prospectus indicates that the fund will seek to achieve these objectives by investing primarily in U.S. government and corporate fixed-income securities of investment grade quality and dividend-paying common stocks. A more detailed explanation of the fund's investment policy is set forth later in the prospectus. Of course, there is no assurance that the fund will meet its stated objectives.

Fund Expenses

How much fund management spends to operate is important to a mutual fund investor. The total operating expenses of mutual funds can run from as little as 0.19 percent of net assets (Vanguard Index Trust 500 Portfolio) to as much as 2.40 percent (Dean Witter World Wide Investment Trust). As an investor, mutual fund expenses affect you directly. For instance, a fund that has a gross total return of 10.0 percent and expenses of 0.25 percent would produce a net return to you as a shareholder of 9.75 percent (10.0 − 0.25 = 9.75). Another fund with a gross return of 10.0 percent and an expense ratio of 2.0 percent would deliver a net return of 8.0 percent.

Each prospectus must include a table illustrating all expenses and fees that you would incur as a shareholder of the fund. The Wellesley Fund provides the following information regarding its expenses:

Shareholder Transaction Expenses

Sales load imposed on purchases	None
Sales load imposed on reinvested dividends	None
Redemption fees	None
Exchange fees	None

Annual Fund Operating Expenses

Management & administrative expenses		0.21%
Investment advisory fees		0.08%
12b-1 fees		None
Other expenses		
Distribution costs	0.02%	
Miscellaneous expenses	0.02%	
Total other expenses		0.04%
Total operating expenses		0.33%

So that you can easily compare costs of one fund to another, each prospectus must also include information on the expenses you would incur on a $1,000 investment over various periods, assuming (1) a 5 percent annual rate of return and (2) redemption at the end of each period. The Wellesley numbers are shown below.

One Year	Two Years	Five Years	Ten Years
$3	$11	$19	$42

Financial Highlights

Every mutual fund prospectus includes a table of financial highlights for a share outstanding during the previous ten years (or for as long as the fund has operated, if less). You can quickly see each year's increase or decrease in NAV, amount of dividend distributions from investment income and realized capital gains and total return of the fund. In addition, the table shows total assets in the fund each year and information on fund expenses and portfolio turnover. (See Figure 12.1.)

Investment Risks

Like any investment program, a mutual fund entails certain risks, and a prospective investor should be aware of them. The Wellesley Fund notes that its shares are subject to the risk that bond or stock prices will decline during short or even extended periods.

The prospectus states that the fund expects to invest most of its assets in longer-term fixed income securities, such as government and corporate bonds, and explains the risk of this policy: bond prices are influenced by changes in interest rate levels. When interest rates rise, bond prices generally fall; conversely, when interest rates fall, bond prices generally rise. Although bonds normally fluctuate less than stocks, extended periods of increases in interest rates have caused significant price declines. For example, bond prices fell 48 percent from December 1976 to September 1981. The risk of bond holdings declining in value, however, may be offset in whole or in part by the high level of income that bonds provide.

After explaining these and other aspects of risk in the portfolio, the prospectus states that from the fund's inception on July 1, 1970, to December 31, 1993, it provided an average annual return of +11.7 percent. During this period, the fund experienced 20 years of positive returns and 3 years of negative returns. Annual returns ranged from +27.4 percent to −6.4 percent. The prospectus notes that the return characteristics are provided to illustrate the risks and returns that the fund has provided in the past and may not be indicative of future results.

Who Should Invest

Is this the right fund for you? The prospectus addresses this question by indicating that the Wellesley Fund is designed for income investors

FIGURE 12.1   Sample Financial Highlights Chart

	Year Ended December 31,									
	1993	1992	1991	1990	1989	1988	1987	1986	1985	1984
Net Asset Value, Beginning of Year	$18.16	$18.08	$16.02	$16.82	$15.26	$14.57	$16.27	$15.31	$13.28	$12.66
Investment Operations										
Net Investment Income	1.14	1.21	1.27	1.30	1.32	1.23	1.24	1.33	1.38	1.37
Net Realized and Unrealized Gain (Loss) on Investments	1.48	.29	2.06	(.72)	1.79	.69	(1.52)	1.43	2.13	.62
Total from Investment Operations	2.62	1.50	3.33	.58	3.11	1.92	(.28)	2.76	3.51	1.99
Distributions										
Dividends from Net Investment Income	(1.14)	(1.21)	(1.27)	(1.30)	(1.31)	(1.23)	(1.04)	(1.33)	(1.38)	(1.37)
Distributions from Realized Capital Gains	(.40)	(.21)	—	(.08)	(.24)	—	(.38)	(.47)	(.10)	—
Total Distributions	(1.54)	(1.42)	(1.27)	(1.38)	(1.55)	(1.23)	(1.42)	(1.80)	(1.48)	(1.37)
Net Asset Value, End of Year	$19.24	$18.16	$18.08	$16.02	$16.82	$15.26	$14.57	$16.27	$15.31	$13.28
Total Return	14.65%	8.67%	21.57%	3.76%	20.93%	13.61%	(1.92)%	18.34%	27.41%	16.64%
Ratios/Supplemental Data										
Net Assets, End of Year (Millions)	$6,011	$3,178	$1,934	$1,022	$788	$567	$495	$510	$224	$115
Ratio of Expenses to Average Net Assets	.33%	.35%	.40%	.45%	.45%	.51%	.49%	.58%	.60%	.71%
Ratio of Net Investment Income to Average Net Assets	5.79%	6.50%	7.08%	7.77%	7.68%	8.14%	7.83%	7.74%	9.36%	10.68%
Portfolio Turnover Rates:										
Common Stocks	26%	16%	19%	12%	10%	19%	27%	18%	32%	35%
Bonds	18%	24%	34%	23%	11%	21%	48%	39%	14%	37%

SOURCE: Vanguard Wellesley Income Fund Prospectus (April 13, 1994). Reprinted by permission of The Vanguard Group.

seeking a high level of current income from a portfolio of bonds and stocks. Because of the risks associated with common stock and bond investments, the fund is intended to be a long-term investment vehicle and is not designed to provide investors with a means of speculating on short-term market movements. The prospectus also explains actions the fund will take to avoid investor transactions that it deems disruptive to efficient portfolio management.

Investment Limitations

Like many mutual funds, the Wellesley Fund has adopted certain limitations on its own investment practices. For example, the fund will *not* do the following:

a. Invest more than 25 percent of its assets in any one industry.
b. With respect to 75 percent of the value of its total assets, purchase the securities of any issuer (except obligations of the U.S. government and its instrumentalities) if as a result the fund would hold more than 10 percent of the outstanding voting securities of the issuer, or more than 5 percent of the value of the fund's total assets would be invested in the securities of such issuer.
c. Borrow money, except that the fund may borrow from banks for temporary or emergency purposes, including the meeting of redemption requests, in an amount not exceeding 10 percent of the value of the funds's net assets.

Fund Management

The prospectus states that the Wellesley Fund is a member of the Vanguard Group of Investment Companies, a family of 32 investment companies with 78 distinct investment portfolios and total assets in excess of $120 billion. It explains how the fund group is organized and that the average expense ratio (annual costs divided by total net assets) for Vanguard funds is approximately 0.30 percent and that this is substantially lower than the 1.02 percent average for the mutual fund industry.

Investment Adviser

According to the prospectus, the Wellington Management Company, an independent professional management advisory firm, manages the investment and reinvestment of the fund's assets and continuously reviews, supervises and administers the fund's investment program. The total advisory fees paid by the fund to the Wellington Company is approximately .08 of 1 percent of the fund's average net assets (which is included in the 0.33 percent total operating expenses of the fund).

Performance Record

This section provides a table of investment results for the Wellesley Fund for several periods throughout the fund's lifetime (see Figure 12.2). It also compares the results to two performance indexes: a Composite Index, comprising the Salomon Brothers High Grade Bond Index (65 percent) and the Standard & Poor's 500 Composite Stock Price Index (35 percent); and the Consumer Price Index, a statistical measure of changes in the prices of goods and services.

Dividends, Capital Gains and Taxes

This section states that the fund expects to pay dividends quarterly from ordinary income and capital gain distributions, if any, annually. Both dividend and capital gain distributions may be automatically reinvested or received by shareholders in cash.

FIGURE 12.2   Sample Investment Results in Prospectus: Average Annual Return for Vanguard/Wellesley Income Fund

Fiscal Periods Ended 12/31/93	Vanguard/Wellesley Income Fund %	Composite Index %	Consumer Price Index %
1 Year	+14.6	+12.1	+2.7
5 Years	+13.7	+13.6	+3.9
10 Years	+14.1	+14.4	+3.7
Lifetime*	+11.7	+11.2	+5.8

*July 1, 1970, to December 31, 1993

Source: Reprinted by permission of The Vanguard Group.

The fund qualifies as a "regulated investment company" under the Internal Revenue Code so that it is not subject to federal income tax to the extent its income is distributed to shareholders. Dividends paid by the fund from net investment income, whether received in cash or reinvested in additional shares, will be taxable to shareholders as ordinary income. Distributions paid by the fund from long-term capital gains, whether received in cash or reinvested in additional shares, are taxable as long-term capital gains, regardless of the length of time an investor has owned shares in the fund.

The prospectus notes that a sale of fund shares is a taxable event and may result in a capital gain or loss. A capital gain or loss may be realized from an ordinary redemption of shares or an exchange of shares between two mutual funds (or portfolios of a mutual fund). Dividend distributions, capital gains distributions, and capital gains or losses from redemptions and exchanges may be subject to federal, state and local taxes.

The Share Price of the Fund

Like all mutual funds, the fund's share price or NAV per share is determined by dividing the total market value of the fund's investments and other assets, less any liabilities, by the number of outstanding fund shares. NAV is determined once daily at the regular close of the New York Stock Exchange (generally 4:00 PM Eastern time) on each day that the Exchange is open for business. The fund's share price appears in the mutual fund listings of most major newspapers.

Directors and Officers

The prospectus provides a list of the 13 directors and officers of the fund and a statement of their present positions and principal occupations during the past five years.

John C. Bogle is listed as Chairman, Chief Executive Officer and Director of The Vanguard Group, Inc., and of each of the investment companies in The Vanguard Group.

Shareholder Guide

This section explains such important things as how to open an account and purchase shares in the Wellesley Fund and how to make additional investments with the minimum transaction amounts.

You will find out how to purchase shares by mail, by wire, by exchange from a Vanguard account, and by Fund Express (moving money from your bank account on your request or automatically on a schedule you select). This portion of the prospectus also discusses how distributions are made. A new shareholder must select from one of three distribution options:

1. *Automatic reinvestment option*: Both dividends and capital gains distributions will be reinvested in additional fund shares.
2. *Cash dividend option*: Your dividends will be paid in cash and your capital gains will be reinvested in additional fund shares.
3. *All cash option*: Both dividend and capital gains distributions will be paid in cash.

Other information in this section relates to such items as these:

- The requirement that signature guarantees are needed for certain written transaction requests.
- Share certificates will be issued upon request.
- If you purchase shares in Vanguard Funds through a registered broker-dealer or investment adviser, the broker-dealer may charge a service fee.
- The fund will not cancel any purchase, exchange or redemption of shares believed to be authentic, received in writing or by telephone, once the transaction has been received.

The prospectus states that you may withdraw in writing or by telephone any portion of the funds in your account by redeeming shares at any time. Your redemption proceeds are normally mailed within two business days. Explicit instructions are given on the requirements for selling shares.

Finally, information is provided on other Vanguard services and administrative procedures the fund applies to such items as delivery of redemption proceeds, minimum account balances, exchange privileges, telephone transactions and transferring the registration of fund shares.

In Your Spare Time ...

Read the prospectus, one of the most important sources of information afforded mutual fund investors. It sets forth concisely the information you need to know about a particular fund before investing.

13

$ $

Investing in
Growth Funds

$ $

Patient investors seeking to build a fortune have been amply rewarded by investing in well-managed mutual funds with an objective of long-term capital appreciation. Some of the best funds have had extraordinary performance records. For example, Fidelity Magellan Fund has the best performance of any fund over the last 20 years. If you had invested $10,000 in that fund in 1975, your money would have grown to $964,626 by August 31, 1994 (assuming you automatically reinvested your dividends and capital gain distributions). Even now, with net assets topping $34 billion, making it the largest mutual fund in the United States, Magellan continues to produce returns that keep it among the leaders in the industry.

Most of the best-performing mutual funds over the long term have been those whose investment objective is growth of capital and where current income is a secondary consideration. Nearly 300 funds have this basic objective and are categorized as "growth" funds by *The Value Line Investment Survey*. As a group, their performance has tended to follow the general stock market (as measured by the S&P 500 Index) quite closely. But the group's average can be misleading; several funds have performed significantly better than the market as a whole.

An interesting aspect of relative performance among funds is that certain funds may do very well for a period of time, then drop from the top rankings, as other funds with different investment styles take over the leadership. For example, AIM Weingarten Fund, which invests in common stocks of seasoned, financially strong companies, earned a 46.9 percent total return for its shareholders in 1991, but in 1992 and 1993 the shares showed losses of 1.4 percent and 0.4 percent respectively. Fidelity Value Fund, on the other hand (using an investment style that seeks undervalued, asset-rich companies), had a 26.2 percent return in 1991 (20.7 percentage points less than AIM Weingarten), but earned 21.2 percent in 1992 and 22.9 percent in 1993.

Total Annual Returns

Year	AIM Weingarten Fund %	Fidelity Value Fund %	S&P 500 %
1991	46.9	26.2	30.5
1992	−1.4	21.2	7.7
1993	−0.4	22.9	10.1

No single investment style is always in favor. Sometimes the market rewards funds that emphasize technology stocks. At other times consumer stocks or financial stocks lead the market. In the same way, stocks with low PE ratios at times outperform stocks with high PE ratios, and vice versa. So, mutual funds leading the pack for a year or two often drop back and are replaced by other funds with different investment approaches. Long-term investors generally do best by hanging on to ably managed funds that have demonstrated consistent performance.

Traditionally, growth funds have been a mainstay for investors wanting to see their capital appreciate in value. Over the past 20 years, these funds have delivered an average total return (capital growth plus dividend distributions) of 15.2 percent per year. This was slightly better than the S&P 500, which had an average return of 14.5 percent during the same period. In more recent periods, the returns of growth mutual funds gradually have been dropping. Growth funds had an average annual return of 14.2 percent over the last 15 years, 13.2 percent over the last 10 years, and 9.3 percent over the last 10 years.

Figure 13.1 shows the annual performance of the growth fund group, as well as that of the S&P 500, from 1980 to August, 1994.

FIGURE 13.1   Total Return of Growth Funds 1980–August 31, 1994
Compared with S&P 500

Year	Group %	S&P 500%	Year	Group %	S&P 500%	Year	Group %	S&P 500%
1980	36.0	32.4	1985	28.4	32.2	1990	−4.7	−3.2
1981	−1.5	−4.9	1986	15.1	18.5	1991	35.7	30.5
1982	25.8	21.4	1987	2.7	5.2	1992	8.1	7.7
1983	21.1	22.6	1988	14.6	16.8	1993	11.5	10.1
1984	−1.5	6.3	1989	26.2	31.5	1994	0.9	3.8

A Recommended Long-Term Growth Fund

Fidelity Magellan Fund
82 Devonshire Street
Boston, MA 02109
800-544-8888

Min. initial investment: $2,500   **Date of inception:** January 1, 1963
Min. subsequent investment: $250   **Portfolio manager:** Jeffrey Vinik

Shares of this low-load fund are purchased with a 3 percent sales charge. Lower sales charges are available for accounts larger than $250,000. With more than 200 funds, Fidelity Investments offers the broadest mutual funds selection in the world. The company manages more than $225 billion in fund assets for about 15 million shareholder accounts.

Investment objective. Fidelity Magellan Fund seeks capital appreciation (increasing the value of the fund's shares). Current income is not a primary consideration. Over the last 15 years, the annual dividend yield has remained less than 2 percent.

Performance.   If you had invested $10,000 in Fidelity Magellan Fund for the 20 years ending August 31, 1994, your funds would have grown to $964,626. A similar investment in the S&P 500 would have resulted in a value of $152,648. During that period, the Magellan

Fund's average annual return was 25.9 percent. In recent years its return has been considerably less, averaging 18.7 percent in the last 10 years, and 13 percent in the last 5 years.

Figure 13.2 shows the year by year performance of the fund from 1980 to August 31, 1994.

Reason for recommendation. The long-term record of the Magellan Fund is matched by few of its peers. Magellan's history of moderate risk and high returns has made it the investment of choice for fund investors, as is evident by its more than $34 billion in assets.

Investment manager Jeffrey Vinik tries to identify stocks he believes have strong long-term earnings potential. He is more concerned with long-term trends than short-term market swings and attempts to position the fund for two to three years ahead. These efforts are supported by Fidelity's extensive research group of more than 200 analysts and portfolio managers. Despite its immense size, the Magellan Fund has not yet shown any signs of being too large to be flexible in its investment style. On the contrary, its nearly 25 percent gain in 1993 was way ahead of most funds' returns in the growth category. The Magellan Fund is an excellent choice as a core holding for investors seeking long-term growth of their capital.

Investment results. Long-term investors in the fund have reason to be extremely pleased with the fund's performance and with their own patience. Figure 13.3 illustrates the results of investing $10,000 in the Magellan fund over various time periods ending August 31, 1994, as well as the results of investing $10,000 plus $200 per month thereafter. The first-year investment totals $12,200 ($10,000 plus 11 months times $200). Income dividends and capital gains distributions have been reinvested.

Investment policy. The Magellan Fund attempts to achieve its objective of capital appreciation by investing primarily in common stock and securities convertible to common stock, of U.S., multinational and foreign companies of all sizes that are considered to offer potential for growth. In selecting foreign securities, management favors large and well-known companies, although it may choose smaller firms that it believes offer unusual value, even if they involve more risk. The fund may also invest in domestic and foreign debt

FIGURE 13.2   Fidelity Magellan Fund Total Return 1980–August 31, 1994
Compared with S&P 500

Year	Fund %	S&P 500%	Year	Fund %	S&P 500%	Year	Fund %	S&P 500%
1980	69.9	32.4	1985	43.1	32.2	1990	−4.5	−3.2
1981	16.4	−4.1	1986	23.7	18.5	1991	41.0	30.6
1982	48.1	21.4	1987	1.0	5.2	1992	7.0	7.7
1983	38.6	22.5	1988	22.8	16.8	1993	24.7	10.1
1984	2.0	6.3	1989	34.6	31.5	1994	1.7	3.8

FIGURE 13.3   Fidelity Magellan Fund Investment Results for Various
Periods Ending August 31, 1994

Time of Investment	Value of $10,000 Invested	Value of $10,000 Invested Plus $200 Per Month	Total Invested
1 Year	$9,941	$ 12,195	$12,200
3 Years	14,124	22,550	17,000
5 Years	17,867	34,895	21,800
10 Years	54,042	109,806	33,800
15 Years	226,304	420,514	45,800
20 Years	964,626	1,802,210	57,800

securities that are believed to have capital appreciation potential, including lower-rated corporate bonds.

10 Largest Common Stock Holdings (as of March 31, 1994)

	Percent of Common Stock Holdings
Intel Corporation	2.6
Motorola, Inc.	2.2
Burlington Northern, Inc.	1.7
CSX Corporation	1.3
Caterpillar, Inc.	1.3
Columbia/HCA Healthcare Corporation	1.2
Burlington Resources	1.1
Texas Instruments	1.1

Entergy Corporation	1.1
International Business Machines Corporation	1.0
	14.6

Cost of ownership. Following is a list of expenses and fees based on the fund's May 20, 1994, prospectus.

Shareholder transaction expenses

Sales charge imposed on purchases: 3.0% (less for accounts over $250,000)
Sales charge imposed on reinvested dividends: None
Deferred sales charge: None
Redemption fees: None
Exchange fees: None

Annual fund operating expenses

Management fees: 0.76%
12b-1 fees: None
Other expenses: 0.23%

Total operating expenses: 0.99%

Example of expenses. The following example illustrates the expenses you would incur on a $1,000 investment in Fidelity Magellan Fund over various time periods, assuming (1) a 5 percent annual rate of return and (2) redemption at the end of each period.

Years	1 Year	3 Years	5 Years	10 Years
Expenses	$40	$61	$83	$148

Five Other Top Performing Funds

During the ten-year period ending August 31, 1994, the following five mutual funds characterized as growth funds led their peers in total return. No-load or low-load funds that you can purchase directly from the mutual fund companies are shown in **bold print**.

Fund	Ten-Year Average Annual Total Return %
CGM Capital Development Fund	21.9
Fidelity Advisor Equity Growth Portfolio	19.6

Fidelity Contrafund   19.0
Berger 100 Fund   18.4
Fidelity Destiny I   18.2

Following are addresses, phone numbers, and investment performance for each fund. The charts illustrate the results of $10,000 invested in each fund over various time periods ending August 31, 1994, as well as the results of a $10,000 investment plus $200 per month thereafter.

CGM Capital Development Fund (closed to new investors)
399 Boylston Street
Boston, MA 02116
800-345-4048

Date of Inception: June 22, 1961

Investment Results

Time of Investment	Value of $10,000 Invested	Value of $10,000 Invested Plus $200 per Month	Total Invested
1 Year	$10,780	$12,950	$12,200
3 Years	16,529	25,185	17,000
5 Years	26,323	47,455	21,800
10 Years	72,706	144,002	33,800
15 Years	215,896	437,838	45,800
20 Years	451,105	1,077,963	57,800

Fidelity Advisor Equity Growth Portfolio
82 Devonshire Street
Boston, MA 02109
800-522-7297

Date of Inception: November 22, 1983

Investment Results

Time of Investment	Value of $10,000 Invested	Value of $10,000 Invested Plus $200 per Month	Total Invested
1 Year	$ 10,604	$12,854	$12,200
3 Years	14,125	22,387	17,000
5 Years	23,791	41,931	21,800
10 Years	60,094	124,722	33,800

Fidelity Contrafund
82 Devonshire Street
Boston, MA 02109
800-544-8888

Date of Inception: May 17, 1967

Investment Results

Time of Investment	Value of $10,000 Invested	Value of $10,000 Invested Plus $200 per Month	Total Invested
1 Year	$ 9,867	$ 12,111	$ 12,200
3 Years	15,076	23,522	17,000
5 Years	22,826	41,444	21,800
10 Years	55,275	120,251	33,800
15 Years	98,272	251,518	45,800
20 Years	240,654	565,106	57,800

Berger 100 Fund
210 University Boulevard
Denver, CO 80206
800-333-1001

Date of Inception: August 1, 1966

Investment Results

Time of Investment	Value of $10,000 Invested	Value of $10,000 Invested Plus $200 per Month	Total Invested
1 Year	$ 10,019	$12,187	$12,200
3 Years	14,730	22,838	17,000
5 Years	23,059	41,423	21,800
10 Years	54,267	118,415	33,800
15 Years	90,875	228,265	45,800
20 Years	137,114	419,914	57,800

Fidelity Destiny I
82 Devonshire Street
Boston, MA 02109
800-544-8888

Date of Inception: July 10,1970

Investment Results

Time of Investment	Value of $10,000 Invested	Value of $10,000 Invested Plus $200 per Month	Total Invested
1 Year	$11,591	$13,965	$12,200
3 Years	16,402	25,668	17,000
5 Years	20,718	39,894	21,800
10 Years	53,144	113,090	33,800
15 Years	129,895	301,483	45,800
20 Years	538,435	1,030,873	57,800

In Your Spare Time ...

Consider growth funds. Some of the best have had extraordinary performance records. Even the average growth fund has provided its investors a return of approximately 15 percent per year over the past 20 years.

14

$ $

Investing in Small-Company Funds

$ $

Investing in mutual funds that specialize in small-company stocks can be rewarding in the long term, but possibly unnerving along the way. If you had invested $10,000 in the Acorn Fund 20 years ago, then added $200 each month thereafter, you would have invested a total of $57,800. By the end of May, 1994, it would have been worth $727,611. But it would have tested your patience a number of times. In 1990 Acorn Fund shares dropped more than 17 percent, and they were down 8 percent during the first five months of 1994. Small-company stocks tend to be more volatile than the market as a whole.

Small-company funds seek long-term growth of capital; current income is generally not an important consideration. When held for the long term, small-company stocks have done better than those of large companies. Small-company funds on average bear this out, having led all other general equity groups in performance over recent three, five and ten year periods. Aggressive growth funds trailed only slightly. The chart illustrates this.

Total Return Performance Through 7/29/94

Fund Group	Three Years %	Five Years %	Ten Years %
Aggressive Growth	10.8	10.3	14.4
Growth	9.0	8.9	13.8
Growth and Income	9.2	8.4	13.5

| Income | 10.0 | 8.2 | 12.7 |
| **Small Company** | 12.3 | 11.1 | 14.5 |

The success of small-company funds has led to impressive gains in asset size for the leaders. Acorn Fund, for example, grew from net assets of $210 million in 1984 to more than $2 billion by the end of 1993. Concerned that it might grow too big and become unwieldy to manage, the fund is now closed to new investors.

Small-company funds have the potential for explosive growth, but are extremely volatile, and hence, risky. Investors with short time horizons run the risk of big losses. Generally, small-company stocks do better than those of large companies in rising markets, but fare worse in declining markets. Figure 14.1 shows the annual calendar year performance of the small-company group, as well as that of the S&P 500, and gives some indication of the group's volatility.

If $1,000 had been invested in the small-fund group on the first business day of 1980, it would have had a value of $7,272 on May 31, 1994. A similar investment in the S&P 500, with less volatility, would have resulted in a value of $7,284. Nevertheless, certain small-company funds have done very well over time. One example is the young PBHG Growth Fund.

A Recommended Small-Company Fund

PBHG Growth Fund
P.O. Box 3167
Houston, TX 77253
800-809-8008

Min. initial investment: $1,000
Min. subsequent investment: No minimum
Date of inception: December 19, 1985
Portfolio manager: Gary L. Pilgrim

Shares of this no-load fund are purchased and redeemed at NAV. There are no sales charges or 12b-1 plan distribution charges. A redemption fee of 2.0 percent is imposed on shares purchased on or after August 15, 1994, and held less than six months.

FIGURE 14.1 Total Return of Small-Company Funds 1980–May 31, 1994
Compared with S&P 500

Year	Group %	S&P 500%	Year	Group %	S&P 500%	Year	Group %	S&P 500%
1980	41.5	32.4	1985	32.2	32.2	1990	−9.7	−3.2
1981	−0.9	−4.9	1986	10.6	18.5	1991	51.1	30.5
1982	31.3	21.4	1987	−1.1	5.2	1992	13.4	7.7
1983	25.7	22.6	1988	20.1	16.8	1993	16.7	10.1
1984	−7.2	6.3	1989	24.3	31.5	1994	−5.4	−0.9

FIGURE 14.2 Total Return of PBHG Growth Fund 1986–May 31, 1994
Compared with S&P 500

Year	Fund %	S&P 500%	Year	Fund %	S&P 500%
1986	23.0	18.5	1991	51.6	30.6
1987	11.6	5.2	1992	28.5	7.7
1988	6.9	16.8	1993	46.6	10.1
1989	29.4	31.5	1994	−8.4	−1.0
1990	−9.7	−3.2			

Investment objectives. PBHG Growth Fund seeks capital appreciation; current dividend or interest income is not an objective. The fund invests principally in common stocks that have an outlook for strong growth in earnings.

Performance. $10,000 invested in the fund during the nearly eight and one half years from 1986 (its first full year of operation) to May 31, 1994 ,would have grown to $44,850. A similar investment in the S&P 500 would have resulted in a value of $28,420. Figure 14.2 shows the year-by-year performance of the fund.

Reason for recommendation. Gary Pilgrim has managed the PBHG Growth Fund by successfully researching companies with high growth rates and sustainable profitability. He has continued to discover new investments and added to existing ones. Pilgrim has been aggressive in buying stocks at or shortly after their initial public offering

(IPO), resulting in some big winners. One example is Callaway Golf. After following the company's progress for about six months after the IPO, the fund bought a small position in the stock, then gradually increased its holdings as more was learned about the golf club-maker's business. It is now one of PBHG Growth Fund's largest and most profitable holdings. Other profitable purchases include Bombay Company and Sunglass Hut. Pilgrim's approach to investing is to "find the fastest growing companies and stick with them."

This fund should continue to deliver excellent returns when the small-capitalization market is doing well. But as with any fund holding small-company stocks, the share value of this fund can be volatile. PBHG Growth is suitable only for investors with a good tolerance for risk.

Investment results.   PBHG Growth Fund investors have been well rewarded during the fund's short history. Figure 14.3 illustrates the results of $10,000 invested in the fund over various time periods ending May 31, 1994, as well as the results of an investment of $10,000 plus $200 per month thereafter. Income dividends and capital gains distributions have been reinvested in additional shares.

Small dividend distributions were made in 1986 and 1989. Because this fund generally invests in young, rapidly growing companies that typically reinvest earnings to finance future growth, expect little or no dividends in future years.

Investment policy of PBHG Growth Fund.   The fund invests mainly in companies with an outlook for strong growth in earnings and the potential for significant capital appreciation. The expected trend of companies' earnings is the primary criterion used in selecting securities. Securities are sold when the manager believes that anticipated appreciation is no longer probable, alternative investments offer superior appreciation prospects or the risk of a decline in market price is too great.

PBHG Growth invests in stocks that are traded in the over-the-counter market as well as in those listed on a stock exchange. Purchases are made in securities issued by small and mid-sized companies, including IPOs. The fund may also invest in convertible securities or cash equivalents when management believes it is prudent. As much as 15 percent of total assets may be invested in foreign securities. Gener-

FIGURE 14.3　PBHG Growth Fund Investment Results: for Various
　　　　　　　　　Periods Ending May 31, 1994

Time of Investment	Value of $10,000 Invested	Value of $10,000 Invested Plus $200 Per Month	Total Invested
1 Year	$11,444	$13,590	$12,200
3 Years	18,497	28,963	17,000
5 Years	23,887	45,811	21,800

ally, a small portion (but not more than 5 percent) of assets will be held in high-quality, short-term debt securities and investment grade corporate or government bonds.

10 Largest Common Stock Holdings (as of June 30, 1994)

	Percent of Common Stock Holdings
Value Health	1.8
Linear Technology Corporation	1.7
Clear Channel Communications, Inc.	1.6
Three-Five Systems Corporation	1.5
Avid Technology, Inc.	1.5
Gentex, Inc.	1.5
ALC Communications, Inc.	1.5
Powersoft Corporation	1.4
Antec Corporation	1.4
Atmel Corporation	1.4
Total	15.3

The fund's portfolio contained about 100 stock issues, with a total market value of $423 million on June 30, 1994. Illustrating the relatively small size of companies purchased for the portfolio, the median market capitalization (number of shares outstanding times market price) of stocks held was $362 million.

Cost of ownership.　PBHG Growth Fund charges no sales loads, deferred sales fees, or 12b-1 distribution fees. However, a 2 percent redemption fee is charged when shares purchased after August 15, 1994, are held less than six months. Following is a list of expenses and fees, based on the fund's June 3, 1994 prospectus.

Shareholder transaction expenses

Sales load imposed on purchases: None
Sales load imposed on reinvested dividends: None
Deferred sales load: None
Redemption fees: 2.0 percent on shares held less than six months.
Exchange fees: None

Annual fund operating expenses

Management fees: 0.85%
12b-1 fees: None
Other expenses: 0.45%
Total operating expenses: 1.30%

Example of expenses. The following example illustrates the expenses you would incur on a $1,000 investment in PBHG Growth Fund over various time periods, assuming (1) a 5 percent annual rate of return and (2) redemption at the end of each period.

Years	1 Year	3 Years	5 Years	10 Years
Expenses	$13	$41	$71	$157

Five Other Top Performing Funds

During the ten-year period ending June 30, 1994, the following five mutual funds characterized as *small-company funds* led their peers in total return. No-load or low-load funds that you can purchase directly from the mutual fund companies are shown in **bold print**.

Fund	*Ten-Year Average Annual Total Return %*
Twentieth Century Giftrust Investors	**24.2**
FPA Capital Fund	18.5
Acorn Fund	**18.4**
Putnam OTC Emerging Growth Fund	17.6
Evergreen Limited Market Fund	**17.3**

Following are addresses, phone numbers and investment performance for each fund. The charts illustrate the results of $10,000 invested in each fund over various time periods ending June 30, 1994, as well as the results of an investment of $10,000 plus $100 per month thereafter.

Twentieth Century Giftrust Investors
4500 Main Street
Kansas City, MO 64141
800-345-2021

Date of Inception: November 25, 1983

Investment Results

Time of Investment	Value of $10,000 Invested	Value of $10,000 Invested Plus $200 per Month	Total Invested
1 Year	$11,710	$13,876	$12,200
3 Years	18,958	28,374	17,000
5 Years	24.866	45,478	21,800
10 Years	87,687	162,485	33,800

The fund enables an investor to make a gift to a charity, an individual or an organization. Shares are held in trust by an independent trustee until the maturity date specified by the investor. The trust duration must be at least ten years from the time the investor makes the first investment in Giftrust or until the recipient reaches the age of maturity.

FPA Capital Fund
11400 West Olympic Boulevard
Los Angeles, CA 90064
800-638-3060

Date of Inception: January 1, 1968

Investment Results

Time of Investment	Value of $10,000 Invested	Value of $10,000 Invested Plus $200 per Month	Total Invested
1 Year	$11,054	$13,390	$12,200
3 Years	15,340	24,478	17,000
5 Years	19,878	39,330	21,800
10 Years	50,974	111,936	33,800
15 Years	84,702	222,336	45,800
20 Years	108,089	369,063	57,800

Acorn Fund (Closed to new investors)
227 West Monroe Street
Chicago, IL 60606
800-922-6769

Date of Inception: June 10, 1970

Investment Results

Time of Investment	Value of $10,000 Invested	Value of $10,000 Invested Plus $200 per Month	Total Invested
1 Year	$10,773	$12,943	$12,200
3 Years	17,701	26,815	17,000
5 Years	20,137	38,903	21,800
10 Years	54,208	111,562	33,800
15 Years	113,083	254,935	45,800
20 Years	324,211	727,611	57,800

Putnam OTC Emerging Growth Fund
One Post Office Square
Boston, MA 02109
800-225-1581

Date of Inception: November 1, 1982

Investment Results

Time of Investment	Value of $10,000 Invested	Value of $10,000 Invested Plus $200 per Month	Total Invested
1 Year	$10,412	$12,562	$12,200
3 Years	14,803	23,611	17,000
5 Years	17,006	34,502	21,800
10 Years	47,831	100,529	33,800

Evergreen Limited Market Fund
2500 Westchester Avenue
Purchase, NY 10577
800-235-0064

Date of Inception: June 1, 1983

Investment Results

Time of Investment	Value of $10,000 Invested	Value of $10,000 Invested Plus $200 per Month	Total Invested
1 Year	$10,764	$12,964	$12,200
3 Years	13,689	21,551	17,000
5 Years	16,321	31,945	21,800
10 Years	49,438	95,683	33,800

In Your Spare Time ...

Check out small-company stock funds. Historically, the stocks of small companies have done better than those of large companies when held for the long term. On average, small-company stock funds have led all other general equity groups in performance over recent three, five and ten-year periods.

15

$ $

Investing for Balance— Growth and Income

$ $

Investors seeking growth of capital, together with current income, often take a "balanced" approach to investing. You can reach this objective by investing in a mutual fund that holds a combination of equity securities (for growth) and debt securities (for income). About 60 funds follow this course and are classified as balanced funds.

Balanced funds generally seek long-term capital growth, preservation of capital and current income. They invest in common stocks, preferred stocks and bonds. Normally, investments will be made in a broad array of securities, diversified not only in terms of companies and industries, but also by type of security as well. The proportions invested in each type of security will change from time to time in accordance with the funds' interpretation of economic conditions and underlying security values. A typical balanced fund holds at least 25 percent of its total assets in fixed-income senior securities, including debt securities and preferred stocks.

Balanced funds represent a good choice for investors looking for long-term, consistent returns, a decent income and below-market risk. According to *The Value Line Mutual Funds Survey*, over the 20-year period ending in mid-1994, balanced funds as a group have produced average annual returns of just 1 percent less than the S&P 500, while usually experiencing only about half the risk. A plus for this group is that it has consistently performed better than the broad market averages during declines.

Figure 15.1 shows the annual calender year performance of the group, as well as that of the S&P 500.

A Recommended Balanced Fund

Dodge & Cox Balanced Fund
1 Sansome Street
San Francisco, CA 94104
415-981-1710

Minimum initial investment: $2,500
Minimum subsequent investment: $100
Date of inception: June 26, 1931
Portfolio manager: Dodge & Cox's Investment Policy Committee

Shares of this no-load fund are purchased and redeemed at NAV. There are no sales, redemption or 12b-1 plan distribution charges.

Investment objectives. This fund's investment objectives are to provide shareholders with regular income, conservation of principal and an opportunity for long-term growth of principal and income. The fund seeks to achieve these objectives by investing in a diversified portfolio of common stocks, preferred stock and bonds.

FIGURE 15.1 Total Return of Balanced Funds 1980–June 30, 1994 Compared with S&P 500

Year	Group %	S&P 500%	Year	Group %	S&P 500%	Year	Group %	S&P 500%
1980	19.3	32.4	1985	27.1	32.2	1990	−0.5	−3.2
1981	3.3	−4.9	1986	16.1	18.5	1991	25.2	30.5
1982	29.0	21.4	1987	2.7	5.2	1992	7.3	7.7
1983	17.2	22.6	1988	11.4	16.8	1993	10.7	10.1
1984	6.5	6.3	1989	18.3	31.5	1994	−3.8	−3.4

Performance. During the 15-year period ending on June 30, 1994, the total average annual return of Dodge & Cox Balanced Fund was 13.6 percent. Figure 15.2 shows the year-by-year performance of the fund, as well as that of the S&P 500.

Reason for recommendation. The Dodge & Cox Balanced Fund has been a consistent long-term performer among mutual funds in the balanced fund group, producing excellent returns with a low degree of risk. During the dismal first half of 1994, while the S&P 500 declined by 3.5 percent, the fund was off just 1.4 percent. Over the five years ending June 30, 1994, the fund outperformed the S&P 500 by almost a full percentage point. Like other funds in the balanced group, Dodge & Cox Balanced performs better than most in years when the market is down. In 1981, it posted a loss of only 2.5 percent when the S&P 500 was down 4.9 percent, and in 1990 when the S&P was down 3.2 percent, the fund was up nearly 1 percent.

The ability of this fund to consistently outperform its peers has attracted funds from many new investors, with net assets growing from less than $20 million in 1983 to more than $580 million by mid-1994. During the last ten years, Dodge & Cox Balanced has outperformed its group every year except one. Significant further growth in assets is likely as more investors recognize that a well-managed partial-equity fund like Dodge & Cox Balanced can pack a wallop, while limiting risk.

With a dividend yield of about 3.5 percent, investors who like current income along with capital growth should find this fund especially attractive.

FIGURE 15.2   Dodge & Cox Balanced Fund Total Return 1980–June 30, 1994 Compared with S&P 500

Year	Group %	S&P 500%	Year	Group %	S&P 500%	Year	Group %	S&P 500%
1980	21.6	32.4	1985	32.5	32.2	1990	0.9	−3.2
1981	−2.5	−4.9	1986	18.8	18.5	1991	20.7	30.5
1982	26.1	21.4	1987	7.2	5.2	1992	10.6	7.7
1983	16.9	22.6	1988	11.5	16.8	1993	16.9	10.1
1984	4.7	6.3	1989	23.0	31.5	1994	−1.4	−3.5

Investment results. Investors in the Dodge & Cox Balanced Fund have enjoyed excellent performance over many years. Figure 15.3 illustrates the results of $10,000 invested in the fund over various time periods ending June 30, 1994, as well as the results of an investment of $10,000 plus $200 per month thereafter. Income dividends and capital gains distributions have been reinvested.

Based on the 3.57 percent dividend yield for the 12 months ending June 30, 1994, annual income of $4,109 would be paid on the 20-year value of $115,116, resulting from a $10,000 investment. An income of $11,725 would be payable on the 20-year value of $328,458, resulting from a $10,000 investment plus an additional $200 invested per month.

Investment policy. To provide shareholders with regular income, conservation of principal and an opportunity for long-term growth of principal and income, the fund invests in a diversified portfolio of common stocks, preferred stock and bonds.

Because flexibility is necessary in managing fund assets under changing economic conditions, the managers revise the proportions held in common and preferred stocks and bonds in light of their appraisal of business and investment prospects.

The fund maintains no more than 75 percent of its total assets in common stocks. In general, bonds are held for stability of principal and income as well as for a reserve that can be used to take advantage of investment opportunities. Normally, bonds purchased are high quality, including those in the top four rating categories by either Moody's Investors Service (Aaa, Aa, A, Baa) or Standard & Poor's Corporation

FIGURE 15.3   Dodge & Cox Balanced Fund Investment Results
for Various Periods Ending June 30, 1994

Time of Investment	Value of $10,000 Invested	Value of $10,000 Invested Plus $200 Per Month	Total Invested
1 Year	$ 10,386	$ 12,572	$12,200
3 Years	13,921	21,917	17,000
5 Years	17,022	32,406	21,800
10 Years	39,962	84,832	33,800
15 Years	67,807	175,085	45,800
20 Years	115,116	328,458	57,800

(AAA, AA, A, BBB). Securities rated in the lowest of the top four (Baa or BBB) may have speculative characteristics.

A substantial portfolio position is maintained in common stocks that are deemed to have a favorable outlook for long-term growth of principal and income. Prospective earnings and dividends are major considerations in these stock selections. Individual securities are selected with an emphasis on financial strength and a sound economic background.

To minimize unforeseen risks in single securities, the Dodge & Cox Balanced Fund seeks adequate diversification. Investments made in any one stock or bond issue, with the exception of U.S. government securities, seldom exceed 2 percent of the total fund assets. The fund generally invests in securities with ready markets, mainly issues listed on national securities exchanges.

10 Largest Common Stock Holdings (as of December 31, 1993)

	Percent of Common Stock Holdings
International Business Machines Corporation	2.9
Dayton Hudson Corporation	2.9
Procter & Gamble Company	2.7
Caterpillar, Inc.	2.6
General Motors Corporation	2.5
American Express Company	2.5
Deere & Company	2.4
Xerox Corporation	2.3
Federal Express Corporation	2.1
Nordstrom, Inc.	2.1
Total	25.0

Cost of ownership.   Dodge & Cox Balanced Fund is a true no-load fund because it is free of any sales loads or redemption charges. The following list of expenses and fees is based on the fund's March 3, 1994 prospectus.

Shareholder transaction expenses

Sales charge imposed on purchases: None
Sales charge imposed on reinvested dividends: None
Deferred sales charge: None
Redemption fees: None
Exchange fees: None

Annual fund operating expenses

Management fees: 0.50%
12b-1 fees: None
Other expenses: 0.10%
Total operating expenses: 0.60%

Example of expenses. The following example illustrates the expenses you would incur on a $1,000 investment in Dodge & Cox Balanced Fund over various time periods, assuming (1) a 5 percent annual rate of return and (2) redemption at the end of each period.

Years	1 Year	3 Years	5 Years	10 Years
Expenses	$6	$19	$33	$75

Five Other Top Performing Funds

During the ten-year period ending June 30, 1994, the following five mutual funds characterized as *balanced funds* led their peers in total return. No-load or low-load funds that you can purchase directly from the mutual fund companies are shown in **bold print**.

Fund	*Ten-Year Average* *Annual Total Return %*
CGM Mutual Fund	**16.9**
T. Rowe Price Balanced Fund	**14.6**
MFS Total Return Fund A	14.3
Phoenix Balanced Fund Series	14.1
IDS Mutual Fund	14.1

Following are addresses, phone numbers, and investment performance for each fund. The charts illustrate the results of $10,000 invested in each fund over various time periods ending June 30, 1994, as well as the results of an investment of $10,000 plus $200 per month thereafter.

CGM Mutual Fund
399 Boylston Street
Boston, MA 02116
800-345-4048

Date of Inception: November 5, 1929

Investment Results

Time of Investment	Value of $10,000 Invested	Value of $10,000 Invested Plus $200 per Month	Total Invested
1 Year	$9,897	$11,977	$12,200
3 Years	14,504	22,322	17,000
5 Years	18,601	34,425	21,800
10 Years	47,522	95,686	33,800
15 Years	81,973	204,269	45,800
20 Years	109,399	349,575	57,800

T. Rowe Price Balanced Fund
P.O. Box 89000
Baltimore, MD 21202
800-225-5132

Date of Inception: November 29, 1938

Investment Results

Time of Investment	Value of $10,000 Invested	Value of $10,000 Invested Plus $200 per Month	Total Invested
1 Year	$ 10,210	$12,348	$12,200
3 Years	13,919	21,663	17,000
5 Years	17,649	32,993	21,800
10 Years	39,237	82,845	33,800
15 Years	61,282	162,472	45,800

MFS Total Return Fund A
500 Boylston Street
Boston, MA 02116
800-343-2829

Date of Inception: October 6, 1979

Investment Results

Time of Investment	Value of $10,000 Invested	Value of $10,000 Invested Plus $200 per Month	Total Invested
1 Year	$9,608	$11,758	$12,200
3 Years	12,851	20,593	17,000

5 Years	15,102	29,860	21,800
10 Years	36,145	78,441	33,800
15 Years	65,231	169,977	45,800
20 Years	117,141	329,011	57,800

Phoenix Balanced Fund Series
1 American Row
Hartford, CT 06115
800-243-4361

Date of Inception: January 30, 1976

Investment Results

Time of Investment	*Value of $10,000 Invested*	*Value of $10,000 Invested Plus $200 per Month*	*Total Invested*
1 Year	$9,332	$11,456	$12,200
3 Years	11,609	18,853	17,000
5 Years	15,453	29,411	21,800
10 Years	35,739	76,499	33,800
15 Years	74,560	182,456	45,800
20 Years	120,955	349,305	57,800

IDS Mutual Fund
IDS Tower 10
Minneapolis, MN 55440
800-437-4332

Date of Inception: January 18, 1940

Investment Results

Time of Investment	*Value of $10,000 Invested*	*Value of $10,000 Invested Plus $200 per Month*	*Total Invested*
1 Year	$9,819	$11,989	$12,200
3 Years	13,104	20,964	17,000
5 Years	14,846	29,924	21,800
10 Years	35,469	77,843	33,800
15 Years	61,994	165,426	45,800
20 Years	95,699	296,555	57,800

In Your Spare Time ...

Consider a balanced approach to investing. Balanced funds invest in bonds, as well as stocks, and represent a good choice for investors looking for above-average returns with below-market risk.

16

$ $

Investing in
International
Growth Funds

$ $

Foreign stock markets have been attracting enormous attention from investors. By early 1994, more than $50 billion was invested in international equity funds—compared with less than $560 million just ten years earlier. Put another way, for every U.S. mutual fund dollar invested overseas in 1983, more than $90 is invested today. Some international funds operate in particular geographical regions, such as Europe, the Far East or Latin America. Other funds invest anywhere in the world, except in the United States. Global funds, with the greatest flexibility, purchase the securities of companies located in any country, including the United States.

On average, long-term investors in mutual funds holding foreign equities have fared significantly better than those sticking entirely with U.S. securities. For example, while the average annual return of U.S. equity securities (as measured by the S&P 500 Index) for the 20-year period ending May 31, 1994, was 13.2 percent, global equity funds averaged 14.7 percent and Pacific area funds averaged 17.4 percent. Figure 16.1 illustrates average annual returns of international mutual fund groups from 1980 to May 1994.

The volatility of some foreign markets can make investing overseas risky. The Morgan Stanley Asian Equity Portfolio, for instance, gained 105.6 percent in 1993, then lost 15.3 percent in the first five months of 1994. Spectacular performances by individual funds are not unusual.

FIGURE 16.1   Total Annual Return of International Fund Groups
1980–May 31, 1994

	Europe[1]	Foreign[2]	Pacific[3]	Global[4]	S&P 500[5]
1980	N/A	30.3	35.8	37.0	32.4
1981	N/A	−2.1	17.6	−0.5	−4.9
1982	N/A	4.3	−2.6	18.2	21.4
1983	N/A	26.0	35.1	25.9	22.5
1984	N/A	−5.1	−3.5	−5.1	6.3
1985	N/A	46.3	31.7	37.2	32.2
1986	21.9	46.7	68.6	29.4	18.5
1987	0.4	10.6	22.6	8.3	5.2
1988	22.3	17.0	35.6	14.0	16.8
1989	21.8	22.2	25.7	20.5	31.5
1990	−5.9	−9.6	−18.3	−10.1	−3.2
1991	7.1	12.9	13.4	19.4	30.6
1992	−5.1	−4.1	−4.4	0.7	7.7
1993	27.6	40.0	58.3	30.1	10.1
1994	0.3	0.0	−3.1	−1.7	−1.0

N/A=Insufficient number of funds operating in these years.

(1) *Europe funds* generally invest in securities of companies located in the British Isles, continental Europe, and Scandinavia.

(2) *Foreign funds* buy securities of companies located in any country worldwide, except for the United States.

(3) *Pacific funds* invest in Pacific Rim securities, generally including Japan, Hong Kong, Australia, Korea, Taiwan and Southeast Asian countries.

(4) *Global funds* invest in the securities of companies worldwide, including the United States.

(5) The *S&P 500* is an index of 500 of the largest U.S. companies and represents about 80 percent of the value of all stocks traded on the New York Stock Exchange and 70 percent of the value of all stocks traded in the United States.

The Newport Tiger Fund had annual returns of 26 percent in 1991, 22 percent in 1992, and 75.3 percent in 1993, before dropping nearly 9 percent in early 1994. You can make money abroad, but the road to long-term riches can be rocky.

Important benefits of investing in mutual funds with a worldwide perspective include access to hundreds of companies in markets such as Europe, South America and the Far East. The United States now accounts for only about a third of the world's total stock market value, so international funds allow you to participate in the other two-thirds, with exposure to markets driven by forces different from those affecting the U.S. markets.

A Recommended International Growth Fund

Templeton Growth Fund
700 Central Avenue
St. Petersburg, FL 33701-3628
800-354-9191

Min. initial investment: $100
Min. subsequent investment: $25
Date of inception: November 19, 1954
Portfolio manager: Mark G. Holowesko

You can purchase fund shares through a broker with a 5.75 percent sales charge. Lower sales charges are available for accounts larger than $100,000.

Investment objective. This fund's objective is long-term capital growth, which it seeks through a flexible policy of investing in stocks and debt obligations of companies and governments of any nation.

Performance. A $10,000 investment in the Templeton Growth Fund on November 29, 1954, would have been worth $2,182,164 on December 31, 1993 (assuming reinvestment of dividends and capital gain distributions).

This fund has been a consistently good performer, often an outstanding one. Its average annual return of 17 percent in the 20-year period ending May 31, 1994, was a healthy 3.8 percentage points better than the S&P 500's 13.2% and 4.1 percentage points better than the Morgan Stanley Capital International World Index (MSCI World).

FIGURE 16.2   Templeton Growth Fund Total Return 1980–May 31, 1994
Compared with MSCI World Index

Year	Fund	MSCI World	Year	Fund	MSCI World	Year	Fund	MSCI World
1980	25.9	25.7	1985	27.8	40.6	1990	-9.1	-8.9
1981	-0.2	-4.7	1986	21.2	41.9	1991	31.3	18.3
1982	10.8	9.7	1987	3.1	16.2	1992	4.2	-5.2
1983	32.9	21.9	1988	23.6	23.3	1993	32.7	22.7
1984	2.2	4.7	1989	22.6	16.4	1994	1.6	4.1

Templeton Growth Fund avoided the extreme volatility common among many international funds during that period.

Since 1980, the fund has had only two down years, losing 0.2 percent in 1981 and 9.1 percent in 1990. Figure 16.2 shows the year-by-year performance of the fund from 1980 to May 31, 1994.

A hypothetical $1,000 invested in Templeton Growth Fund from the first business day of 1980 and held until May 31, 1994, would have been worth $7,672. The same $1,000 invested in the MSCI World Index would have grown to $6,267.

Reason for recommendation.   Like most Templeton funds, Templeton Growth Fund takes a value-oriented bottom-up approach. The manager searches for the most undervalued companies worldwide. About a third of the fund's portfolio was invested in U.S. companies in early 1994, followed by the United Kingdom and Hong Kong, each with 6 percent of the portfolio's value. Nearly 80 percent of the portfolio was invested in common stocks, 8 percent was in bonds and 13 percent in cash equivalents.

This fund is an excellent choice for an investor who wants to invest worldwide. Good selection of well-researched U.S. and foreign stocks has been the key to the fund's success. It has soundly beaten its peers in recent years.

Investment results.   Patient investors in this fund have enjoyed steady growth of their money over the years, with few setbacks. Figure 16.3 illustrates the results of $10,000 invested in Templeton Growth over various time periods ending May 31, 1994, as well as the results

FIGURE 16.3   Templeton Growth Fund Investment Results for Various
Periods Ending May 31, 1994

Time of Investment	Value of $10,000 Invested	Value of $10,000 Invested Plus $200 Per Month	Total Invested
1 Year	$11,284	$13,634	$12,200
3 Years	14,307	23,283	17,000
5 Years	17,566	34,824	21,800
10 Years	41,747	92,789	33,800
15 Years	83,803	297,869	45,800
20 Years	216,412	534,040	57,800

of an investment of $10,000 plus $200 per month thereafter. Income dividends and capital gains distributions have been reinvested in additional shares.

Investment policy. The Templeton Growth Fund attempts to achieve its objective of long-term capital growth by investing in stocks and debt obligations of companies and governments of any nation. Any income realized will be incidental.

Although the fund invests primarily in common stock, it may also invest in preferred stocks and certain debt securities, rated or unrated, such as convertible bonds and bonds selling at a discount. Whenever the investment manager decides that market or economic conditions warrant, the fund may invest in U.S. government securities, bank time deposits in the currency of any major nation and commercial paper.

The fund may invest no more than 5 percent of its total assets in securities issued by any one company or government, exclusive of U.S. government securities. The fund invests for long-term growth of capital and does not intend to emphasize short-term trading profits. As a result, the fund expects to have a portfolio turnover rate of less than 50 percent.

The fund may also purchase and sell stock index futures contracts up to an amount not exceeding 20 percent of its total assets. To increase its return or to hedge all or a portion of its portfolio investments, the fund may purchase and sell put and call options on securities indexes.

Cost of ownership. This front-end load mutual fund carries a maximum sales charge of 5.75 percent of the offering price. Reduced charges are available for purchases of $100,000 and greater. The following list of expenses and fees is based on the fund's January 1, 1994, prospectus.

Shareholder transaction expenses

Sales charge imposed on purchases: 5.75% (less for accounts
    over $250,000)
Sales charge imposed on reinvested dividends: None
Deferred sales charge: None
Redemption fees: None
Exchange fees: None

Annual fund operating expenses

Management fees: 0.63%
12b-1 fees: 0.17%
Other expenses: 0.29
Total operating expenses: 1.09%

Example of expenses. The following example illustrates the expenses you would incur on a $1,000 investment in Templeton Growth Fund over various time periods, assuming (1) a 5 percent annual rate of return and (2) redemption at the end of each period.

Years	1 Year	3 Years	5 Years	10 Years
Expenses	$68	$90	$114	$183

Fourteen Other Top Performing Funds

In recent years, the following funds led their peers in each of the major groups of international equity funds: Europe, Foreign, Global, and Pacific. No-load or low-load funds that you can purchase directly from the mutual fund companies are shown in **bold print**.

Each major group lists addresses, phone numbers, and investment performance for each fund in the group. The charts illustrate results of $10,000 invested in each fund over various time periods ending May 31, 1994, as well as the results of an investment of $10,000 plus $200 per month thereafter.

Europe Funds

Funds included in the Europe group seek capital appreciation and generally invest at least 65 percent of their assets in the equity securities of companies located in the British Isles, continental Europe and Scandinavia. None of the top-performing Europe funds was established before 1990, so only one and three-year average return numbers are listed for this group.

Fund	Three-Year Average Annual Total Return %
Dean Witter European Growth Fund	12.9
Alliance New Europe Fund	11.2
Putnam Europe Growth Fund	10.9

Dean Witter European Growth Fund
Two World Trade Center
New York, NY 10048
800-869-3863

Date of Inception: May 31, 1990

Investment Results

Time of Investment	Value of $10,000 Invested	Value of $10,000 Invested Plus $200 per Month	Total Invested
1 Year	$12,279	$14,633	$12,200
3 Years	14,376	23,350	17,000

Alliance New Europe Fund
1345 6th Avenue
New York, NY 10105
800-221-5672

Date of Inception: April 2, 1990

Investment Results

Time of Investment	Value of $10,000 Invested	Value of $10,000 Invested Plus $200 per Month	Total Invested
1 Year	$11,001	$13,305	$12,200
3 Years	12,979	21,559	17,000

Putnam Europe Growth Fund
One Post Office Square
Boston, MA 02109
800-225-1581

Date of Inception: September 7, 1990

Investment Results

Time of Investment	Value of $10,000 Invested	Value of $10,000 Invested Plus $200 per Month	Total Invested
1 Year	$11,318	$13,644	$12,200
3 Years	12,849	21,379	17,000

Foreign Funds

Funds in this group generally seek long-term growth of capital by investing their assets in securities of companies located outside the Unites States. Depending on each fund's investment policy, investments may be concentrated in particular regions of the world.

Fund	Ten-Year Average Annual Total Return %
Templeton Foreign Fund	18.4
T. Rowe Price International Stock Fund	**18.1**
EuroPacific Growth Fund	17.9
Vanguard Trustees Equity International Portfolio	**16.9**
Scudder International Fund	**16.6**

Templeton Foreign Fund
700 Central Avenue
St. Petersburg, FL 33701
800-237-0738

Date of Inception: October 5, 1982

Investment Results

Time of Investment	Value of $10,000 Invested	Value of $10,000 Invested Plus $200 per Month	Total Invested
1 Year	$11,462	$13,838	$12,200
3 Years	13,929	22,869	17,000

5 Years	18,421	35,093	21,800
10 Years	51,050	108,066	33,800

T. Rowe Price International Stock Fund
P.O. Box 89000
Baltimore, MD 21202
800-225-5132

Date of Inception: December 28, 1988

Investment Results

Time of Investment	*Value of $10,000 Invested*	*Value of $10,000 Invested Plus $200 per Month*	*Total Invested*
1 Year	$12,210	$14,584	$12,200
3 Years	13,130	22,050	21,800
5 Years	17,631	33,223	33,800

EuroPacific Growth Fund
333 South Hope Street
Los Angeles, CA 90071
800-421-4120

Date of Inception: April 16, 1984

Investment Results

Time of Investment	*Value of $10,000 Invested*	*Value of $10,000 Invested Plus $200 per Month*	*Total Invested*
1 Year	$11,430	$13,770	$12,200
3 Years	13,893	22,809	21,800
5 Years	18,091	34,897	33,800
10 Years	48,996	103,730	45,800

Vanguard Trustees Equity International Portfolio
P.O. Box 2600
Valley Forge, PA 19482
800-662-7447

Date of Inception: May 16, 1983

Investment Results

Time of Investment	Value of $10,000 Invested	Value of $10,000 Invested Plus $200 per Month	Total Invested
1 Year	$11,378	$13,726	$12,200
3 Years	13,006	21,594	17,000
5 Years	14,745	29,563	21,800
10 Years	47,848	95,234	33,800

Scudder International Fund
Two International Place
Boston, MA 02110
800-225-2470

Date of Inception: January 1, 1953

Investment Results

Time of Investment	Value of $10,000 Invested	Value of $10,000 Invested Plus $200 per Month	Total Invested
1 Year	$11,745	$14,069	$12,200
3 Years	13,405	22,101	17,000
5 Years	15,826	31,234	21,800
10 Years	46,425	93,971	33,800
15 Years	84,336	205,638	45,800
20 Years	117,325	371,617	57,800

Global Funds

Mutual funds in this category buy stocks of companies anywhere in the world, but normally invest at least 65 percent of their assets in securities of issuers located outside the United States. Their investment objective generally is to seek long-term capital appreciation.

Fund	Ten-Year Average Annual Total Return %
Putnam Global Growth Fund	17.3
Oppenheimer Global Fund	17.0
New Perspective Fund	16.5

Putnam Global Growth Fund
One Post Office Square
Boston, MA 02109
800-225-1581

Date of Inception: August 15, 1967

Investment Results

Time of Investment	Value of $10,000 Invested	Value of $10,000 Invested Plus $200 per Month	Total Invested
1 Year	$10,805	$13,085	$12,200
3 Years	12,396	20,880	17,000
5 Years	15,443	30,889	21,800
10 Years	46,318	92,692	33,800
15 Years	87,685	213,051	45,800
20 Years	175,148	460,906	57,800

Oppenheimer Global Fund
P.O. Box 5270
Denver, CO 80217
800-525-7048

Date of Inception: January 1, 1969

Investment Results

Time of Investment	Value of $10,000 Invested	Value of $10,000 Invested Plus $200 per Month	Total Invested
1 Year	$12,189	$14,603	$12,200
3 Years	13,263	22,135	17,000
5 Years	17,836	34,062	21,800
10 Years	45,389	99,177	33,800
15 Years	114,444	244,660	45,580
20 Years	181,379	512,589	57,800

New Perspective Fund
333 South Hope Street
Los Angeles, CA 90071
800-421-4120

Date of Inception: March 13, 1973

Investment Results

Time of Investment	Value of $10,000 Invested	Value of $10,000 Invested Plus $200 per Month	Total Invested
1 Year	$11,072	$13,398	$12,200
3 Years	13,357	21,979	17,000
5 Years	17,347	33,641	21,800
10 Years	43,520	93,744	33,800
15 Years	93,083	219,911	45,800
20 Years	173,903	470,073	57,800

Pacific Funds

Mutual funds in this category generally invest in Pacific Basin countries, including Japan, Hong Kong, Australia, Korea, Taiwan, India, Thailand, Singapore, Malaysia, New Zealand, Indonesia, China, Pakistan and Sri Lanka. Some funds will invest mainly in just one portion of the Pacific Basin. For instance, Japan Fund invests primarily in Japanese companies, and Newport Tiger Fund buys stocks of Hong Kong, Singapore, South Korea, Taiwan, and Southeast Asian companies. Capital appreciation is the primary investment objective.

Fund	Five-Year Average Annual Total Return %
Newport Tiger Fund	18.2
GAM Pacific Basin Fund	17.8
Merrill Lynch Pacific Fund	12.4

Newport Tiger Fund
P.O. Box 8687
Richmond, VA 23226
800-527-9500

Date of Inception: May 30, 1989

Investment Results

Time of Investment	Value of $10,000 Invested	Value of $10,000 Invested Plus $200 per Month	Total Invested
1 Year	$12,550	$15,038	$12,200
3 Years	18,832	29,636	17,000
5 Years	21,953	43,283	21,800

GAM Pacific Basin Fund
135 E. 57th Street
New York, NY 10022
800-356-5740

Date of Inception: May 6, 1987

Investment Results

Time of Investment	Value of $10,000 Invested	Value of $10,000 Invested Plus $200 per Month	Total Invested
1 Year	$12,348	$14,888	$12,200
3 Years	15,973	26,259	17,000
5 Years	21,509	40,617	21,800

Merrill Lynch Pacific Fund
P.O. Box 45289
Jacksonville, FL 32232
800-637-3863

Date of Inception: August 5, 1976

Investment Results

Time of Investment	Value of $10,000 Invested	Value of $10,000 Invested Plus $200 per Month	Total Invested
1 Year	$10,616	$12,998	$12,200
3 Years	13,216	22,226	17,000
5 Years	16,756	33,164	21,800
10 Years	62,650	118,176	33,800
15 Years	135,278	314,010	45,800

In Your Spare Time ...

Take a look at international equity funds. On average, long-term investors in funds holding foreign stocks have fared significantly better than those with only U.S. securities.

17

$ $

Investing in the
Whole Market—
Index Funds

$ $

Mutual fund investors can now invest in a replication of the whole stock market, or in segments of the market, by buying shares in a single fund. Any investor, even with very limited funds, can invest in a fund that holds all 500 of the largest U.S. companies, a representation of all small capitalization companies, a representation of the total U.S. stock market or a representation of foreign stock markets through a recently developed strategy known as indexing.

Many individual investors, pension funds and institutional investors choose indexing. According to The Vanguard Investment Group, one leading provider of index funds, by 1994 individual investors held more than $10 billion in index funds.

Indexing describes the investment approach of attempting to parallel the investment returns of a specific stock (or bond) market index. A market *index* measures changes in the stock, bond and commodities markets, reflecting market prices and the number of shares outstanding for the companies in the index. Well-known market indexes include Standard & Poor's 500 Composite Stock Price Index (S&P 500), the New York Stock Exchange Index and the Value Line Index.

An index fund manager tries to replicate the target index investment results by holding all or a representative sample of the securities in the index. Indexing is a passive approach to investing. No attempt is made to use traditional active money management techniques in selecting individual stocks or industry sectors in an effort to outperform the indexes. The result is an investment approach emphasizing broad diversification and low portfolio trading activity.

Indexing is based on a simple truth: It is impossible for all stock market investors in the aggregate to have superior performance than the overall stock market. Why? Studies have shown that the stock market has had an average return of 10 percent per year. Some investors, as a result of luck or skill, have earned more than 10 percent; others have earned less. But the 10 percent historical return is the average amount that all investors can achieve as a group.

But that 10 percent is the gross return, before expenses (such as management fees, commissions and other costs). The net return can be significantly less, resulting in a number well below the market return. Here's how it works: Most mutual funds have costs such as advisory fees, distribution charges, operating expenses and portfolio transaction costs. According to Lipper Analytical Services, these costs, on average, total approximately 2 percent of investor assets. Thus, the net average return to investors is 8 percent, not the 10 percent provided by the market average.

In contrast, one key advantage of an index fund should be its low cost. A properly run index fund pays no advisory fees (because there is no active investment management), keeps operating expenses at a very low level and keeps portfolio transactions costs at the minimum. The lower the expenses a fund incurs, the closer will be the fund's performance to the index it tracks.

Figure 17.1 shows the ten-year total return (capital change plus income) through July 29, 1994, of U.S. equity funds compared with the Standard & Poor's 500 Composite Stock Price (S&P 500) Index (a measure representing about 80 percent of the market value of all issues traded on the New York Stock Exchange) and foreign equity funds compared with the Morgan Stanley Capital International Europe, Australia, Far East (MSCI-EAFE) Index.

No group of U.S. general equity funds on average performed better than the S&P Index during the ten-year period. The average return of the five groups was 13.8 percent—1.9 percentage points less than the unmanaged S&P 500. In the foreign market, the average annual return of 74 foreign equity funds was 1.4 percentage points less than the index of foreign stocks.

FIGURE 17.1   Ten-Year Average Annual Return Performance for the
Period Ending July 29, 1994

Objective	Number of Funds in Group	Annual Return %
U.S. general equity funds		
Aggressive growth funds	80	14.4
Growth funds	296	13.8
Growth and income funds	202	13.5
Income funds	63	12.7
Small company funds	96	14.5
S&P 500 Index		15.7
Foreign equity funds	74	17.8
MSCI EAFE Index		19.2

Investing in Index Funds

An index fund invests in common stocks (or bonds) in an attempt to match the investment performance of a distinct market index. As a result, the fund achieves its goal over the long term. According to Lipper Analytical Services, the Wilshire 5000 Index (a measure of the total U.S. Stock Market) has equaled or surpassed the average equity fund in eight out of ten years since 1984. And because of its consistency (it was never a poor performer), the Wilshire 5000 outperformed 72 percent of general equity funds over this period.

Indexing's main appeal is to long-term investors who seek a very competitive investment return through broadly diversified portfolios. Index funds provide investors with a high degree of *relative predictability* in an uncertain stock market. Nothing can assure absolute returns, but these investors can feel confident that their investment should not be a dramatic underperformer relative to other funds investing in the same type of securities and, over the long term, index funds should deliver a very competitive relative performance.

Investors wanting to buy into particular segments of the securities market now have an increasing selection of indexes to choose from. Although most of the focus on index investing has been on funds that attempt to replicate the S&P 500, you can now find funds that seek to match other indexes, both in the U.S. market and abroad. Here are some of your choices:

- *Dow Jones World Stock Index.* Consists of approximately 2,600 stocks of U.S. and foreign companies, located in 25 countries. The index has approximately 120 industry groups and sub-groups grouped into 9 broad market sectors.
- *Lehman Brothers Aggregate Bond Index.* Consists of more than 6,000 individual investment-grade, fixed-income securities, including U.S. Treasury and Government agency securities, corporate debt obligations and mortgage-backed securities.
- *Morgan Stanley Capital International—Select Emerging Markets Free Index* is a broadly diversified index consisting of approximately 460 common stocks of companies located in the countries of 12 emerging markets in Southeast Asia, Latin America and Europe.
- *Morgan Stanley Capital International Europe (Free) Index* is a diversified index comprising approximately 575 companies located in 13 European countries. The *Free* index includes only the shares of companies that U.S. investors are "free to purchase."
- *Morgan Stanley Capital International Pacific Index* is a diversified index consisting of approximately 425 companies located in Australia, Japan, Hong Kong, New Zealand and Singapore. The index is dominated by the Japanese stock market, which represents about 85 percent of its market capitalization.
- *Russell 2000 Small Stock Index* is a broadly diversified, small capitalization index consisting of approximately 2,000 common stocks. The average market capitalization of stocks in this index is about $200 million.
- *Standard & Poor's 500 Index.* Measures the total investment return of 500 common stocks, most of which trade on the NYSE and represent about 70 percent of the market value of all U.S. common stocks.
- *Wilshire 4500 Index.* Consists of all U.S. stocks that are not in the S&P 500 Index and that trade regularly on the NYSE and AMEX as well as in the Nasdaq OTC market. More than 5,000 stocks of midsize and small-capitalization companies are included in the index.

- *Wilshire 5000 Index.* Consists of *all* regularly and publicly traded U.S. stocks, providing a complete proxy for the U.S. stock market. More than 6,000 stocks, including large, medium-size and small capitalization companies are included in the index. It represents the value of all NYSE, AMEX and OTC stocks for which quotes are available.

Investors have wide-ranging interests and index funds are available for different market sectors. The recommended fund in this chapter has been chosen for two reasons: (1) It is exceptionally well run, with low costs and a history of consistently coming very close to meeting its stated objective. (2) It replicates the S&P 500, which has attracted the most attention from investors interested in an index fund investment. Information about several other index funds is presented later in this chapter.

 A Recommended Index Fund

Vanguard Index Trust 500 Portfolio
P.O. Box 2600
Valley Forge, PA 19482
800-662-7447

Minimum initial investment: $3,000
Minimum subsequent investment: $100
Date of inception: August 31, 1976
Portfolio manager: George U. Sauter

Fund shares are purchased and redeemed at NAV. There are no sales, redemption or 12b-1 plan distribution charges. You can purchase the fund directly from the Vanguard Group.

Investment objective. The Vanguard Index Trust 500 Portfolio seeks to match the investment performance of the Standard & Poor's 500 Composite Stock Price Index, which emphasizes large-capitalization stocks.

Performance. During the 15-year period ending on April 30, 1994, the total average annual return of Vanguard Index Trust 500

Portfolio was 14.5 percent. Figure 17.2 shows the year-by-year perfor-mance of the fund, as well as that of the S&P 500, its target index.

Reason for recommendation. Only expenses separate Vanguard Index Trust 500 Portfolio from its target, the S&P 500. An index fund's expense ratio (advisory fees, operating expenses and transac-tions costs) accounts for most of the difference between the fund's returns and those generated by its target index, so expenses are very important in assessing these passively managed funds. The 500 Portfo-lio has more nearly matched the S&P 500 than any of its peers because its expenses are lower than those of any other publicly avail-able index fund.

Some index funds contain only a representative sampling of the S&P 500, but the Vanguard 500 Portfolio holds all 500 stocks in its portfolio. The fund invests in each stock in approximately the same proportion as that stock is represented in the index. As a result the fund's returns in tracking the S&P 500 are highly accurate. An exception was 1983, when the fund trailed the index by 1.2 percentage points.

Vanguard Index Trust 500 Portfolio is an excellent choice if you are seeking both growth of capital and current income. Its total returns and dividend yield are essentially a mirror image of the large capital-ization stock market. Very low expenses and the lack of sales charges (other than an annual $10 account maintenance fee, deducted from the portfolio's dividend) add to the fund's appeal.

Investment results. The Vanguard Index Trust 500 Portfolio has delivered returns consistent with those of the S&P 500 and has treated

FIGURE 17.2 Total Return of Vanguard Index Trust 500 Portfolio 1980–April 30, 1994 Compared with S&P 500

Year	Fund %	S&P 500%	Year	Fund %	S&P 500%	Year	Fund %	S&P 500%
1980	31.6	32.4	1985	31.2	32.2	1990	−3.3	−3.2
1981	−5.2	−4.9	1986	18.1	18.5	1991	30.2	30.5
1982	21.0	21.4	1987	4.7	5.2	1992	7.4	7.7
1983	21.3	22.6	1988	16.2	16.8	1993	9.9	10.1
1984	6.2	6.3	1989	31.4	31.5	1994	−2.6	−2.6

long-term investors very well. Figure 17.3 shows the results of a $10,000 investment in the fund over various time periods ending April 30, 1994, as well as the results of an investment of $10,000 plus $200 per month thereafter. Income dividends and capital gains distributions have been reinvested in additional shares.

Investment policy.　The 500 Portfolio is not managed according to traditional methods of active investment management, which involve the buying and selling of securities based upon economic, financial and market analysis, as well as investment judgment. Instead, the fund attempts to duplicate the investment performance of the S&P 500 Index through statistical procedures, utilizing a *passive* or *indexing* investment approach. The 500 Portfolio invests in all 500 stocks in the S&P 500 Index in approximately the same proportions as they are represented in the index.

The 500 Portfolio attempts to remain fully invested in common stocks, and under normal circumstances it will invest at least 95 percent of its assets in the common stocks of the S&P 500. The fund may invest in short-term fixed-income securities as cash reserves, although cash or cash equivalents normally represent less than 1 percent of the fund's assets.

20 Largest Common Stock Holdings Ranked By Market Value

General Electric Company	E.I. du Pont de Nemours & Company
Exxon Corporation	Ford Motor Company
AT & T Corporation	IBM Corporation
Wal-Mart Stores, Inc.	GTE Corporation
Royal Dutch Petroleum Company	Mobile Corporation
The Coca-Cola Company	PepsiCo, Inc.
Philip Morris Companies, Inc.	Bristol-Myers Squibb Company
Merck & Company, Inc.	Chevron Corporation
General Motors Corporation	Johnson & Johnson
Procter & Gamble Company	Intel Corporation

Cost of ownership.　The Vanguard Index Trust 500 Portfolio assesses no sales charge, 12b-1 fee or redemption fee. A $10 annual maintenance fee is deducted from the fund's dividend. The following

FIGURE 17.3 Vanguard Index Trust 500 Portfolio Investment Results for Various Periods Ending April 30, 1994

Time of Investment	Value of $10,000 Invested	Value of $10,000 Invested Plus $200 Per Month	Total Invested
1 Year	$10,514	$12,698	$12,200
3 Years	13,054	20,784	17,000
5 Years	16,888	31,760	21,800
10 Years	38,663	83,713	33,800
15 Years	76,692	187,446	45,800

table illustrates all expenses and fees incurred by a shareholder, based on the fund's March 3, 1994, prospectus.

Shareholder transaction expenses

Sales charge imposed on purchases: None
Sales charge imposed on reinvested dividends: None
Deferred sales load: None
Redemption fees: None
Exchange fees: None

Annual fund operating expenses

Management fees: 0.15%
12b-1 fees: None
Other expenses: 0.04%
Total operating expenses: 0.19%
Account maintenance fee: $10

Other Mutual Funds and the Market Indexes They Target

Mutual fund companies have established funds that track a number of market indexes, both in the United States and overseas. Because expenses account for most of the difference between an index fund's returns and those generated by the target index, you should carefully note the operating expenses of any index fund you're considering purchasing.

Following are some of the companies offering index funds and the indexes targeted by each fund.

Index Fund	*Target Index*

The Benham Group
1665 Charleston Road
Mountain View, CA 94043
800-331-8331

Benham Global Natural Resources Index Fund	Combined Basic Materials and Energy sectors of the Dow Jones World Stock Index

Dreyfus Corporation
144 Glen Curtiss Boulevard
Uniondale, NY 11556
800-645-6561

Peoples Index Fund	S&P 500 Index
Peoples S&P Midcap Index Fund	S&P Midcap 400 Index

Fidelity Investments
82 Devonshire Street
Boston, MA 02109
800-544-8888

Fidelity Market Index Fund	S&P 500 Index

T. Rowe Price
100 East Pratt Street
Baltimore, MD 21202
800-225-5132

T. Rowe Price Equity Index Fund	S&P 500 Index

Charles Schwab
101 Montgomery Street
San Francisco, CA 94104
800-266-5623

The Schwab International Index Fund	Schwab International Index
The Schwab 1000 Fund	Schwab 1000 Index

SEI Financial Services
680 E. Swedesford Road
Wayne, PA 19087
800-342-5734

SEI S&P 500 Index Fund	S&P 500 Index

The Vanguard Group of Investment Companies
P.O. Box 2600
Valley Forge, PA 19482
800-662-7447

Vanguard Balanced Index Fund	Wilshire 5000 Index & Lehman Brothers Aggregate Bond Index
Vanguard Bond Index Fund	
Total Bond Market Portfolio	Lehman Brothers Aggregate Bond Index
Short-Term Bond Portfolio	Lehman Brothers Mutual Fund Short (1–5) Government/ Corporate Index
Intermediate-Term Bond Portfolio	Lehman Brothers Mutual Fund Short (5–10) Government/ Corporate Index
Long-Term Bond Portfolio	Lehman Brothers Mutual Fund Short (10+) Government/ Corporate Index
Vanguard Index Trust	
Extended Market Portfolio	Wilshire 4500 Index
Total Stock Market Portfolio	Wilshire 5000 Index
Small Capitalization Stock Portfolio	Russell 2000 Small Stock Index
International Equity Index Fund	
Emerging Markets Portfolio	Morgan Stanley Emerging Markets Free Index
European Portfolio	Morgan Stanley Europe (Free) Index
Pacific Portfolio	Morgan Stanley Pacific Index

In Your Spare Time ...

$\mathbf{Y}$ou can invest in the whole stock market, or important segments of it, by purchasing an index fund. Indexing has become the investment strategy of choice among many individual investors, as well as for many pension funds and institutional investors.

18

$ $

Investing for
Income in
Bond Funds

$ $

Investors are attracted to bond funds for two primary reasons. The first is income: bond funds generally provide higher and steadier income than cash reserve investments such as money market funds or bank passbook accounts. Unlike stable cash reserves, however, bond funds fluctuate in value as interest rates change. The second reason investors like bond funds is diversification: bond funds have investment characteristics that are quite different from stock funds. Though sometimes volatile, bond funds are usually considered less risky than stock funds and can balance a portfolio heavy in stock funds.

In this chapter, you will find out about the major types of bond mutual funds and how they differ from one another. You can use bond funds to earn immediate income from your capital (most bond funds pay income distributions monthly) or you can let your money accumulate in bond funds for possible income purposes at a later time.

Bond funds are divided into four principal classifications: U.S. government, corporate, municipal and international.

U.S. Government bond funds hold three types of issues offered by the U.S. Treasury: U.S. Treasury bills (T-bills), which have maturities from 90 days to 1 year; U.S. Treasury notes (T-notes), which have maturities from 1 to 10 years; and U.S. Treasury bonds (T-bonds), which have maturities from 10 to 30 years. Treasury securities are deemed the most creditworthy of all debt instruments because they are backed by the full faith and credit of the U.S. government.

Government bond funds also hold U.S. agency obligations. These are debt securities of agencies of the U.S. government, such as the Government National Mortgage Association (GNMA). Some agency securities are explicitly guaranteed by the U.S. government, and others carry a less formal backing.

Corporate bond funds hold debt obligations issued by corporations in various maturities ranging from short-term (maturing between 1 and 5 years) to long-term (maturing in more than 15 years).

Municipal bond funds invest in bonds issued by states and municipalities to finance schools, highways, airports, bridges, hospitals, water and sewer works and other public projects. In most cases, income earned from these securities is exempt from federal income tax, but may be subject to state and local taxes.

International bond funds invest in the debt securities of companies and countries throughout the world, including the United States.

Investment Returns on Bond Funds

If you invest in a bond fund, your return comes in two forms: income return (yield) and capital return. Together they form your *total return.*

Income return (yield) is a bond fund's interest income expressed as a percentage of its purchase price. For instance, if you invest $10,000 in a bond fund and it pays you $800 a year, it provides an 8 percent yield.

Capital return is a measure of the increase or decrease in a bond-fund's market price. For instance, if your $10,000 bond fund drops in price to $9,700, your capital return would be −3 percent.

Total return is the total of income return plus capital return. Thus, an 8 percent yield less a 3 percent decline in principal results in a 5 percent total return.

Your income return on a bond fund is based primarily on two factors: credit quality and maturity of bonds in the portfolio.

Credit quality

Credit quality assessments are made by independent agencies such as Moody's Investors Service, Inc.; Standard & Poor's Corporation; Duff & Phelps; and Fitch's Investors Service. These firms analyze the financial strength of each bond's issuer, whether a corporation or a government body. These agencies assign ratings that help you determine the suitability of a particular instrument for investment purposes. Following is a brief description of the letter codes used by Moody's Investors Service, Inc.

Moody's Investors Service, Inc. credit quality ratings

Aaa Judged to be the best quality, carrying the smallest degree of investment risk. U.S. Government and Agency Securities have Aaa ratings.

Aa Judged to be of high quality by all standards. Together with the Aaa group, they are known as high-grade bonds.

A Possess many favorable investment attributes and are considered as high, medium-grade obligations.

Baa Considered medium-grade obligations (i.e., they are neither highly protected nor poorly secured).

Ba Judged to have speculative elements (i.e., their future cannot be considered well assured).

B Generally lack characteristics of a desirable investment.

Caa Poor standing; may be in default.

NR Not rated.

Note: Moody's applies numerical modifiers (1, 2, and 3) in each rating classification from Aa through Baa in its corporate bond rating system. The modifier 1 indicates that the security ranks in the higher end of its category; 2 indicates a mid-range ranking; and 3 indicates a low ranking.

You can generally earn higher yields from lower-quality bonds. Government bonds, which carry the highest credit ratings and therefore the lowest risk of default, offer the lowest yields. Investment-grade bonds (Baa and above) provide somewhat higher yields. Noninvestment grade, often called *high-yield* or *junk* bonds (Ba and below) produce the highest levels of income, but have the greatest potential for default.

Bond Maturity

A bond's maturity is set by its issuer and is expressed in days or years. For bonds of similar credit quality, a bond with a longer maturity will generally pay a higher yield. For instance, a 30-year Baa corporate bond generally provides a higher yield than a 3-year Baa corporate bond.

Capital return, the gain or loss you experience as a result of changes in a bond fund's price, is mainly determined by changes in interest rates. In general, bond prices move inversely with interest rates. When interest rates go up, bond prices go down; when rates go down, bond prices go up. Another factor is maturity; longer-maturity bonds will have greater price volatility in response to interest rate changes than will bonds with shorter maturities.

Figure 18.1 shows how the prices of bonds with varying maturities would respond following a 1 percent change in interest rates.

Risk

Before investing in a bond fund, assess these two basic risks:

- *Market risk*: The degree to which the bond fund's price fluctuates as a result of changes in interest rates. Bond funds with longer maturities usually offer higher yields, but also tend to have more volatile price swings than those with shorter maturities.
- *Credit risk*: The chance that bonds in the portfolio will default (fail to make payment of principal and interest). Bond funds holding lower-quality bonds usually offer higher yields, but also carry greater risk of bonds in the portfolio defaulting.

FIGURE 18.1   Effect of Interest Rate Changes on Bond Prices

	Initial Principal: $10,000 Yield: 10%			
Bond Maturity	**1% Rate Rise**		**1% Rate Decline**	
	Bond Value	**Percentage Change**	**Bond Value**	**Percentage Change**
Short-term (2.5-year maturity)	$9,790	−2.1%	$10,220	+2.2%
Intermediate-term (7-year maturity)	9,520	−4.8%	10,510	+5.1%
Long-term (20-year maturity)	9,200	−8.0%	10,920	+9.2%

During the last three years, *total returns* (yield plus change in value) from the major classifications of bond funds have been about what one would expect. High-yield (and risky) corporate bond funds led the way in total returns, while U.S. government bond funds had the lowest returns. But the last ten year period showed much less difference, as the following chart illustrates.

Total Returns of Bond Funds for Periods Ending August 31, 1994

	Three Years %	Ten Years %
General corporate bond funds	7.4	10.0
Government bond funds	6.3	9.7
High yield corporate bond funds	12.9	10.7
Municipal (tax-free) bond funds	7.1	9.1
Worldwide bond funds	5.9	10.1

General Corporate Bond Funds

Mutual funds in this category usually keep about 65 percent of their assets in investment-grade (Baa or higher) fixed-income securities. Most also invest in U.S. government securities, lower-grade corporate issues and, in some cases, foreign securities. Like other bond funds, corporate funds seek to maximize income over the long term while providing reasonable safety of shareholder investment. Capital appreciation is normally a secondary consideration.

Although many investors think of bonds and bond funds as providing a relatively safe haven for their money, these investments can be quite volatile (see Figure 18.1). For example, the first six months of 1994 was a period of rapidly rising interest rates. The total return of the general corporate bond group during the six months ending June 30, 1994, was −4.1 percent. This decline included interest income, which for many funds contributed about 3.5 percent toward the return.

Over time, however, the general corporate bond fund group has done pretty much what investors have expected. During the 20 years ending June 30, 1994, at least eight such funds had average annual total returns in excess of 10 percent, and in the 10-year period ending

FIGURE 18.2   Total Return of General Corporate Bond Funds
1980–June 30, 1994, Compared with LEH AGI

Year	Group %	LEH AGI %	Year	Group %	LEH AGI %	Year	Group %	LEH AGI %
1980	1.6	2.7	1985	20.3	22.1	1990	6.5	8.3
1981	5.3	6.2	1986	13.5	15.2	1991	16.1	16.0
1982	31.4	32.6	1987	1.9	2.7	1992	7.2	7.4
1983	8.6	8.3	1988	8.2	7.9	1993	10.0	9.7
1984	12.2	15.6	1989	11.0	14.6	1994	−4.1	−2.8

on that date, the top ten funds produced average annual returns of more than 11 percent. Figure 18.2 shows the total return of general corporate bond funds from 1980 to June 30, 1994, as well as the Lehman Brothers Aggregate Bond Index (LEH AGI), an index representing more than 6,000 fixed-income securities.

 A Recommended Corporate Bond Fund

FPA New Income Fund
11400 West Olympic Boulevard
Los Angeles, CA 90060
800-638-3060

Minimum initial investment: $1,500
Minimum subsequent investment: $100
Date of inception: January 1, 1969
Portfolio manager: Robert L. Rodriguez

Investment objective.   The objective is to seek a high level of current income consistent with the preservation of capital.

Performance.   FPA New Income Fund outpaced its bond fund rivals in nine of the last ten years, with an average annual total return of 13 percent. Its dividend yields have been near the top of its peers, while maintaining quality and increasing share value. During the first six months of 1994, during which most bond funds had negative total returns, FPA New Income increased 1.3 percent, more than 5 percentage points better than the average bond fund.

Figure 18.3 shows the year-by-year performance of the fund from 1980 to June 30, 1994.

Reason for recommendation. During the last ten years, FPA New Income Fund has consistently ranked among the top funds in the corporate income group and has never had a losing year during that period.

Manager Rodriguez has the contrarian philosophy that although investing with the consensus may be comfortable, it is not the most profitable way to go. The fund usually invests in what management deems undervalued segments of the taxable fixed-income market. Its flexible approach permits investment in a broad range of securities, such as Treasuries, mortgages, corporate high-yields and convertibles. It thus can avoid pitfalls that can hurt single-sector funds. If a particular segment comes under pressure, these funds have few options.

Normally, FPA New Income has about 70 percent of its assets in Aaa rated securities, with 30 percent invested in lower-rated, higher-yielding issues. The fund emphasizes a total-return approach because Rodriguez believes that funds set on providing income alone are destined to underperform their peers because they focus on the market segments least likely to provide increases in value.

The fund has a bias toward capital preservation, which has contributed to its strong performance. When management believes interest rates will rise, maturities are shortened and cash reserves are increased. Although such a position has not always been conventional wisdom at the time, such conservatism has paid off. For instance, the fund posted a 1.3 percent positive return in the first six months of 1994 when almost every other fixed-income fund showed a loss.

Based on FPA New Income Fund's historical performance, and management's apparent command of the fixed-income markets, the fund should be a good choice for any fixed-income investor seeking maximum returns with minimum risk.

Investment results. Ten-year total returns averaging 13 percent during the last ten years have placed the fund consistently near the top of its fixed-income group. Figure 18.4 illustrates the results of $10,000 invested in FPA New Income over various time periods ending June

FIGURE 18.3   New Income Fund Total Return and Dividend Yield: 1980–June 30, 1994

Year	Total Return %	Dividend Yield %	Year	Total Return %	Dividend Yield %	Year	Total Return %	Dividend Yield %
1980	5.2	8.8	1985	21.3	8.6	1990	7.5	8.3
1981	1.3	10.4	1986	11.4	8.4	1991	7.7	16.0
1982	27.8	10.9	1987	7.7	8.6	1992	6.2	7.4
1983	6.1	10.8	1988	8.5	5.4	1993	5.8	9.7
1984	16.4	10.1	1989	12.2	7.3	1994	7.7	3.8

FIGURE 18.4   FPA New Income Fund Investment Results for Various Periods Ending June 30, 1994

Time of Investment	Value of $10,000 Invested	Value of $10,000 Invested Plus $200 Per Month	Total Invested
1 Year	$9,965	$12,201	$12,200
3 Years	13,011	20,901	17,000
5 Years	15,661	30,913	21,800
10 Years	32,368	73,948	33,800
15 Years	44,897	135,823	45,800
20 Years	70,141	229,891	57,800

30, 1994, as well as the results of an investment of $10,000 plus $200 per month thereafter. Income dividends and capital gains distributions have been reinvested in additional shares.

Investment policy.   FPA New Income Fund generally invests at least 50 percent of assets in debt obligations issued or guaranteed by the U.S. government and its agencies and instrumentalities, including the GNMA. The fund will also invest in nonconvertible debt securities rated either Aa or Aaa, repurchase agreements, short-term obligations and cash equivalents. In addition, the fund may invest as much as 25 percent of assets in convertible debt securities and preferred stocks (in an amount not exceeding 5 percent of its assets). As much as 30 percent of the fund's assets may be invested, or committed for investment, in securities offered on a delayed delivery basis.

10 Largest Taxable Bond Holdings (as of March 31, 1994)

Security/Coupon	Maturity	% of Net Assets
GNMA Pool 9.75%	2006	6.5
U.S. Treasury Note 4.25%	1995	5.7
Merrill Lynch Mortgage 8.3%	2012	3.8
GNMA Pool 9.5%	2011	3.7
U.S. Treasury Note 4.5%	1996	3.5
Tennessee Valley Authority 8.38%	1999	3.3
FHLMC 7%	2020	2.6
ADT Ltd. 6%	2002	2.4
Seagate Technology	2012	2.4
FHLMC 7%	2018	2.3
Total		36.2

Cost of ownership.   Fund shares carry a maximum sales charge of 4.5 percent. Sales charges are reduced for purchases of $25,000 or more. Fund expenses are about 30 percent less than those of its peers in the general corporate bond fund group, helping provide an outstanding total return among bond funds. Dividends are paid quarterly.

Shareholder transaction expenses

Sales charge imposed on purchases: 4.5% (less for accounts over
    $250,000)
Sales charge imposed on reinvested dividends: None
Deferred sales charge: None
Redemption fees: None
Exchange fees: None

Annual fund operating expenses

Management fees: 0.50%
12b-1 fees: None
Other expenses: 0.25%
Total operating expenses: 0.99%

Other Top Performing General Corporate Bond Funds

During the ten-year period ending June 30, 1994, the following five mutual funds characterized as general corporate bond funds led their peers in total return. No-load or low-load funds that you can purchase directly from the mutual fund companies are shown in **bold print**.

Fund	Ten-Year Average Annual Total Return %
Alliance Corporate Bond Fund	13.2
Smith Barney Shearson Investment Grade Bond Fund	12.2
Bond Fund of America	12.0
IDS Bond Fund	11.9
Vanguard Fixed Income Long-Term Corporate Bond Fund	**11.8**

Following are addresses, phone numbers, and investment performance for each fund. The charts show the year-by-year total return and dividend yield of the funds from 1980 to June 30, 1994.

Alliance Corporate Bond Fund

1345 6th Avenue
New York, NY 10105
800-221-5672

Date of Inception: March 1, 1974

Investment Results 1980–June 30, 1994

	Total Return %	Dividend Yield %		Total Return %	Dividend Yield %		Total Return %	Dividend Yield %
1980	−4.0	11.4	1985	22.3	9.9	1990	5.5	10.4
1981	1.3	12.9	1986	14.0	8.9	1991	18.1	8.5
1982	40.0	10.7	1987	3.4	10.0	1992	13.3	9.3
1983	10.0	11.0	1988	8.2	9.1	1993	31.1	7.2
1984	15.2	10.9	1989	13.1	9.1	1994	−12.2	4.3

Smith Barney Shearson Investment Grade Bond Fund

53 State Street
Boston, MA 02109
800-451-2010

Date of Inception: January 4, 1982

Investment Results 1983–June 30, 1994

	Total Return %	Dividend Yield %		Total Return %	Dividend Yield %		Total Return %	Dividend Yield %
1983	7.6	10.9	1987	−2.8	9.8	1991	22.5	7.4
1984	14.6	10.8	1988	6.4	8.5	1992	8.6	7.4
1985	26.4	11.5	1989	15.6	7.9	1993	18.1	6.4
1986	19.5	8.4	1990	3.0	8.3	1994	−10.5	3.3

Bond Fund of America
333 South Hope Street
Los Angeles, CA 90071
800-421-4120

Date of Inception: May 28, 1974

Investment Results 1980–June 30, 1994

	Total Return %	*Dividend Yield %*		*Total Return %*	*Dividend Yield %*		*Total Return %*	*Dividend Yield %*
1980	3.5	11.6	1985	26.6	9.8	1990	3.3	9.5
1981	6.6	13.5	1986	15.2	9.4	1991	21.0	8.2
1982	32.9	11.6	1987	2.0	9.7	1992	11.3	7.9
1983	9.5	11.0	1988	10.7	9.1	1993	14.1	6.9
1984	11.9	11.1	1989	10.1	9.4	1994	−5.2	3.7

IDS Bond Fund
IDS Tower 10
Minneapolis, MN 55440
800-437-4332

Date of Inception: September 30, 1974

Investment Results 1980–June 30, 1994

	Total Return %	*Dividend Yield %*		*Total Return %*	*Dividend Yield %*		*Total Return %*	*Dividend Yield %*
1980	1.4	13.1	1985	24.0	11.3	1990	4.7	8.0
1981	3.7	14.2	1986	19.5	8.4	1991	20.7	7.6
1982	36.0	12.1	1987	−0.1	9.0	1992	10.6	7.8
1983	14.9	11.8	1988	10.1	8.9	1993	15.4	7.0
1984	9.2	12.2	1989	10.6	8.7	1994	−5.2	3.9

Vanguard Fixed Income Long-Term Corporate Bond Fund
P.O. Box 2600
Valley Forge, PA 19482
800-662-7447

Date of Inception: July 9, 1973

Investment Results 1980–June 30, 1994

	Total Return %	*Dividend Yield %*		*Total Return %*	*Dividend Yield %*		*Total Return %*	*Dividend Yield %*
1980	4.4	10.8	1985	22.0	11.9	1990	6.2	9.0
1981	9.0	12.4	1986	14.3	10.1	1991	20.9	8.0

1982	28.5	11.6	1987	0.2	9.7	1992	9.8	7.6
1983	6.7	12.2	1988	9.7	9.5	1993	11.1	6.3
1984	14.1	12.7	1989	15.2	8.9	1994	−6.2	3.3

Government Securities Funds

Funds in this category generally hold at least 75 percent of their assets in U.S. government and government-agency debt instruments. Many income-seeking investors choose government securities funds as a way of assuring the safety of their principal, but rising interest rates can severely depress the value of these funds. For example, the average government securities fund showed a 4.2 percent *total return loss* (change in value plus dividends paid) in the first six months of 1994, as interest rates moved upward. Because the average fund paid dividends of 2.8 percent in the period, the average loss in value per share was 7 percent.

Rising interest rates in 1994 took a particularly sharp toll on U.S. Treasury issues, especially those with long maturities. Funds with heavy stakes in Treasuries were hard hit during the rate rise. Nevertheless, well-managed government funds have treated their long-term investors well. The average government securities fund had an average total annual return of 10 percent during the 10 years ending June 30, 1994.

Figure 18.5 shows the total return of government securities bond funds from 1980 to June 30, 1994, as well as the Lehman Brothers Aggregate Bond Index (LEH AGI), an index representing more than 6,000 fixed-income securities.

FIGURE 18.5   Total Return of Government Securities Bond Funds 1980–June 30, 1994, Compared with LEH AGI

Year	Group %	LEH AGI %	Year	Group %	LEH AGI %	Year	Group %	LEH AGI %
1980	6.2	2.7	1985	21.9	22.1	1990	7.8	8.3
1981	9.0	6.3	1986	15.0	15.2	1991	14.1	16.0
1982	22.7	32.6	1987	0.0	2.7	1992	5.9	7.4
1983	6.8	8.3	1988	6.8	7.9	1993	8.6	9.7
1984	12.4	15.6	1989	12.4	14.6	1994	−4.2	−2.8

A Recommended Government Securities Fund

Fidelity Government Securities Fund
82 Devonshire Street
Boston, MA 02109
800-544-8888

Minimum initial investment: $2,500
Minimum subsequent investment: $250
Date of inception: April 4, 1979
Portfolio manager: Curt Hollingsworth

You can purchase shares at NAV. There are no sales charges and there is no 12b-1 fee. Fund expenses are slightly less than average for the industry, which helps maintain high long-term returns. Dividends are paid monthly.

Investment objective.   The objective is to seek a high level of current income, consistent with the preservation of capital.

Performance.   Even after a dismal first six months in 1994, when the fund's share value was down 8.8 percent, long-term investors have much to celebrate. Total returns over the last 10- and 15-year periods averaged more than 10 percent. Long-term share value has been maintained, despite fluctuations along the way. Figure 18.6 shows the fund's year-by-year performance from 1980 to June 30, 1994.

Reason for recommendation.   Portfolio manager Curt Hollingsworth uses an investment approach called *duration averaging,* in which the fund buys long-term bonds when their prices fall because interest rates rise, and sells long bonds when rates fall and prices go up. Thus, the fund aggressively buys bonds when prices are low and takes a defensive position when prices are high. This strategy has worked well over the years and benefits investors with a long-term perspective.

Fidelity Government Securities Fund does not invest in mortgage-backed securities. Instead, it invests entirely in government agency bonds and Treasury issues. In mid-1994 the fund had about 40 percent

FIGURE 18.6   Fidelity Government Securities Fund Total Return and
Dividend Yield: 1980–June 30, 1994

Year	Total Return %	Dividend Yield %	Year	Total Return %	Dividend Yield %	Year	Total Return %	Dividend Yield %
1980	6.7	12.9	1985	17.7	10.0	1990	9.5	8.6
1981	10.5	13.2	1986	14.6	8.8	1991	16.0	7.8
1982	26.1	11.4	1987	1.1	9.0	1992	8.0	7.1
1983	6.0	9.9	1988	6.4	9.1	1993	11.7	5.8
1984	11.3	10.9	1989	12.6	8.2	1994*	-6.1	2.7

FIGURE 18.7   Investment Results for Various Periods Ending
June 30, 1994

Time of Investment	Value of $10,000 Invested	Value of $10,000 Invested Plus $200 Per Month	Total Invested
1 Year	$9,653	$11,751	$12,200
3 Years	12,730	20,100	17,000
5 Years	15,057	29,095	21,800
10 Years	26,697	63,393	33,800
15 Years	42,319	119,645	45,800

of its assets in agency notes and 60 percent in Treasuries, with the fund's average maturity at roughly 11 years. The fund seemed positioned to ride out the difficult interest rate environment.

During the current turbulence in interest rates, the fund may not do as well as some of its peers, but its long-term strategy has proven to be a solid source of income and appreciation.

Investment results.   With greater than 10 percent total returns during the last 10- and 15-year periods and having preserved principal, Fidelity Government Securities Fund has pretty much delivered what its investors sought. Figure 18.7 shows what investing $10,000 would have earned you over various time periods ending June 30, 1994, as well as the results of investing $10,000 plus $200 per month thereafter. Income dividends and capital gains distributions have been reinvested in additional shares.

Investment policy.   Fidelity Government Securities Fund attempts to achieve a high level of current income and preserve principal by investing in securities issued by the U.S. government, its agencies or instrumentalities and in certain options and futures contracts. The fund limits its investments to those securities whose interest is exempt from state and local income taxes for most shareholders. Under normal conditions, at least 65 percent of total assets will be invested in U.S. government securities which may or may not be backed by the full faith and credit of the U.S. government. The fund has no restrictions or targets relating to maturities of securities in its portfolio.

10 Largest Taxable Bond Holdings (as of March 31, 1994)

Security/Coupon	Maturity	% of Net Assets
U.S. Treasury 12%	8/15/13	10.1
U.S. Treasury 8.13%	8/15/19	9.6
Tennessee Valley Authority 8.25%	11/15/96	9.5
Tennessee Valley Authority 7.25%	7/15/03	6.0
Tennessee Valley Authority 8.38%	10/01/99	5.7
U.S. Treasury 8.38%	8/15/00	5.1
Financing Corporation 9.8%	4/06/18	5.0
U.S. Treasury Strip 0%	2/15/11	4.1
Financing Corporation 10.35%	8/03/18	3.2
U.S. Treasury 7.25%	2/15/23	2.4
Total		60.7

Cost of ownership.   Shares are sold with no sales or redemption charges.

Shareholder transaction expenses

Sales charge imposed on purchases: None
Sales charge imposed on reinvested dividends: None
Deferred sales charge: None
Redemption fees: None
Exchange fees: None

Annual fund operating expenses

Management fees: 0.46%
12b-1 fees: None
Other expenses: 0.23%
Total operating expenses: 0.69%

Other Top Performing Government Securities Bond Funds

During the ten-year period ending June 30, 1994, the following five mutual funds characterized as government securities bond funds led their peers in total return. These funds are available for purchase through a brokerage firm.

Fund	Ten-Year Average Annual Total Return %
Lord Abbett U.S. Government Securities Fund	10.9
Colonial Federal Securities Fund	10.4
Fortis U.S. Government Securities Fund	10.2
John Hancock Limited-Term Government Fund	9.4
Prudential Government Securities Intermediate Series	9.4

Following are addresses, phone numbers, and investment performance for each fund. The charts show the year-by-year total return and dividend yield of the funds from 1980 to June 30, 1994.

Lord Abbett U.S. Government Securities Fund
767 Fifth Avenue
New York, NY 10153
800-426-1130

Date of Inception: January 1, 1932

Investment Results 1980–June 30, 1994

	Total Return %	Dividend Yield %		Total Return %	Dividend Yield %		Total Return %	Dividend Yield %
1980	4.1	12.8	1985	22.5	10.1	1990	9.3	10.0
1981	13.4	11.4	1986	15.0	10.0	1991	16.9	8.6
1982	28.0	11.1	1987	2.1	11.5	1992	7.1	8.4
1983	10.0	11.1	1988	7.8	10.7	1993	7.7	8.0
1984	12.9	11.1	1989	12.7	10.1	1994	-4.8	4.5

Colonial Federal Securities Fund
1 Financial Center
Boston, MA 02111
800-345-6611

Date of Inception: March 30, 1984

Investment Results 1985–June 30, 1994

	Total Return %	Dividend Yield %		Total Return %	Dividend Yield %		Total Return %	Dividend Yield %
1985	19.6	8.3	1988	8.7	7.7	1991	15.2	7.0
1986	15.7	7.0	1989	13.4	7.8	1992	6.2	6.9
1987	0.1	6.8	1990	6.7	7.9	1993	11.5	7.0
						1994	−6.3	3.5

Fortis U.S. Government Securities Fund
500 Bielenberg Drive
Woodbury, MN 55125
800-800-2638

Date of Inception: March 1, 1973

Investment Results 1980–June 30, 1994

	Total Return %	Dividend Yield %		Total Return %	Dividend Yield %		Total Return %	Dividend Yield %
1980	5.8	9.8	1985	21.0	10.3	1990	10.4	8.9
1981	12.5	11.6	1986	12.4	9.2	1991	13.9	8.3
1982	31.2	10.1	1987	3.7	9.0	1992	5.6	8.1
1983	4.9	10.7	1988	7.3	9.1	1993	8.3	7.3
1984	9.9	11.2	1989	12.5	9.1	1994	−5.9	3.8

John Hancock Limited-Term Government Fund
101 Huntington Avenue
Boston, MA 02199
800-225-5291

Date of Inception: January 1, 1968

Investment Results 1980–June 30, 1994

	Total Return %	Dividend Yield %		Total Return %	Dividend Yield %		Total Return %	Dividend Yield %
1980	17.5	6.0	1985	20.0	10.1	1990	7.7	8.3
1981	−3.8	7.3	1986	14.6	8.2	1991	12.5	7.1
1982	20.6	9.2	1987	−0.5	8.9	1992	4.2	5.8
1983	6.4	10.7	1988	5.7	8.5	1993	6.7	4.8
1984	13.4	9.3	1989	11.6	8.7	1994	−1.0	2.2

Prudential Government Securities Intermediate Series
1 Seaport Plaza
New York, NY 10292
800-225-1852

Date of Inception: September 22, 1982

Investment Results 1983–June 30, 1994

	Total Return %	*Dividend Yield %*		*Total Return %*	*Dividend Yield %*		*Total Return %*	*Dividend Yield %*
1983	6.1	9.9	1987	2.6	8.4	1991	13.2	8.2
1984	14.4	10.1	1988	6.3	10.5	1992	6.1	7.5
1985	17.1	9.6	1989	10.9	8.8	1993	7.2	7.0
1986	13.7	8.9	1990	8.0	8.8	1994	-3.4	3.4

High-Yield Corporate Bond Funds

Funds in this category invest in high-yielding, lower-quality corporate bonds that should be considered speculative. These funds carry the highest yield and the highest risk of the various bond fund groups. Although high-yield bond fund share prices will move up and down with changing interest rates, fund prices may react more to news about the perceived credit quality of bond issuers in each portfolio and to events in the high-yield market than to changes in interest rates. Share prices of high-yield bond funds typically are less sensitive to interest rate changes than are other bond fund groups.

The high income available from funds in this group makes them attractive for aggressive income investors who are willing to shoulder the additional risk. In mid-1994, the average fund in the group had a yield of 9.0 percent, compared with 6.0 percent for funds in the general corporate bond group, 5.6 percent for government securities funds and 6.3 percent for funds in the international group.

Figure 18.8 shows the total return of high-yield corporate bond funds from 1980 to June 30, 1994, as well as the Lehman Brothers Aggregate Bond Index (LEH AGI).

FIGURE 18.8   High-Yield Corporate Bond Funds: Total Return
1980–June 30, 1994, Compared with the LEH AGI

Year	Group %	LEH AGI %	Year	Group %	LEH AGI %	Year	Group %	LEH AGI %
1980	4.5	2.7	1985	21.3	22.1	1990	−9.6	8.3
1981	6.1	6.3	1986	13.1	15.2	1991	35.2	16.0
1982	30.3	32.6	1987	2.0	2.7	1992	16.4	7.4
1983	15.5	8.3	1988	12.7	7.9	1993	16.6	9.7
1984	8.5	15.6	1989	−2.2	14.6	1994	−3.4	−2.8

 A Recommended High-Yield Corporate Bond Fund

Fidelity Capital & Income Fund
82 Devonshire Street
Boston, MA 02109
800-544-8888

Minimum initial investment: $2,500
Minimum subsequent investment: $250
Date of inception: November 1, 1977
Portfolio manager: David Breazzano

Shares are purchased at NAV. There are no sales charges and no 12b-1 fee. Fund expenses are slightly less than average for the industry. Dividends are paid monthly.

Investment objective.   The objective is to provide a combination of income and capital growth.

Performance.   Fidelity Capital & Income has produced outstanding results for its shareholders, leading its peers with an average total annual return of 13.5 percent for the ten years ending June 30, 1994. Until recent years, the dividend yield was well over 10 percent. Share values have gradually moved upward, with some slips along the way, and long-term investors have seen their principal grow in value. Figure 18.9 illustrates the year-by-year performance of the fund from 1980 to June 30, 1994.

FIGURE 18.9   Total Return and Dividend Yield: 1980 to 1994

Year	Total Return %	Dividend Yield %	Year	Total Return %	Dividend Yield %	Year	Total Return %	Dividend Yield %
1980	4.4	14.2	1985	25.5	12.1	1990	−4.0	12.2
1981	6.9	15.9	1986	18.0	10.9	1991	29.8	10.1
1982	35.7	13.5	1987	1.3	11.9	1992	28.0	7.7
1983	18.5	12.4	1988	12.6	11.7	1993	24.9	8.5
1984	10.5	13.5	1989	−3.1	14.8	1994	−4.1	3.7

Reason for recommendation.   This fund invests in the securities of distressed companies trading at deep discounts and in lower-quality securities with high yields. The fund's dual objective is to provide capital growth plus current income. The fund uses a team of specialists to analyze the fundamentals of troubled companies and seek those securities that offer the greatest potential for capital appreciation. The fund's managers also analyze the high-yield market, seeking the best income-producing opportunities with the lowest degree of default risk. A portfolio of some 200 securities diversified across broad market sectors reduces risk in the volatile lower-quality securities market.

Fund management believes that distressed companies provide emerging opportunities for growth, and that the high-yield markets offer possibilities for capital appreciation as well as current income. Although Fidelity Capital & Income carries fairly high risk relative to all taxable fixed-income funds, long-term investors have been amply compensated for the fund's moderately high volatility with solid total returns.

Investment results.   Fidelity Capital & Income has been a standout performer among the high-yield group. In the three-year period ending in mid-1994, the fund had an average total annual return of 19.2 percent, 5.5 percentage points more than the group average. Figure 18.10 illustrates the results of investing $10,000 in the fund over various time periods ending June 30, 1994, as well as the results of investing $10,000 plus $200 per month thereafter. Income dividends and capital gains distributions have been reinvested in additional shares.

Investment policy.   Fidelity Capital & Income Fund follows an aggressive investment program and may invest in any type or quality of debt or equity security that the manager judges to have potential for

FIGURE 18.10   Investment Results for Various Periods Ending
June 30, 1994

Time of Investment	Value of $10,000 Invested	Value of $10,000 Invested Plus $200 Per Month	Total Invested
1 Year	$10,261	$12,401	$12,200
3 Years	16,935	25,371	17,000
5 Year	17,590	35,122	21,800
10 Years	35,561	80,727	33,800
15 Years	59,636	165,510	45,800

income or capital growth. The fund has no fixed policy on allocating its assets between debt and equity investments. However, management expects that the fund will invest the majority of its assets in bonds and other interest-bearing debt instruments, with particular emphasis on lower-rated debt securities (which may be in default). The fund may make investments solely for earning income or solely for capital gains.

To achieve the fund's objective, the manager actively seeks opportunities for income and capital growth from companies whose financial circumstances may be perceived to be troubled or uncertain. The success of the fund's aggressive investment style depends on management's financial analysis and research, particularly investments in companies experiencing financial difficulties.

10 Largest Taxable Bond Holdings (as of April 30, 1994)

Security/Coupon	Maturity	% of Net Assets
NexTel Communications 9%	8/15/04	3.4
TransTexas Gas Corporation 10.5%	9/01/00	3.3
USG Corporation 9.25%	9/15/01	1.9
Resorts International 6%	4/15/96	1.7
Zale Corporation 11%	7/30/00	1.1
Bally's Gaming Corporation 10.7%	9/03/03	1.1
Bally's Grand 10.38%	12/15/03	1.0
El Paso Funding Corporation 10%	4/01/13	1.0
Barry's Jewelers 11%	12/22/00	0.9
Argentina Republic BOCON 4%	4/01/01	0.9
Total		16.3

Cost of ownership. Shares of this fund are sold with no sales charges. There is a redemption fee of 1.5 percent for shares held less than 365 days.

Shareholder transaction expenses

Sales charge imposed on purchases: None
Sales charge imposed on reinvested dividends: None
Deferred sales charge: None
Redemption fees: None (except on shares held less than 365 days)
Exchange fees: None

Annual fund operating expenses

Management fees: 0.72%
12b-1 fees: None
Other expenses: 0.37%
Total operating expenses: 1.09%

Other Top Performing High-Yield Corporate Bond Funds

During the ten-year period ending June 30, 1994, the following five mutual funds characterized as high-yield corporate bond funds led their peers in total return. The five funds listed are all load funds that must be purchased through a broker.

Fund	Ten-Year Average Annual Total Return %
Eaton Vance Traditional Income Fund	13.4
Kemper High-Yield Fund	13.4
AIM High Yield Fund	13.3
Merrill Lynch Corporate Bond Fund High Income Portfolio	13.2
Delaware Delchester Fund	12.9

Following are addresses, phone numbers, and investment performance for each of these funds. The charts show the year-by-year total return and dividend yield of the funds from 1980 to June 30, 1994.

Eaton Vance Traditional Income Fund
24 Federal Street
Boston, MA 02110
800-225-6265

Date of Inception: June 15, 1972

Investment Results: 1980–June 30, 1994

	Total Return %	Dividend Yield %		Total Return %	Dividend Yield %		Total Return %	Dividend Yield %
1980	10.6	8.3	1985	25.0	9.8	1990	−15.5	17.7
1981	5.5	9.6	1986	14.9	9.7	1991	42.8	13.0
1982	25.8	9.4	1987	3.4	15.8	1992	18.3	11.2
1983	11.4	10.2	1988	15.2	10.8	1993	18.0	10.1
1984	14.7	10.5	1989	4.2	12.3	1994	−0.1	5.1

Kemper High-Yield Fund
120 South LaSalle Street
Chicago, IL 60603
800-621-1048

Date of Inception: January 26, 1978

Investment Results: 1980–June 30, 1994

	Total Return %	Dividend Yield %		Total Return %	Dividend Yield %		Total Return %	Dividend Yield %
1980	−0.9	13.6	1985	23.3	11.6	1990	−13.0	17.6
1981	7.3	13.3	1986	18.3	10.5	1991	46.8	12.5
1982	39.4	12.3	1987	9.0	11.1	1992	17.1	9.8
1983	17.6	11.9	1988	14.4	12.0	1993	21.2	8.7
1984	10.2	12.4	1989	−1.1	13.6	1994	−2.6	4.6

AIM High Yield Fund
11 Greenway Plaza
Houston, TX 77046
800-347-1919

Date of Inception: July 11, 1978

Investment Results: 1980–June 30, 1994

	Total Return %	Dividend Yield %		Total Return %	Dividend Yield %		Total Return %	Dividend Yield %
1980	1.0	12.9	1985	23.5	12.0	1990	−9.0	15.1
1981	7.1	15.0	1986	16.0	11.2	1991	42.2	11.2
1982	31.8	13.3	1987	3.1	11.8	1992	18.6	10.6
1983	17.5	12.4	1988	16.4	11.2	1993	18.4	9.5
1984	9.8	12.9	1989	1.2	12.9	1994	−0.9	4.8

Merrill Lynch Corporate Bond Fund High Income Portfolio
P.O. Box 45289
Jacksonville, FL 32232
800-637-3863

Date of Inception: November 10, 1978

Investment Results: 1980–June 30, 1994

	Total Return %	*Dividend Yield %*		*Total Return %*	*Dividend Yield %*		*Total Return %*	*Dividend Yield %*
1980	2.7	12.5	1985	21.6	11.7	1990	−4.6	16.4
1981	6.7	14.9	1986	12.9	11.2	1991	39.8	11.9
1982	23.1	12.9	1987	4.9	11.7	1992	20.6	10.6
1983	18.3	12.0	1988	12.7	11.7	1993	17.4	8.8
1984	8.7	12.7	1989	4.3	12.9	1994	−2.3	4.4

Delaware Delchester Fund
1818 Market Street
Philadelphia, PA 19103
800-523-4640

Date of Inception: August 20, 1970

Investment Results: 1980–June 30, 1994

	Total Return %	*Dividend Yield %*		*Total Return %*	*Dividend Yield %*		*Total Return %*	*Dividend Yield %*
1980	0.7	9.4	1985	23.3	14.1	1990	−11.9	16.1
1981	1.0	12.9	1986	16.8	12.1	1991	43.9	11.9
1982	37.5	12.1	1987	5.2	12.1	1992	17.2	10.9
1983	12.9	11.6	1988	14.0	11.7	1993	16.5	10.2
1984	8.7	12.9	1989	1.1	13.1	1994	−1.6	5.4

Municipal (Tax-Free) Bond Funds

Mutual funds in the municipal bond fund group seek income by investing primarily in tax-free bonds issued by any state or municipality. These municipal bonds, similar to bonds issued by a corporation or the U.S. government, obligate the issuer to pay bondholders a fixed amount of interest periodically and to repay the principal value of the bond on a specific maturity date. Like corporate bonds, municipal bonds are considered fixed-income securities; they offer a steady rate of interest income. They are often called debt obligations because they represent a loan to the bond issuer.

Municipal bond funds appeal to investors mainly because they provide income that is exempt from federal income taxes and, in some cases, from state and local taxes. Like other mutual funds, municipal bond funds deliver an investment return in two forms: income return (yield) and capital return. Together, they provide the total return. Note: Only the dividend income from interest paid by bonds in a mutual fund portfolio is tax exempt. Capital gains distributions *are* subject to tax.

Not considered in this chapter are single state municipal bond funds. Single state funds invest in municipal bonds of a particular state and are sold to residents of that state. For instance, the Fidelity New York Tax-Free Insured Portfolio invests only in municipal bonds issued by New York State and New York City. Single state funds have the added advantage of being exempt from taxes of the state in which the bonds are issued, as well as from federal income taxes.

Figure 18.11 shows the total return of nationally distributed municipal bond funds from 1980 to July 31, 1994, as well as the Lehman Brothers Municipal Bond Index (LEH MUNI).

A Recommended Municipal Bond Fund

Vanguard Municipal High-Yield Fund
P.O. Box 2600
Valley Forge, PA 19482
800-662-7447

Minimum initial investment: $3,000
Minimum subsequent investment: $100
Date of inception: December 27, 1978
Portfolio managers: Ian MacKinnon & Jerome Jacobs

Shares of this no-load fund are available from Vanguard with no sales charge. Total expenses are extremely low: 0.20 percent of assets. This is important if you are an income-minded investor, because the expenses of running a mutual fund are deducted from its income, which has a direct impact on shareholder returns.

Investment objective.   This fund seeks to provide a high level of income that is exempt from federal income tax and consistent with preservation of capital.

Performance.   This fund has outperformed its peers in both short- and long-term periods ending July 31, 1994, beating the average municipal bond fund by nearly 2 percentage points in total return over 1 year, 3 years and 10 years and doing nearly 1 percentage point better over 15 years. Figure 18.12 illustrates the year-by-year performance of the fund from 1980 to July 31, 1994.

Reason for recommendation.   Vanguard Municipal High-Yield Fund has limited its losses during periods of rising interest rates, and its annual return has been better than its peers in 12 of the last 15 years. Because of its low expense ratio, dividend yields are also very competitive in the tax-exempt fund group. Over nearly any time

FIGURE 18.11   Municipal Bond Funds: Total Return 1980–July 31, 1994 Compared with LEH MUNI

Year	Group %	LEH MUNI %	Year	Group %	LEH MUNI %	Year	Group %	LEH MUNI %
1980	−10.7	−11.0	1985	17.9	20.0	1990	6.1	7.3
1981	−5.5	−10.2	1986	16.7	19.3	1991	11.4	12.2
1982	34.5	40.7	1987	−0.4	1.5	1992	8.3	8.8
1983	9.8	8.0	1988	10.4	10.2	1993	11.3	12.3
1984	8.3	10.5	1989	9.2	10.8	1994	−3.0	−2.6

FIGURE 18.12   Total Return and Dividend Yield: 1980–July 31, 1994

Year	Total Return %	Dividend Yield %	Year	Total Return %	Dividend Yield %	Year	Total Return %	Dividend Yield %
1980	−15.1	9.6	1985	21.7	8.6	1990	5.9	7.3
1981	−4.9	12.3	1986	19.7	7.6	1991	14.8	6.9
1982	36.1	9.9	1987	−1.6	7.9	1992	9.9	6.5
1983	10.4	9.4	1988	13.8	7.4	1993	12.7	5.8
1984	9.7	9.7	1989	11.1	7.3	1994	−2.1	2.9

period the fund has outperformed both the average municipal bond fund and the Lehman Brothers Municipal Bond Index.

Careful credit analysis of the bonds included in the portfolio, together with wide diversification, gives the fund a less risky stance than you would expect in a high-yield fund. More than 90 percent of the bonds are rated BBB or better by Standard & Poor's Investors Service.

This fund is an attractive choice for the typical municipal bond investor. Nearly half of the fund is in noncallable issues, which protects the fund against issuers calling away the bonds when rates go down. Management avoids risky issues such as zero-coupon bonds and other instruments that have brought considerable losses to many other municipal bond funds.

Investment results.   Vanguard Municipal High-Yield Fund has performed well for its shareholders. Figure 18.13 shows the results of investing of $10,000 plus $200 per month thereafter in the fund from 1980 to July 31, 1994.

Investment policy.   This fund invests in municipal securities of varying maturities, but tries to keep the dollar-weighted average maturity between 15 and 20 years, with no limit to any individual maturity length. The fund invests at least 80 percent of its assets in investment-grade securities and as much as 20 percent in lower-rated or unrated municipal securities.

Compared with other funds in its group, the fund's portfolio is high-quality oriented. Only 25 percent of the fund's assets are rated below A, whereas the typical high-yield fund holds more than 50 percent of assets in BBBs and below. Vanguard's high-yield municipal fund has

FIGURE 18.13   Investment Results for Various Periods Ending
July 31, 1994

Time of Investment	Value of $10,000 Invested	Value of $10,000 Invested Plus $200 Per Month	Total Invested
1 Year	$10,289	$12,489	$12,200
3 Years	13,008	20,710	17,000
5 Years	15,015	29,575	21,800
10 Years	28,130	66,770	33,800
15 Years	32,397	113,887	45,800

found success more through interest-rate sensitive securities (those of good quality and longer maturities) than through credit-quality bets. Its higher-quality bonds adjust more quickly to rate shifts than do low-quality bonds.

Although total returns are the fund's primary focus, management tries to keep call protection high to help maintain the fund's income stream. The fund owns premium-priced bonds (priced above face value) that it believes will be more valuable than discounts because some appreciation on discounts is subject to income taxes, making them less attractive. High-coupon bonds should also temper the fund's volatility, as these issues are less sensitive to interest rate changes.

Cost of ownership. Shares of this fund are sold with no sales or redemption charges.

Shareholder transaction expenses

Sales charge imposed on purchases: None
Sales charge imposed on reinvested dividends: None
Deferred sales charge: None
Redemption fees: None
Exchange fees: None

Annual fund operating expenses

Management fee: 0.15%
12b-1 fees: None
Other expenses: 0.05%
Total operating expenses: 0.20%

Other Top Performing Municipal Bond Funds

During the ten-year period ending July 31, 1994, the following five national municipal bond funds led their peers in total return. No-load funds that may be purchased directly are listed in **bold** print.

Fund	Ten-Year Average Annual Total Return %
United Municipal Bond Fund	11.4
Smith Barney Shearson Managed Municipals Fund	11.0
Delaware Group Tax-Free USA Fund	10.8
Pioneer Tax-Free Income Fund	10.7
SAFECO Municipal Bond Fund	**10.7**

Following are addresses, phone numbers, and investment performance for each of these funds. The charts show the year-by-year total return and dividend yield of the funds from 1980 to July 31, 1994.

United Municipal Bond Fund
P.O. Box 29217
Shawnee Mission, KS 66201
800-366-5465

Date of Inception: September 29, 1976

Investment Results: 1980–July 31, 1994

	Total Return %	Dividend Yield %		Total Return %	Dividend Yield %		Total Return %	Dividend Yield %
1980	−16.3	8.8	1985	24.3	7.6	1990	5.6	6.6
1981	−10.4	11.5	1986	22.0	6.6	1991	13.5	5.8
1982	36.0	8.9	1987	−1.6	6.9	1992	9.5	5.5
1983	8.5	8.3	1988	15.0	6.5	1993	14.3	4.8
1984	9.9	8.6	1989	11.1	6.6	1994	−4.0	2.5

Smith Barney Shearson Managed Municipals Fund
P.O. Box 9134
Boston, MA 02205
800-451-2010

Date of Inception: March 4, 1981

Investment Results: 1982–July 31, 1994

	Total Return %	Dividend Yield %		Total Return %	Dividend Yield %		Total Return %	Dividend Yield %
1982	41.1	9.2	1986	18.7	7.0	1990	5.2	7.1
1983	12.3	8.7	1987	0.5	7.3	1991	14.3	6.6
1984	10.5	8.8	1988	11.6	7.1	1992	9.4	6.1
1985	20.8	7.8	1989	10.1	6.8	1993	15.4	5.1
						1994	−0.1	2.5

Delaware Group Tax-Free USA Fund
1818 Market Street
Philadelphia, PA 19103
800-523-4640

Date of Inception: January 11, 1984

Investment Results: 1985–July 31, 1994

	Total Return %	Dividend Yield %		Total Return %	Dividend Yield %		Total Return %	Dividend Yield %
1985	22.7	8.4	1988	14.2	7.1	1991	12.4	6.2
1986	21.9	7.3	1989	10.5	6.9	1992	9.7	5.9
1987	–1.8	7.6	1990	3.9	7.9	1993	11.6	5.6
						1994	–1.8	2.7

Pioneer Tax-Free Income Fund
60 State Street
Boston, MA 02109
800-225-6292

Date of Inception: January 18, 1977

Investment Results: 1980–July 31, 1994

	Total Return %	Dividend Yield %		Total Return %	Dividend Yield %		Total Return %	Dividend Yield %
1980	13.4	9.1	1985	21.2	7.7	1990	7.4	6.3
1981	8.6	11.4	1986	22.7	6.7	1991	12.5	5.8
1982	34.7	9.2	1987	–1.6	7.2	1992	8.7	5.5
1983	7.2	8.3	1988	12.3	6.8	1993	13.0	4.9
1984	9.4	8.6	1989	10.1	6.6	1994	–3.5	2.7

SAFECO Municipal Bond Fund
P.O. Box 34890
Seattle, WA 98124
800-426-6730

Date of Inception: November 15, 1981

Investment Results: 1982–July 31, 1994

	Total Return %	Dividend Yield %		Total Return %	Dividend Yield %		Total Return %	Dividend Yield %
1982	42.1	9.3	1986	19.8	7.1	1990	6.7	6.7
1983	10.4	9.1	1987	0.2	7.4	1991	13.8	6.2
1984	10.1	9.4	1988	13.9	7.1	1992	8.7	5.9
1985	21.6	8.3	1989	10.1	6.6	1993	12.7	5.3
						1994	–4.7	2.8

International Bond Funds

International bond funds invest in the debt securities of companies and countries throughout the world, including the United States. They seek current income for their shareholders, while attempting to protect principal.

Currency fluctuations are an additional concern for investors in funds that hold foreign securities. For example, the European currency crisis in 1992 aggravated an already difficult year for income investors. Shares of the average international bond fund in that year gained just 2.3 percent, trailing the domestic bond market by nearly 5 percentage points.

At times the international bond markets provide better returns than their U.S. counterparts. In 1987, the average international bond fund posted a total return of 15.9 percent, compared with a total return of 1.9 percent for the average U.S. corporate bond fund. The reverse can also be true, such as in 1984 when the average U.S. corporate bond fund returned 12.2 percent to investors, compared with 4.7 percent for international bond funds.

Figure 18.14 shows the average total returns of international bond funds and U.S. general corporate bond funds from 1982 to July 31, 1994.

A Recommended International Bond Fund

Scudder International Bond Fund
Two International Place
Boston, MA 02110
800-225-2470

Minimum initial investment: $1,000
Minimum subsequent investment: $100
Date of inception: July 6, 1988
Portfolio managers: Adam M. Greshin & Lawrence Teitelbaum

Fund shares are available from Scudder with no sales charge. Total expenses of the fund are 1.25 percent of assets, a little lower than the expense ratio of its average competitor. Expenses of international mutual funds tend to be somewhat higher than U.S. funds.

FIGURE 18.14 International Bond Funds and U.S. Corporate Bond Funds: Total Returns 1982–July 31, 1994

Year	International Funds Group%	U.S. Corporate Funds Group%	Year	International Funds Group%	U.S. Corporate Funds Group%
1982	21.7	31.4	1988	6.4	8.2
1983	10.1	8.6	1989	6.0	11.0
1984	4.7	12.2	1990	9.5	6.5
1985	23.9	20.3	1991	12.7	16.1
1986	13.6	13.5	1992	2.2	7.2
1987	15.9	1.9	1993	12.8	10.0
			1994	−4.2	−4.1

FIGURE 18.15 Total Return and Dividend Yield: 1989–July 31, 1994

Year	Total Return %	Dividend Yield %	Year	Total Return %	Dividend Yield %	Year	Total Return %	Dividend Yield %
1989	7.2	8.7	1991	22.2	8.2	1993	15.8	6.6
1990	21.1	8.8	1992	7.6	7.9	1994	−7.3	3.8

Investment objective. The objective is to provide current income. As a secondary objective, the fund seeks protection and possible enhancement of principal.

Performance. In its short history, Scudder International Bond Fund has outperformed its peers in both the three- and five-year periods ending July 31, 1994, with more than a 5 percent advantage in the longer period. Figure 18.15 illustrates the year-by-year performance of the fund from 1989 to July 31, 1994.

Reason for recommendation. Despite its lagging performance in 1994, Scudder International Bond Fund has been the best performing fund in its group over the longer term, substantially beating its peers in the most recent three- and five-year periods. The fund has a stake in the debt of emerging markets and holds positions in debt securities issued in Mexico, Argentina and Venezuela. The managers believe that

FIGURE 18.16   Investment Results for Periods Ending July 31, 1994

Time of Investment	Value of $10,000 Invested	Value of $10,000 Invested Plus $200 Per Month	Total Invested
1 Year	$9,721	$11,813	$12,200
3 Years	13,608	21,060	17,000
5 Years	17,992	32,964	21,800

those bonds will experience strong total return as investors recognize the improved creditworthiness of the issuing countries.

The fund is somewhat risky; it has been 40 percent more volatile than the average international bond fund. But investors with time horizons that are long enough to even out its performance swings should find this a rewarding investment.

Investment results. This fund has provided reasonably good returns for its shareholders during a difficult time in bond investments. Figure 18.16 shows the results of investing $10,000 plus $200 per month for various periods ending July 31, 1994.

Investment policy.   The fund invests primarily in high-grade international bonds denominated in foreign currencies and in the European Currency Unit. Its investments may include debt securities issued or guaranteed by foreign national governments, their agencies, instrumentalities or political subdivisions. It may also invest in debt securities issued or guaranteed by supranational organizations, corporate debt securities and bank debt securities. The fund's high-grade debt securities are rated in the three highest rating categories. As much as 5 percent of its assets may be invested in securities rated BBB or lower.

Cost of ownership.   Fund shares are sold with no sales or redemption charges.

Shareholder transaction expenses

Sales charge imposed on purchases: None
Sales charge imposed on reinvested dividends: None
Deferred sales charge: None
Redemption fees: None

Annual fund operating expenses

Management fee: 0.85%
12b-1 fees: None
Other expenses: 0.40%
Total operating expenses: 1.25%

Other Top Performing International Bond Funds

During the five-year period ending July 31, 1994, the following five national municipal bond funds led their peers in total return. No-load funds that may be purchased directly are listed in **bold** print.

Fund	Five-Year Average Annual Total Return %
T. Rowe Price International Bond Fund	**10.9**
Merrill Lynch World Income Fund	10.2
Putnam Diversified Income Trust	10.2
IDS Global Bond Fund	9.8
Merrill Lynch Global Bond Fund for Investment and Retirement	9.5

Following are addresses, phone numbers, and investment performance for each fund. The charts show the year-by-year total return and dividend yield of the funds from 1980 to July 31, 1994.

T. Rowe Price International Bond Fund
100 East Pratt Street
Baltimore, MD 21202
800-225-5132

Date of Inception: September 10, 1986

Investment Results: 1987–July 31, 1994

	Total Return %	Dividend Yield %		Total Return %	Dividend Yield %		Total Return %	Dividend Yield %
1987	28.1	2.8	1990	16.1	8.6	1993	19.4	6.3
1988	-1.3	8.7	1991	17.6	7.5	1994	-1.7	3.1
1989	-3.2	8.2	1992	2.9	8.5			

Merrill Lynch World Income Fund
P.O. Box 45289
Jacksonville, FL 32232
800-637-3863

Date of Inception: September 29, 1988

Investment Results: 1989–July 31, 1994

	Total Return %	Dividend Yield %		Total Return %	Dividend Yield %		Total Return %	Dividend Yield %
1989	6.9	11.7	1991	23.4	11.4	1993	13.8	7.8
1990	9.8	16.5	1992	6.2	10.7	1994	−4.4	3.9

Putnam Diversified Income Trust
One Post Office Square
Boston, MA 02109
800-225-1581

Date of Inception: October 3, 1988

Investment Results: 1989–July 31, 1994

	Total Return %	Dividend Yield %		Total Return %	Dividend Yield %		Total Return %	Dividend Yield %
1989	5.1	9.9	1991	23.6	8.3	1993	15.9	6.1
1990	5.0	9.8	1992	12.3	7.9	1994	−3.9	3.6

IDS Global Bond Fund
IDS Tower
Minneapolis, MN 55440
800-437-4332

Date of Inception: March 20, 1989

Investment Results: 1990–July 31, 1994

	Total Return %	Dividend Yield %		Total Return %	Dividend Yield %		Total Return %	Dividend Yield %
1990	13.0	8.8	1992	6.5	5.9	1994	−5.1	3.1
1991	15.3	6.6	1993	16.4	5.9			

Merrill Lynch Global Bond Fund for Investment and Retirement
P.O. Box 45289
Jacksonville, FL 32232
800-637-3863

Date of Inception: August 29, 1986

Investment Results: 1987–July 31, 1994

	Total Return %	Dividend Yield %		Total Return %	Dividend Yield %		Total Return %	Dividend Yield %
1987	23.2	11.8	1990	14.7	12.0	1993	12.3	5.7
1988	3.8	8.0	1991	15.2	9.3	1994	−5.6	2.6
1989	6.5	10.8	1992	6.9	12.1			

In Your Spare Time ...

Consider bond funds if you are interested in high and steady income. Although bond funds fluctuate in value, they are considered less risky than stock funds and can balance a portfolio heavy in stock funds.

Appendix A

$ $

Sources of
Investment Analysis
and Information

$ $

A host of research and statistical services, newsletters and other sources of information are available to investors. Many publications offer special introductory rates and are advertised regularly in *BARRON'S*, *The Wall Street Journal*, and *Investor's Business Daily*. You can find a complete list of just about all the major publications that can help keep you informed about developments in finance and investment in *BARRON'S Finance & Investment Handbook* by Jordan Goodman and John Downes.

Check your local public library for many widely used services. This appendix describes some of the most useful investment sources and organizations.

Individual Securities Analysis and Information

American Association of Individual Investors (AAII)
625 North Michigan Avenue
Chicago, IL 60611-3110
312-280-0170

AAII is a nonprofit corporation recognized under Section 501(C)(3) of the Internal Revenue Code as a public educational organization. Membership in the organization entitles you to several important benefits. All members receive the *AAII Journal,* the *AAII Year-End Tax Strategy, AAII Quoteline,* a listing of companies with dividend investment plans (DRIPs) and an annual stock brokerage survey. Other services include investment seminars, home study programs, a computer users' newsletter and local chapter membership.

Morningstar, Inc.
225 West Wacker Drive
Chicago, IL 60606
800-876-5005

Morningstar offers a variety of thoroughly documented services, including Morningstar ADRs (information on actively traded foreign stocks traded on U.S. exchanges in the form of American Depositary Receipts), and Morningstar Closed-End Funds (complete profiles on 284 of the most actively traded closed-end funds).

Securities Research Company
101 Prescott Street
Wellesley Hills, MA 02181
617-235-0900

For investors interested in using technical analysis to predict future price movements, this company produces SRC Chart Books covering both listed and over-the-counter (OTC) stocks. Charts plot pure market performance. You get a picture of past price action and how it may repeat or break with prior patterns, resistance levels, turning points, major formations and volume of buying or selling. All Security Research charts are plotted on semi-logarithmic scales, showing percentage changes rather than ordinary numerical changes.

Standard & Poor's Corporation
25 Broadway
New York NY 10004
212-208-8000

Standard & Poor's Corporation's highly respected publications cover virtually the full spectrum of investor needs. Some of the most widely used include *Bond Guide, Corporation Records, Daily Action Stock Charts, Daily Stock Price Record, Dividend Record, Growth Stocks Handbook, Mutual Fund Profiles, OTC Handbook, Register of Corporations, Stock Guide* and *Stock Reports.*

TeleChart 2000 Software Bundle
Worden Brothers, Inc.
4905 Pine Cone Drive
Durham, NC 27707
800-776-4940

TC2000 is a fully integrated technical analysis service that provides an advanced charting module and inexpensive toll-free price data 24 hours a day. The service provides free daily information on symbol changes, company name changes, stock split dates and ratios, new issues, and so on, for more than 10,000 stocks and mutual funds, alphabetized by both symbol and company name. *TC2000* requires an IBM-PC compatible, modem, hard disk and EGA or VGA color monitor.

Value Line Publishing, Inc.
711 Third Avenue
New York, NY 10017-4064
800-833-0046

The Value Line Investment Survey presents every week, for each of 1,700 stocks, the up-to-date rank for probable relative price performance, rank for investment safety, estimated yield in the next 12 months, estimated appreciation potentiality in the next 3 to 5 years, current price and estimated PE ratios, and the latest available quarterly earnings and dividends. The service includes a 2,000 page *Investors Reference Library*. The weekly *Selection & Opinion* section gives Value Line's opinion of the business prospect, the stock market outlook and the advisable investment strategy.

Mutual Funds Analysis and Information

CDA Investment Technologies, Inc.
1355 Piccard Drive
Rockville, MD 20850
800-232-2285

CDA/Wiesenberger Investment Companies Service includes the annual volume *Investment Companies* and the monthly *Mutual Funds Update*. *Investment Companies* is a 1,200-page hard-cover reference volume published each spring. The "bible" of the industry for more than 50 years, *Investment Companies* is considered by many to be the most complete single source of information on investment companies. It covers more than 4,500 mutual funds, money market funds, unit investment trusts, variable annuity separate accounts and closed-end funds. It also includes *Panorama*, an annual directory and guide to mutual funds, which features ten years of performance information and shareholder data, including fees and expenses, investment minimums, special services, addresses, telephone numbers and investment advisers.

Dearborn Financial Publishing, Inc.
155 North Wacker Drive
Chicago, IL 60606
800-829-7934, ext. 650

The Mutual Fund Encyclopedia, an annual by Gerald W. Perritt, profiles more than 3,000 no-load, low-load and load funds. Each profile gives a detailed statement of objectives and strategies and provides key financial statistics, including assets under management, current yield, portfolio turnover ratio, risk factors, and year-by-year and five-year total returns. The minimum initial investment for each fund is noted, as well as the cost of investing in each fund and the company address and toll-free number.

IBC/Donoghue
290 Eliot Street
Ashland, MA 01721-9104
800-343-5413

Donoghue's Mutual Funds Almanac is designed for individual and corporate investors. It includes a directory, toll-free numbers and ten-year performance on more than 1,100 funds and has a special section on betas and investment risk. The service provides information on no-load funds, low-load funds and load funds. No closed-end funds are included.

Investment Company Institute
1401 H Street NW, Suite 1200
Washington, DC 20005
202-326-5800

The Investment Company Institute is the national association of the American mutual fund industry. It produces several publications that you will find helpful, especially *Mutual Fund Fact Book* and *Directory of Mutual Funds.* The *Fact Book* is a basic guide to the mutual fund industry, providing annually updated facts and figures on the U.S. mutual fund industry, including trends in sales, assets and performance. It outlines the history and growth of the fund industry and its policies, operations, regulation, services and shareholders. In addition to mutual fund names, addresses and telephone numbers (many are toll-free), the annual *Directory* lists each fund's assets, initial and subsequent investment requirements, fees charged, where to buy shares and other pertinent details. An extensive introductory text serves as a short course in mutual fund investing.

Johnson's Charts, Inc.
175 Bridle Path
Williamsville, NY 14221
716-626-0845

Johnson's publishes graphs and charts analyzing long-term performance of individual mutual funds, including information on historical income and capital gains payment, share price trends, and total returns with and without dividend reinvestments.

Lipper Analytical Services, Inc.
47 Maple Street
Summit, NY 07901
908-273-2772

Lipper provides statistical services on the mutual fund industry, which are widely quoted and used by other financial publications.

Morningstar, Inc.
225 West Wacker Drive
Chicago, IL 60606
800-876-5005

Morningstar Mutual Funds ranks among the most comprehensive, timely and useful sources for mutual fund information. Vital information for tracking, analyzing, comparing and choosing mutual funds is condensed on a single page for each of more than 1,200 mutual funds and is presented in one hard-cover binder. Every two weeks Morningstar provides subscribers with a 32-page report summarizing the current performance of all funds covered, plus a new issue of more than 120 updated full-page fund reports. Morningstar also publishes *Mutual Fund Sourcebook, Mutual Fund Performance Report, Morningstar Mutual Fund 500, 5-Star Investor, Morningstar Closed-End Funds, Closed-End Fund Sourcebook, Mutual Fund Styles of Investing Chart, Variable Annuity/Life Sourcebook, Variable Annuity/Life Performance Report, Morningstar Japan* and a variety of computer disk products.

Standard & Poor's Corporation
25 Broadway
New York, NY 10004
800-221-5277
212-208-8812

Mutual Fund Profiles is jointly produced with Lipper Analytical Services, Inc. Individual mutual fund profiles include statistical data; investment policy, performance and evaluation; and comparison with S&P 500 results and top holdings.

Value Line Publishing, Inc.
220 E. 42nd Street
New York, NY 10017
800-284-7607

The Value Line Mutual Funds Survey, produced in two binders, covers 2,000 funds encompassing a wide range of investment objectives, from aggressive growth to tax-free income. Full-page analyses are provided for 1,500 established mutual funds through biweekly ratings and reports, which include performance data, portfolio data, tax data and so on. Every fund is updated three times a year.

In Your Spare Time ...

Be informed. Most people will find it surprisingly easy to become successful investors by using the information in this book and selecting one or more other sources of investment analysis and information that are readily available.

Appendix B

$ $ $ $ $ $ $ $ $ $ $ $ $ $ $ $ $ $ $ $

Corporations with Dividend Reinvestment Plans (DRIPs)

$ $ $ $ $ $ $ $ $ $ $ $ $ $ $ $ $ $ $ $

This directory lists most of the companies that now offer dividend reinvestment plans. In some cases, shares purchased under the plans are offered at a discount from the market price. Detailed information on how each plan works may be obtained by calling the stockholder relations department of the companies in which you have an interest.

Company	Telephone	Company	Telephone
AAR Corporation	404-953-8300	AMAX, Inc.	800-243-4000
Abbott Laboratories	617-575-2900	Amcast Indutrial	513-298-5251
Acme-Cleveland	216-737-5742	Corporation	
Corporation		AMCORE Financial,	815-961-7098
Aetna Life and	203-273-3945	Inc.	
Casualty Company		Amerada Hess	800-647-4273
AFLAC, Inc.	800-235-2667	Corporation	
Air Products &	215-481-8101	American Brands, Inc.	203-698-5440
Chemicals, Inc.		American Business	404-953-8300
Albany International	518-445-2284	Products, Inc.	
Allegheny Ludlum	412-394-2813	American Colloid	708-392-4600
Corporation		Company	
Allegheny Power	212-752-2121	American Cyanamid	201-831-3586
System, Inc.		Company	
ALLIED Group, Inc.	515-280-4211	American Electric	800-237-2667
Allied Signal, Inc.	800-255-4332	Power Co. Inc.	
Aluminum Company	412-553-4708	American Express	212-640-5693
of America		Company	

American Filtrona Corporation	804-346-2401	Avery Dennison Corporation	818-304-2032
American General Corporation	800-446-2617	Avnet, Inc.	516-466-7000
American Greetings Corporation	216-253-7300	Avon Products, Inc.	212-456-6786
American Heritage Life Investors	904-359-2545	Baker Hughes, Inc.	713-439-8668
		Baldwin Technology	617-575-2900
		Ball Corporation	317-747-6170
American Home Products Corporation	212-878-6139	Baltimore Bancorporation	800-435-7016
American Recreation Centers	916-852-8005	Baltimore Gas & Electric Company	800-258-0499
American Telephone & Telegraph	800-348-8288	Banc One Corporation	800-753-7107
American Water Works Company, Inc.	609-346-8290	Bancorporation Hawaii, Inc.	808-537-8239
Ameritech	800-233-1342	Bancorporation of Mississippi, Inc.	601-680-2000
Amoco Corporation	800-638-5672		
AMP, Inc.	717-780-4869	Bangor Hydro- Electric Company	207-990-6936
AmSouth Bancorporation	205-583-4439		
		Bank of Boston Corporation	617-929-5445
AmVestors Financial Corporation	913-232-6945	Bank of Granite Corporation	704-396-3141
Anheuser-Busch Companies	314-577-2309	Bank of New York Company, Inc.	800-524-4458
Aon Corporation	800-446-2617	BankAmerica Corporation	800-642-9880
Apache Corporation	713-296-6504		
Aquarion Company	800-526-0801	Bankers Trust New York Corporation	800-221-4096
ARCO Chemical	215-359-3382		
Arkla, Inc.	318-429-2925	Banta Corporation	414-287-3920
Armstrong World Industries, Inc.	717-396-2029	Bard (CR), Inc.	908-277-8221
		Barnes Group, Inc.	203-583-7070
Arrow Financial Corporation	518-745-1000	Barnett Banks, Inc.	904-791-7093
		Bausch & Lomb, Inc.	617-575-2900
Arvin Industries, Inc.	312-461-2549		
		Baxter International, Inc.	708-948-2886
Asarco, Inc.	800-524-4458		
Ashland Coal	304-526-3750	Bay State Gas Company	508-836-7313
Associated Banc- Corporation	800-236-2722		
		Bay View Capital Corporation	415-312-7272
Atlanta Gas Light Company	404-584-3819		
		BayBanks, Inc.	617-482-1040
Atlantic Energy, Inc.	609-645-4507	BB&T Financial Corporation	919-399-4248
Atlantic Richfield Company	212-791-6422		
		Becton, Dickinson & Company	212-791-6422
Atmos Energy Corporation	800-382-8667		

Bell Atlantic Corporation	800-631-2355	Cabot Corporation	617-575-2900
BellSouth Corporation	800-631-6001	Cadmus Communications Corporation	804-287-5680
Bemis Company, Inc.	612-376-3011	California Financial Holding Company	800-524-4458
Beneficial Corporation	302-792-4753	California Water Service Company	408-451-8200
Berkshire Gas Company	413-442-1511	Campbell Soup Company	609-342-5919
Black & Decker Corporation	212-791-6422	Capital Holding Corporation	512-560-2391
Black Hills Corporation	605-348-1700	Carlisle Companies, Inc.	315-474-2500
Block (H&R), Inc.	816-932-8468	Carolina Freight Corporation	704-435-6811
Blount, Inc.	205-244-4000	Carolina Power & Light Company	800-662-7232
BMJ Financial Corporation	609-291-2841	Carpenter Technology Corporation	212-791-6422
Boatman's Bancshares, Inc.	314-466-7720	Cascade Natural Gas Corporation	206-624-3900
Bob Evans Farms	614-491-2225	Caterpillar, Inc.	309-675-4621
Boise Cascade Corporation	208-384-7056	CB&T Financial Corporation	304-367-2375
Borden, Inc.	800-524-4458	CBI Industries, Inc.	708-572-7366
Boston Bancorporation	800-524-4458	CBS, Inc.	212-975-4321
Boston Edison Company	617-424-2658	CCB Financial Corporation	800-829-8432
Bowater, Inc.	203-656-7206	Centel Corporation	800-446-2617
Braintree Savings Bank	617-843-9100	Centerbank	203-573-6630
Briggs & Stratton Corporation	414-259-5480	Centerior Energy Corporation	800-433-7794
Bristol-Myers Squibb Company	212-546-3309	Central & South West Corporation	800-527-5797
British Airways plc	212-648-3212	Central Bancshares of the South	205-933-3960
British Petroleum Company	800-428-4237	Central Fidelity Banks, Inc.	804-697-6942
Brooklyn Union Gas Company	718-403-3334	Central Holding Company	800-257-1770
Brown Group, Inc.	314-854-4122	Central Hudson Gas & Electric	800-428-9578
Brown-Forman Corporation	502-774-7688	Central Jersey Bancorporation	908-294-4121
Browning-Ferris Industries, Inc.	713-870-7893	Central Louisiana Electric Company	800-253-2652
Brunswick Corporation	708-470-4293		
Brush Wellman, Inc.	216-486-4200		
BSB Bancorporation, Inc.	607-779-2552		

Central Maine Power Company	800-695-4267	CNB Bancshares, Inc.	812-464-3400
Central Vermont Public Service	802-747-5406	Coca-Cola Company	404-676-2777
Centura Banks, Inc.	800-633-4236	Coca-Cola Enterprises	404-676-7052
Century Telephone Enterprises	800-833-1188	Colgate Palmalive Company	212-310-2575
Champion International Corporation	203-358-7000	Colonial BancGroup (Ala.)	205-240-5182
Charter One Financial, Inc.	800-442-2001	Colonial Gas Company	508-458-3171
Chase Manhattan Corporation	800-526-0801	Colorado National Bankshares	303-629-1968
Chemed Corporation	513-762-6900	Comerica	800-551-6161
Chemical Banking Corporation	800-647-4273	Commercial Intertech Corporation	216-746-8011
Chemical Financial Corporation	216-737-5745	Commonwealth Edison Company	800-950-2377
Chemical Waste Management	312-461-2543	Commonwealth Energy System	800-447-1183
Chesapeake Corporation	804-697-1166	Communications Satellite Corporation	202-863-6200
Chesapeake Utilities Corporation	302-734-6716	Community Bank System, Inc.	315-445-2282
Chevron Corporation	800-547-9794	COMSTAT Corporation	301-214-3200
Chrysler Corporation	313-956-3007	ConAgra, Inc.	402-595-4000
Chubb Corporation	908-580-3579	Connecticut Energy Corporation	203-382-8156
CIGNA Corporation	215-761-3516		
CILCORP, Inc.	800-622-5514	Connecticut Natural Gas Corporation	203-727-3203
Cincinnati Bell	800-345-6301		
Cincinnati Financial Corporation	513-870-2000	Connecticut Water Service, Inc.	203-669-8636
Cincinnati Gas & Electric Company	513-287-1940	Consolidated Edison Company of N.Y.	800-221-6664
Cincinnati Milacron, Inc.	513-841-8782	Consolidated Natural Gas Company	412-227-1183
CIPSCO, Inc.	312-427-2953	Consolidated Rail Corporation	215-209-5099
Citicorp	800-342-6690		
Citizens Bancorporation	301-206-6243	Consumers Water Company	800-292-2925
Citizens Banking Corporation	313-257-2593	Cooper Industries	212-791-6422
CLARCOR, Inc.	212-791-6422	CoreStates Financial Corporation	215-973-2836
Cleveland-Cliffs, Inc.	216-694-5459		
Clorox Company	510-271-2927	Coming, Inc.	312-461-4834
CMS Energy Corporation	517-788-1867	CPC International, Inc.	201-894-2460

CPI Corporation	314-231-1575	Dreyfus Corporation	800-524-4458
Crane Company	203-363-7239	Duke Power Company	800-488-3853
Crestar Financial Corporation	804-782-5769	Duriron Company	513-476-6183
Crompton & Knowles Corporation	203-353-5400	E'Town Corporation	908-654-1234
		Eastern Company	203-729-6183
CRSS, Inc.	713-552-2000	Eastern Enterprises	800-524-4458
CSX Corporation	800-521-5571	Eastern Utilities Associates	617-357-9590
Cummins Engine Company, Inc.	800-446-2617	Eastman Kodak Company	800-253-6057
Curtice-Burns Foods, Inc.	716-383-1850	Eaton Corporation	216-737-5745
Cyprus Minerals Company	303-643-5046	Ecolab, Inc.	212-791-6422
		EG&G, Inc.	617-431-4143
		E. I. duPont de Nemours & Company	800-526-0801
Dana Corporation	419-535-4633	Elco Industries, Inc.	815-397-5151
Dauphin Deposit Corporation	717-255-2369	EMC Insurance Group, Inc.	515-280-2836
Dayton Hudson Corporation	800-446-2617	Emerson Electric Company	314-553-2197
Dean Foods Company	708-678-1680	Empire District Electric Company	417-623-4700
Deere & Company	309-765-4539		
Delmarva Power & Light Company	800-365-6495	Energen Corporation	800-654-3206
Delta Air Lines, Inc.	404-715-2391	EnergyNorth, Inc.	603-625-4000
Delta Natural Gas Company	606-744-6171	EngelhardCorporation	908-205-6065
		Engraph, Inc.	404-329-0332
Detroit Edison Company	313-237-8757	Enron Corporation	713-853-5455
		ENSERCH Corporation	214-651-8700
Dexter Corporation	203-627-9051		
Dial Corporation	800-453-2235	Equifax, Inc.	404-888-5003
Dominion Bankshares Corporation	703-563-6226	Equitable Resources, Inc.	412-553-5892
Dominion Resources, Inc.	800-552-4034	Essex County Gas Company	508-388-4000
Donaldson Company, Inc.	800-551-6161	E-Systems, Inc.	214-661-1000
		Ethyl Corporation	312-461-6834
Donnelley (R.R.) & Sons Company	312-326-7189	E'Town Corporation	908-654-1234
		Excel Bancorportion, Inc.	617-575-2900
Dow Chemical Company	517-636-1463		
Dow Jones & Company	212-416-2600	Exxon Corporation	214-444-1157
DPL, Inc.	800-322-9244	F&M National Corporation (Virginia)	703-665-4387
DQE Company	800-247-0400	Fay's, Inc.	315-451-8000
Dresser Industries, Inc.	214-740-6888	Federal National Mortgage Association	800-647-4273

Federal Paper Board Company, Inc.	201-391-1776	First Mississippi Corporation	601-948-7550
Federal Signal Corporation	708-954-2000	First National Bancorporation (GA)	706-503-2114
Federal-Mogul Corporation	800-257-1770	First National Bank Corporation (MI)	313-225-2996
Ferro Corporation	216-575-2658	First Northern Savings Bank (WI)	414-437-7101
Fifth Third Bancorporation	513-762-8613	First of America Bank Corporation	800-782-4040
Figgie International, Inc.	800-345-1505	First Security Corporation (UT)	801-350-5292
Fina, Inc.	212-791-6422	First Tennessee National Corporation	901-523-5630
First Alabama Bancshares, Inc.	205-832-8450	First Union Corporation	704-374-6782
First Bancorporation of Ohio	216-384-7347	First Virginia Banks, Inc.	703-241-3669
First Bank System, Inc.	612-973-0334	First Western Bancorporation, Inc.	412-652-8550
First Central Financial Corporation	718-921-8283	Firstar Corporation	414-765-4985
First Chicago Corporation	312-732-4812	Firstbank of Illinois Company	217-753-7371
First Colonial Bankshares Corporation	312-419-9891	Fleet/Norstar Financial Group, Inc.	401-278-5149
First Colonial Group, Inc.	610-746-7317	Fleming Companies, Inc.	405-841-8127
First Commerce Corporation	504-582-2917	Florida Progress Corporation	800-352-1121
First Commercial Corporation	501-371-6666	Florida Public Utilities	407-838-1729
First Eastern Corporation	717-826-4682	Flowers Industries, Inc.	912-226-9110
First Empire State Corporation	716-842-5445	Food Lion, Inc.	800-633-4236
First Fidelity Bancorp	800-524-4450	Foote, Cone & Belding	800-446-2617
First Financial Holdings, Inc.	803-724-0800	Ford Motor Company	212-613-7147
First Harrisburg Bancorp	717-232-6660	Foster Wheeler Corporation	800-526-0801
First Interstate Bancorp	800-522-6645	Fourth Financial Corporation	316-261-4155
First Michigan Bank Corporation	616-396-9325	FPL Group, Inc.	407-694-4704
First Midwest Bancorp, Inc.	312-427-2953	Franklin Resources	415-312-3033
		Freeport-McMoRan, Inc.	504-582-4490

Fuller (H.B.) Company	612-647-3666	Grumman Corporation	516-575-5287
Fulton Financial Corporation	800-626-0255	GTE Corporation	800-225-5160
		Guardsman Products, Inc.	616-957-2600
Gannett Company, Inc.	703-284-6962	Gulf States Utilities Company	800-231-9266
GATX Corporation	312-621-6200		
GenCorp	216-869-4453		
General Electric Company	203-326-4040	Handleman Company	800-257-1770
		Handy & Harman	212-661-2400
General Mills, Inc.	800-245-5703	Hanna (M.A.) Company	800-688-4259
General Motors Corporation	212-791-3909		
		Hannaford Brothers Company	207-883-2911
General Public Utilities Corporation	201-263-6600	Harcourt General, Inc.	617-232-8200
General Reinsurance Corporation	203-328-5000	Harland (John H.) Company	800-568-3476
General Signal Corporation	203-329-4321	Harleysville Group, Inc.	215-256-5392
Genuine Parts Company	404-953-1700	Harris Corporation	800-542-7792
		Harsco Corporation	717-763-7064
Georgia Pacific Corporation	404-521-5210	Hartford Steam Boiler	617-575-2900
Gerber Products Company	616-928-2000	Hartmarx Corporation	312-372-6300
Giant Food, Inc.	800-934-5449	Haverfield Corporation	216-226-0510
Glaxo Holdings plc ADR	800-524-4458	Hawaiian Electric Industries, Inc.	808-532-5841
Goodrich (B.F.) Company	216-374-2613	Heinz (H.J.) Company	800-253-3399
Goodyear Tire & Rubber Company	216-796-3457	Hercules, Inc.	800-647-4273
		Hershey Foods Corporation	717-534-7527
Gorman-Rupp Company	419-755-1322		
Goulds Pumps, Inc.	800-937-5449	Hexcel Corporation	510-828-4200
Grace (W.R.) & Company	800-647-4273	Hibernia Corporation	504-586-5552
		Home Depot, Inc. (The)	800-633-4236
Graco, Inc.	612-623-6701		
Great Falls Gas Company	406-791-7500	Homestake Mining Company	800-442-2001
Great Western Financial Corporation	818-775-3741	Honeywell, Inc.	612-870-6887
		Hormel (George A.)	800-551-6161
Green Mountain Power Corporation	802-660-5785	Houghton Mifflin Company	617-725-5128
Grenada Sunburst System Corporation	601-960-2602	Household International, Inc.	312-461-5754

Houston Industries, Inc.	800-231-6406	Iowa-Illinois Gas & Electric Company	800-373-4443
Hubbell, Inc.	212-613-7147	IPALCO Enterprises, Inc.	317-261-8394
HUBCO, Inc.	201-348-2326		
Huntington Bancshares, Inc.	614-463-3878	ITT Corporation	201-601-4202
		IWC Resources Corporation	317-263-6358
IBP, Inc.	402-241-2559		
Idaho Power Company	800-635-5406	Jefferson Bankshares, Inc.	804-972-1115
IES Industries	800-247-9785	Jefferson-Pilot Corporation	800-829-8432
Illinois Power Company	800-800-8220	Johnson & Johnson	212-791-6422
IMCERA Group, Inc.	800-446-2617	Johnson Controls, Inc.	414-228-2363
Imperial Bancorporation	800-522-6645	Joslyn Corporation	312-454-2900
Inco, Ltd.	212-612-5846	Jostens, Inc.	800-551-6161
Independence Bancorporation (PA)	215-453-3005	Justin Industries, Inc.	817-336-5125
Independence Bancorporation (NJ)	201-825-2676	Kaman Corporation	800-647-4273
		Kellogg Company	800-323-6138
Independent Bank Corp. (MA)	617-982-6457	Kellwood Company	314-576-3100
		Kemper Corporation	708-540-2000
Independent Bank Corp. (MI)	800-968-8876	Kennametal, Inc.	412-539-5204
Indiana Energy, Inc.	317-321-0440	Kerr-McGee Corporation	800-624-9541
Ingersoll-Rand Company	800-524-4458	Key Centurion Bancshares, Inc.	800-633-4236
Inland Steel Industries, Inc.	312-461-4075	KeyCorp	518-486-8254
Insteel Industries, Inc.	704-383-5183	Keystone Financial, Inc.	718-921-8200
Integra Financial Corporation	412-644-8400	Keystone Heritage Group, Inc.	717-274-6845
Intel Corporation	800-442-2001	Keystone International, Inc.	713-937-5301
Intermark, Inc.	619-459-1000		
International Business Machines	212-791-4208	Kimberly-Clark Corporation	800-442-2001
International Multifoods Corporation	800-468-9716	K-Mart Corporation	313-643-1040
		KN Energy, Inc.	303-989-1740
International Paper Company	914-397-1500	Knight-Ridder, Inc.	305-376-3938
		Kollmorgen Corporation	617-575-2404
Interpublic Group of Companies, Inc.	212-791-6422	Kuhlman Corporation	606-224-4300
		KU Energy	606-288-1188
Interstate Power Company	319-582-5421	Kysor Industrial Corporation	616-779-2200

La-Z-Boy Chair Company	313-241-4414	May Department Stores Company	800-524-4458
Laclede Gas Company	800-456-9852	Maytag Company	515-791-8344
Lafarge Corporation	800-633-4236	McCormick & Company, Inc.	800-424-5855
Lakeland First Financial Group	201-584-6666	McDermott International, Inc.	800-446-2617
Lance, Inc.	704-554-1421	McDonald's	800-621-7825
LG&E Energy Corporation	502-627-2000	Corporation	
Liberty National Bancorporation (KY)	502-566-1771	McGraw-Hill, Inc.	212-512-4150
		McKesson Corporation	415-983-9470
Lilly (Eli) & Company	800-833-8699	MCN Corporation	800-257-1770
Limited (The), Inc.	800-446-2617	MDU Resources Group, Inc.	701-222-7621
Lincoln National Corporation	219-455-2056	Mead Corporation	513-495-3710
Lincoln Telecommunications Company	402-476-5277	Media General, Inc.	804-649-6619
		Medusa Corporation	216-371-4000
Liz Claiborne, Inc.	212-791-6422	Mellon Bank Corporation	412-236-8000
Loctite Corporation	617-575-2900		
Louisiana-Pacific Corporation	503-221-0800	Mercantile Bancorp, Inc.	314-241-4002
Lowe's Companies, Inc.	919-651-4631	Mercantile Bankshares Corporation	401-237-5211
Luby's Cafeterias, Inc.	512-654-9000	Merck & Company, Inc.	908-594-6627
Lukens, Inc.	215-383-2601	Mercury Finance Company	708-564-3720
Lyondell Petrochemical Company	800-524-4458	Meridian Bancorporation, Inc.	215-655-2438
MacDermid, Inc.	203-575-5813	Merrill Lynch & Company, Inc.	800-637-3766
Madison Gas & Electric Company	800-356-6423	Merry Land & Investment Company	706-722-6756
Magna Group, Inc.	618-233-2120	Metropolitan Financial Corporation	612-928-5000
MAPCO, Inc.	212-701-7607		
Marion Merrell Dow, Inc.	212-791-6422	Michigan National Corporation	800-426-5754
Mark Twain Bancshares, Inc.	314-889-0708	Middlesex Water Company	908-634-1500
Marsh & McLennan Companies, Inc.	800-457-8968	Midwest Resources, Inc.	800-247-5211
Marsh Supermarkets, Inc.	317-594-2647	Millipore Corporation	617-275-9200
Martin Marietta Corporation	212-791-6422	Minnesota Mining & Manufacturing	800-468-9716
MASSBANK Corporation	617-942-8120		

Minnesota Power & Light Company	800-535-3056	New Jersey Resources Corporation	800-438-1230
Mobil Corporation	703-846-3901	New York State Electric & Gas Corporation	800-225-5643
Mobile Gas Service Corporation	205-476-2720	New York Times Company	212-791-6422
Modine Manufacturing Company	414-636-1361	Newell	800-446-2617
Monsanto Company	314-694-5353	Niagara Mohawk Power Corporation	315-428-6750
Montana Power Company	800-245-6767	NICOR, Inc.	708-305-9500
Morgan (J.P.) & Company	212-791-6422	NIPSCO Industries, Inc.	800-348-6466
Morrison Knudsen Corporation	208-386-5000	Nordson Corporation	216-892-1580
Motorola, Inc.	312-461-2339	Norfolk Southern Corporation	804-629-2600
		North Carolina Natural Gas Corporation	919-483-0315
Nalco Chemical Company	708-305-1000	North Fork Bancorporation, Inc.	212-791-6422
Nash Finch Company	612-832-0534	Northeast Utilities	800-999-7269
Nashua Corporation	603-880-2323	Northern States Power Company	612-330-5560
National City Corporation	216-575-2532	Northrop Corporation	212-613-7147
National Commerce Bancorp (TN)	404-588-7822	Northwest Illinois Bancorporation	800-288-9541
National Community Banks (NJ)	201-357-7164	Northwest Natural Gas Company	503-220-2591
National Data Corporation	800-633-4236	Northwestern Public Service Company	800-245-6977
National Fuel Gas Company	212-541-7533	Norwest Corporation	612-667-9799
National Medical Enterprises, Inc.	310-998-8434	Nucor Corporation	704-374-2697
National Service Industries, Inc.	919-770-6000	NUI Corporation	908-781-0500
National-Standard Company	616-683-8100	NYNEX Corporation	212-370-7500
NationsBank Corporation	704-386-7804	Occidental Petroleum Corporation	800-622-9231
NBD Bancorporation, Inc.	313-225-3578	Ohio Casualty Corporation	513-867-3904
NBSC Corporation	803-778-8213	Ohio Edison Company	800-736-3403
Neiman-Marcus Group	617-575-2900	Oklahoma Gas & Electric Company	800-395-2662
Nevada Power Company	800-344-9239	Old Kent Financial Corporation	616-771-5482
New England Electric System	508-366-9011	Old National Bancorp (IN)	812-464-1434

Old Republic International Corporation	212-791-6422	PepsiCo, Inc.	212-613-7147
		Perkin-Elmer Corporation	203-762-1485
Olin Corporation	212-613-7147	Pfizer, Inc.	212-573-3087
Omnicare, Inc.	513-762-6967	Phelps Dodge Corporation	602-234-8100
One Valley Bancorp of West Virgina	304-348-7023	Philadelphia Electric Company	800-626-8729
Oneida, Ltd.	312-461-7763		
ONEOK, Inc.	918-588-7159	Philadelphia Suburban Corporation	215-527-8000
Orange and Rockland Utilities, Inc.	212-613-7147	Philip Morris Companies, Inc.	800-442-0077
Otter Tail Power Company	218-739-8481	Phillips Petroleum Company	800-356-0066
Outboard Marine Corporation	617-575-2900	Piccadilly Cafeterias, Inc.	504-293-9440
Pacific Enterprises	800-722-5483	Piedmont Natural Gas	704-364-3120
Pacific Gas & Electric Company	800-367-7731	Pinnacle West Capital Corporation	800-457-2983
Pacific Telesis Group	415-394-3074	Pioneer Hi-Bred International, Inc.	617-575-2900
Pacific Western Bancshares, Inc.	800-522-6645	Pitney Bowes, Inc.	203-356-5000
Pacificorp	800-233-5453	PNC Financial Corporation	800-982-7652
Paine Webber Group, Inc.	212-713-2722	Polaroid Corporation	617-577-3963
		Portland General Corporation	503-464-8599
Pall Corporation	516-484-5400		
Panhandle Eastern Corporation	800-225-5838	Portsmouth Bank Shares, Inc.	603-436-6630
Paramount Communications, Inc.	212-373-8100	Potlatch Corporation	415-576-8806
		Potomac Electric Power Company	800-527-3726
Parker-Hannifin Corporation	216-531-3000		
		PPG Industries, Inc.	412-434-3312
Penney (J.C.) Company, Inc.	800-842-9470	Premier Industrial Corporation	216-391-8300
Pennsylvania Enterprises, Inc.	717-829-8843	Preston Corporation	212-613-7147
		Procter & Gamble Company	800-742-6253
Pennsylvania Power & Light Company	800-345-3085		
		PSI Resources, Inc.	800-446-2617
Pennzoil Company	713-546-4000	Public Service Company of Colorado	303-294-2617
Pentair, Inc.	800-551-6161		
Peoples Bancorporation of Worcester	800-937-5449	Public Service Company of North Carolina	704-864-6731
Peoples Energy Corporation	800-228-6888	Public Service Enterprise Group	800-242-0813
Pep Boys-Manny, Moe & Jack	215-227-9208	Puget Sound Power & Light Company	206-462-3719

Quaker Oats Company	800-344-1198
Quaker State Corporation	814-676-7806
Quanex Corporation	800-231-8176
Quantum Chemical Corporation	212-949-5000
Questar Corporation	801-534-5885
Ralston Purina Company	314-982-3000
Raymond Corporation	607-656-2466
Raytheon Company	617-575-2900
Regional Bancorporation, Inc.	617-395-7700
Reynolds & Reynolds Company	513-443-2000
Reynolds Metals Company	800-526-0801
Rhone-Poulenc Rorer, Inc.	215-454-3850
Rite Aid Corporation	212-701-7608
Roadway Services, Inc.	216-258-2467
Roanoke Electric Steel	919-770-6000
Rochester Gas & Electric Corporation	716-546-2700
Rochester Telephone Corporation	800-836-0342
Rockwell International Corporation	412-565-7120
Rollins Environmental Services, Inc.	800-525-7686
Rollins, Inc.	800-568-3476
Rollins Truck Leasing Corporation	800-525-7686
Roosevelt Financial Group, Inc.	314-532-6200
Rose's Stores, Inc.	919-770-6000
Rouse Company	410-992-6546
RPM, Inc.	216-273-5090
Rubbermaid, Inc.	216-264-6464

Russell Corporation	205-329-4832
Ryder System, Inc.	305-593-4053
Rykoff-Sexton, Inc.	213-622-4131
Safety-Kleen Corporation	708-697-8460
Salomon, Inc.	212-791-6422
San Diego Gas & Electric Company	800-522-6645
Santa Fe Pacific Corporation	212-791-6422
Sara Lee Corporation	312-558-8450
Savannah Foods & Industries, Inc.	912-651-4901
SCANA Corporation	800-763-5891
SCE Corporation	800-347-8625
Schering-Plough Corporation	201-822-7477
Schwab (Charles) & Company, Inc.	312-461-2288
Scott Paper Company	800-752-0771
Seafield Capital Corporation	816-842-7000
Sears, Roebuck & Company	212-791-3357
Selective Insurance Group	201-948-1762
Shawmut National Corp	203-728-2028
Sherwin Williams Company	216-737-2736
Sierra Pacific Resources	800-662-7575
SIFCO Industries, Inc.	216-575-2532
Signet Banking Corporation	800-451-7392
Simpson Industries, Inc.	313-540-6200
Smith (A.O.) Corporation	414-359-4150
SmithKline Beecham plc	800-428-4237
Smucker (J.M.) Company	216-682-3000
Snap-on-Tools	800-524-0687
Society Corporation	800-542-7792

Society for Savings Bancorporation	617-575-2900	Star Banc Corporation	513-632-4610
Sonat, Inc.	212-613-7147	State Street Boston	617-575-2900
Sonoco Products Company	803-383-7740	Corporation	
		Stone & Webster, Inc.	800-647-4273
South Jersey Industries, Inc.	609-561-9000	Stride Rite Corporation	617-575-2900
Southeastern Michigan Gas	800-255-7647	Suffolk Bancorp	516-727-5667
Southern California Water Company	714-394-3710	Summit Bancorp (NJ)	201-701-2512
Southern Company	404-668-3168	Sun Company, Inc.	800-888-8494
Southern Indiana Gas & Electric	800-227-8625	Sundstrand Corporation	815-226-2136
Southern National Corporation	919-671-2273	SunTrust Banks, Inc.	800-568-3476
		Super Valu Stores, Inc.	612-450-4075
Southern New England Telecom	203-771-2058	Susquehanna Bancshares, Inc.	717-626-4721
SouthTrust Corporation	205-254-6764	Synovus Financial Corporation	404-649-2387
Southwest Gas Corporation	800-331-1119	Sysco Corporation	713-584-1390
Southwest Water Company	818-918-1231		
		Tambrands, Inc.	914-696-6060
Southwestern Bell Corporation	314-235-6380	TCF Financial Corporation	612-370-1789
Southwestern Electric Service Co.	214-741-3125	TECO Energy, Inc.	813-228-1326
		Telephone and Data Systems, Inc.	312-630-1900
Southwestern Energy Company	312-407-4880	Temple-Inland, Inc.	800-446-2617
Southwestern Public Service Company	806-378-2841	Tenneco, Inc.	800-446-2617
		Texaco, Inc.	800-283-9785
Sprint Corporation	913-624-2541	Texas Utilities Company	800-828-0812
SPX Corporation	616-724-5572		
St. Joseph Light & Power Company	816-233-8888	Textron, Inc.	212-791-6422
		Thomas & Betts Corporation	908-707-2363
St. Paul Bancorporation	312-804-2283	Thomas Industries, Inc.	502-893-4600
St. Paul Companies, Inc.	612-221-7788		
		Tidewater, Inc.	800-647-4273
Standard Commercial Corporation	919-291-5507	Time Warner, Inc.	212-484-6971
		Times Mirror Company	213-237-3955
Standard Products Company	216-281-8300		
		Timken Company	216-471-3376
Stanhome, Inc.	413-562-3631	TNP Enterprises Company	817-731-0099
Stanley Works (The)	800-288-9541		

Torchmark Corporation	312-407-2258	UNITIL Corporation	603-772-0775
Toro Company	612-450-4004	Universal	804-254-1303
Total Petroleum (North America)	303-291-2003	Corporation	
		Universal Foods	414-347-3827
Transamerica Corporation	800-446-2617	Corporation	
		Unocal Corporation	800-647-4273
Travelers Corporation	203-277-2819	Upjohn Company	800-323-1849
		Upper Peninsula Energy Corporation	906-487-5020
Tribune Company	312-222-4144		
TRINOVA	800-446-2617	USF&G Corporation	301-547-3000
TRW, Inc.	216-291-7654	USLICO Corporation	703-875-3600
Twin Disc, Inc.	414-634-1981	USLIFE Corporation	212-709-6230
Tyco Laboratories, Inc.	412-236-8143	UST Corporation	617-726-7262
		UST, Inc.	203-622-3656
		USX-Marathon Group	412-433-4815
U.S. Bancorporation (Oregon)	503-275-6472		
		USX-U.S. Steel	412-433-4815
U.S. Trust Corporation	212-425-4500	UtiliCorp United, Inc.	800-487-6661
U.S. West, Inc.	800-537-0222		
UGI Corporation	215-337-1000	Valley Bancorporation (Wisconsin)	414-738-3829
UJB Financial Corporation	609-987-3442		
Union Bank	213-239-0672	Valley National Bancorporation (NJ)	201-777-1800
Union Camp Corporation	201-628-2000		
Union Carbide Corporation	203-794-2212	Valley Resources	617-774-3119
		Varian Associates, Inc.	617-575-2900
Union Electric Company	314-554-3502	Vermont Financial Services Corp.	802-257-7151
Union Pacific Corporation	212-791-6422		
		VF Corporation	215-378-1151
Union Planters Corporation	901-523-6980	Vulcan Materials Company	212-791-6422
United Carolina Bancshares Corp.	919-642-1140		
		Wachovia Corporation	919-770-5787
United Cities Gas Company	615-373-0104		
		Walgreen Company	·312-461-5535
United Illuminating Company	203-777-7050	Warner-Lambert Company	201-540-3498
United Mobile Homes, Inc.	908-542-4927	Washington Energy Company	206-622-6767
United States Shoe Corporation	513-527-7480	Washington Gas Light Company	202-624-6688
United Water Resources, Inc.	201-767-2811	Washington Mutual Savings Bank	206-461-3184

Washington National Corporation	708-570-3208	Winn-Dixie Stores, Inc.	904-783-5433
Washington Water Power Company	800-727-9170	Wisconsin Energy Corporation	800-558-9663
Waste Management, Inc.	708-572-8826	Wisconsin Public Service Corporation	800-236-1551
Weis Markets, Inc.	717-286-4571	Wisconsin Southern Gas Company, Inc.	414-248-8861
Wells Fargo & Company	800-446-2617	Witco Corporation	212-791-6422
Wendy's International, Inc.	614-764-3251	Woolworth Corporation	212-791-6422
West One Bancorporation	208-383-7245	Worthington Industries, Inc.	800-441-2001
WestAmerica Bancorporation	415-257-8011	WPL Holdings, Inc.	800-356-5343
Westinghouse Electric Corporation	412-244-3654	Wrigley (Wm.) Jr. Company	312-644-2121
Westvaco Corporation	212-318-5288	Xerox Corporation	800-828-6396
Weyerhaeuser Company	800-647-4273	York Financial Corporation	717-846-8777
Whirlpool Corporation	312-461-2543	Zero Corporation	213-629-7000
Whitman Corporation	708-818-5015	Zions Bancorporation	801-524-4849
WICOR, Inc.	800-236-3453	Zurn Industries, Inc.	814-452-2111
Wilmington Trust Company	302-651-1448		

Glossary

$ $

Account executive: a brokerage firm employee, also called registered representative, who advises and handles orders for clients and has the legal powers of an agent.

Accumulated dividend: the dividend due, but not paid, usually to holders of cumulative preferred stock. It is carried on the books of the corporation as a liability until paid.

Adjusted basis: the base price from which to calculate capital gains or losses upon sale of a security. The cost of commissions is deducted when net proceeds are used for tax purposes. To arrive at the adjusted basis, the price must be adjusted to account for any stock splits that have occurred since the initial purchase.

American Depositary Receipts (ADRs): receipts for the shares of a foreign-based corporation held in the vault of a U.S. bank that entitling the shareholder to all dividends and capital gains, thereby eliminating the need to buy shares of those foreign-based companies in overseas markets.

American Stock Exchange (AMEX): the stock exchange located at 86 Trinity Place in New York City. Stocks and bonds traded on the AMEX are generally those of small to medium-size companies.

American Stock Exchange Composite Index: a market-capitalization weighted index of the prices of the stocks traded on the American Stock Exchange.

Appreciation: the increase in the value of an asset such as a stock, bond or option.

Asked price: the price at which a security or commodity is offered for sale on an exchange or in the over-the-counter market. It is usually the lowest round lot price at which a dealer will sell. Also, the price at which a buyer may purchase shares of a mutual fund (the net asset value per share plus the sales charge, if any).

At the market: an order to buy or sell a security at the best available price.

Average: an appropriately weighted and adjusted mean of selected securities designed to represent market behavior in general or for important segments of the market. Among the most familiar averages are the Dow Jones Industrials and the Standard & Poor's 500.

Back-end load: a redemption fee charged to an investor in certain mutual funds when shares are redeemed within a specified number of years after purchase.

Balanced fund: a mutual fund that at all times holds bonds or preferred stocks in varying ratios to common stocks to maintain relatively greater stability of both capital and income.

Basis point: the smallest measure used in quoting yields on bonds and notes. One basis point is 0.01 percent of yield. Thus, a bond's yield that changes from 7.54 percent to 8.44 percent is said to have gone up 90 basis points.

Basis price: the price an investor uses to calculate capital gains when selling a stock or bond.

Bear: a person who thinks the market will fall.

Bear market: a prolonged period of falling prices.

Bid and asked: a bid is the highest price a prospective buyer is prepared to pay for a security at a particular time, and asked is the lowest price a seller is willing to take for the same security.

Bid price: the price at which the holders of open-end mutual fund shares may redeem their shares. In most cases it is the net asset value (NAV) per share. For closed-end fund shares, it is the highest price then offered for stock in the public market. It may be more or less than the NAV per share.

Blue chip: common stock of a well-known established company that has a long record of profit growth and dividend payment and a reputation for high quality management, products and services.

Bond: an interest-bearing or discounted government or corporate security that obligates the issuer to pay the bondholder a specified sum of money, usually at specific intervals and to repay the principal amount of the loan at maturity.

Bond rating: a method of evaluating the possibility of default by a bond issuer.

Break-point: in the purchase of mutual fund shares, the dollar value level at which the percentage of the sales charge becomes lower. A sales charge schedule typically contains five or six break-points.

Broker: a person who acts as an agent for a buyer or seller of securities, usually charging a commission, and who must be registered with the exchange where the securities are traded.

Bull: a person who thinks prices will rise.

Bull market: a prolonged rise in the prices of stocks, bonds or commodities. A bull market is characterized by high trading volume and usually lasts at least a few months.

Buy and hold strategy: a strategy that calls for accumulating shares in a company over years, allowing an investor to pay favorable long-term capital gains tax on profits and needs much less attention than a move active trading strategy.

Buying on margin: buying securities with credit through a margin account held with a broker.

Capital gain: the difference between an asset's purchase price and selling price, when the difference is positive.

Capital stock: common and preferred stock authorized by a company's charter and having par value, stated value, or no par value.

Cash equivalents: instruments or investments of such high liquidity and safety that they are virtually as good as cash. Examples would include money market funds and Treasury bills.

Cash reserve securities: see Cash equivalents.

Churning: excessive trading of a customer's account. Churning is illegal under SEC and exchange rules, but is difficult to prove.

Closed-end fund: a type of fund that has a fixed number of shares. Unlike open-end mutual funds, it does not stand ready to issue and redeem shares on a continuous basis. Closed-end funds are generally listed on major stock exchanges.

Closing price: the price of the last transaction completed during a day of trading on a stock exchange.

Commercial paper: short-term obligations with maturities ranging from 2 to 270 days issued by banks, corporations and other borrowers.

Commission: the fee paid to a broker for executing a trade based on the number of shares traded or the dollar amount of the trade.

Common stock: units of ownership of a public corporation, usually with the right to vote and to receive dividends.

Common stock fund: a mutual fund whose portfolio consists primarily of common stocks. Such a fund may at times take defensive positions in cash, bonds and other senior securities.

Company risk: the risk that has to do with the unique characteristics of any one stock and the industry in which it operates. It represents about 70 percent of the total risk faced by securities investors.

Compound return: the return that is earned on principal plus the return that was earned earlier. If $100 is deposited in an interest-bearing account at 10 percent, the investor will be credited with $110 at the end of the first year and $121 at the end of the second year. The extra $1, earned on the $10 interest from the first year, is the annual compound return. Returns can also be compounded on a daily, quarterly, half-yearly or other basis.

Constant dollar investing: a system of accumulating assets by investing a fixed amount of dollars in securities at set intervals. Also called dollar cost averaging.

Consumer price index: a measure of change in consumer prices, as determined by a monthly survey of the U.S. Bureau of Labor Statistics.

Conversion price: the dollar value at which convertible bonds, debentures or preferred stock can be converted into common stock.

Conversion ratio: the relationship that determines how many shares of common stock will be received in exchange for each convertible bond or preferred share when the conversion takes place.

Convertibles: preferred stock or bonds that are exchangeable for a set number of another form of securities (usually common stock) at a prestated price.

Corporate bond: a debt instrument issued by a private corporation, as distinct from a governmental agency or municipality.

Corporate (master or prototype) retirement plan: a plan and trust agreement that qualifies for special tax treatment available to a corporation or other organization whereby it can purchase securities for the benefit of plan participants.

Cost basis: the original price of an asset, used in determining capital gains.

Coupon: the interest rate on a debt security the issuer promises to pay to the holder until maturity, expressed as an annual percentage of face value.

Crash: a precipitate drop in stock prices and economic activity, usually brought on by a loss in investor confidence following periods of high inflation.

Credit rating: a formal evaluation of a company's credit history and capability of repaying obligations.

Cumulative preferred: preferred stock whose dividends accumulate until paid out, if they have been omitted for any reason.

Current market value: present worth of a customer's portfolio at today's market price, as listed in a brokerage statement.

Current yield: the annual interest on a bond divided by the market price.

Custodian: the bank or trust company that holds all cash and securities owned by a mutual fund.

Cyclical stock: a stock that tends to rise when the economy turns up and to fall when the economy turns down, such as those of the housing, automobile and paper industries.

Date of record: the date on which a shareholder must own shares to be entiteld to a dividend. Also called the record date.

Debenture: a general debt obligation backed only by the integrity of the borrower and documented by an agreement called an indenture.

Debt instrument: a written promise to repay a debt such as a bill, note, bond, banker's acceptance, certificate of deposit or commercial paper.

Deep discount bond: a bond selling for a discount of more than about 20 percent from its face value.

Default: the failure of a debtor to make timely payments of interest and principal as they come due or to meet some other provision of a bond indenture.

Depression: an economic condition characterized by falling prices, reduced purchasing power, an excess of supply over demand, rising unemployment, deflation, public fear and caution and a general decrease in business activity.

Derivative: a financial instrument that derives its market value from some specified benchmark such as a currency, commodity, interest rate or any number of combined benchmarks.

Direct purchase fund: a mutual fund whose shares are purchased directly from the fund at a low charge or no charge at all. The investor deals directly with the fund rather than through a broker or dealer.

Discount: the percentage below net asset value at which the shares of a closed-end mutual fund sell.

Discount bond: a bond selling below its redemption value.

Discount broker: a brokerage firm that executes orders to buy and sell securities at commission rates lower than those charged by full service brokers.

Distributions: dividends paid from net investment income, and payments made from realized capital gains, by mutual funds.

Diversification: spreading risk by placing assets in several categories of investments, such as stocks, bonds, mutual funds, and so on.

Dividend: a distribution of earnings to shareholders, paid in the form of cash, stock, scrip, or even company products or property.

Dividend payout ratio: the percentage of earnings paid to shareholders in cash.

Dividend reinvestment plan: automatic reinvestment of shareholder dividends in more shares of the company's stock.

Dollar cost averaging: a method of accumulating assets by investing a fixed amount of dollars in securities at set intervals. Also known as constant dollar investing.

Dow Jones Industrial Average: a price-weighted index of 30 actively traded blue chip stocks.

Dow Theory: a theory that a major trend in the stock market must be confirmed by a similar movement in the Dow Jones Industrial Average and the Dow Jones Transportation Average.

Earnings per share: the portion of a company's profit allocated to each outstanding share of common stock.

Equivalent taxable yield: comparison of the taxable yield on a corporate bond and the tax-free yield on a municipal bond.

Exchange privilege: the right to exchange the shares of one open-end mutual fund for those of another under the same fund group at a nominal charge (or no charge) or at a reduced sales charge. For tax purposes, such an exchange is considered a taxable event.

Ex-dividend: interval between the announcement and the payment of the next dividend. An investor who buys shares during that interval is not entitled to the dividend.

Ex-dividend date: the date on which a stock goes ex-dividend, usually about three weeks before the dividend is paid to stockholders of record.

Execution: transacting a trade. A broker who buys or sell shares has executed an order.

Expense ratio: the proportion that annual expenses, including all costs of operation, bear to average net assets for the year.

Face value: the value of a bond, note, mortgage or other security as given on the certificate or instrument.

Fannie Mae: nickname for the Federal National Mortgage Association.

Federal National Mortgage Association (FNMA):   a publicly owned, government-sponsored corporation chartered in 1938 to purchase mortgages from lenders and resell them to investors.

Fiscal year: an accounting period covering 12 consecutive months, 52 consecutive weeks, 13 four-week periods, or 365 consecutive days, after which the books are closed and profit or loss is determined.

Fixed income investment: a security that pays a fixed rate of return.

401(k) plan: a plan whereby an employee may elect to contribute pre-tax dollars to a qualified tax-deferred retirement plan, as an alternative to receiving taxable cash in the form of compensation or a bonus.

Front-end load: a sales fee charged investors in certain mutual funds at the time shares are purchased.

Full coupon bond: a bond with a coupon rate that is near or above current market interest rates.

Full-service broker: a broker who provides a wide range of services to customers, including advice on which securities to buy and sell.

Fully valued: said of a stock that has reached a price at which analysts think the underlying company's earning power has been recognized by the market.

General obligation bond (GO):   a municipal bond backed by the full faith and credit of a municipality.

Ginnie Mae: nickname for the Government National Mortgage Association and the certificate issued by that agency.

Government National Mortgage Association (GNMA):   a goverment-owned corporation, which is an agency of the U.S. Department of Housing and Urban Development, GNMA guarenttees monthly principal and interest payments on mortgage-backed securities of registered holders.

Growth stock: a stock that has shown better than average growth in earnings and is expected to continue to do so as a result of additional resources, new products or expanded markets.

High-grade bond: a bond rated triple-A or double-A by Standard & Poor's or Moody's rating services.

Holder of record: owner of a company's securities as recorded on the books of the issuing company or its transfer agent as of a particular date.

Income fund: a mutual fund whose primary objective is current income.

Income shares: one of two kinds or classes of stock issued by a dual-purpose fund, holders of which receive all the interest and dividends produced by the portfolio.

Index: a statistical composite that measures changes in the economy or in financial markets, often expressed in percentage changes from one period to another.

Index fund: a mutual fund whose portfolio matches that of a broad-based index and whose performance mirrors the market as a whole.

Indexing: weighting one's portfolio to match a broad-based index such as Standard & Poor's 500 and match its performance.

Indicated yield: the coupon or dividend rate as a percentage of the current market price.

Individual retirement account (IRA):   a personal, tax-deferred retirement account that an employed person can set up.

Initial public offering: a corporation's first offering of stock to the public.

Investment company: a firm that invests the pooled funds of small investors in securities appropriate for its stated investment objectives.

Investment grade: a term used to describe bonds suitable for purchase by prudent investors.

Investment objective: the goal of an investor or investment company. It may be growth of capital, current income, relative stability of capital, or some combination of these aims.

Junk bond: a bond with a credit rating of BB or lower by rating agencies.

Keogh plan: a tax-deferred pension account for employees of unincorporated businesses or for persons who are self-employed.

Listed security: a stock or bond that has been accepted for trading by one of the organized and registered securities exchanges in the United States.

Load: an amount that, when added to the net asset value of mutual fund shares, determines the offering price. It covers commissions and other costs and is generally stated as a percentage of the offering price.

Long bond: 30-year U.S. Treasury bonds or any bond that matures in more than ten years.

Margin: the amount a customer deposits with a broker when borrowing from the broker to buy securities.

Margin account: a brokerage account allowing a customer to buy securities with money borrowed from the broker.

Margin requirement: the minimum amount that a customer must deposit in the form of cash or eligible securities in a margin account as spelled out in Regulation T of the Federal Reserve Board.

Marketable securities: securities that may be easily sold.

Market capitalization: the value of a corporation as determined by the market price of its issued and outstanding common stock, calculated by multiplying the number of outstanding shares by the current market price per share.

Market price: the last reported price at which a security was sold on an exchange or the combined bid and asked prices for securities traded over the counter.

Market timing: decisions on when to buy or sell securities considering economic factors or technical indications such as the direction of stock prices and the volume of trading.

Maturity date: the date on which the principal amount of a debt instrument becomes due and payable.

Medium-term bond: a bond with a maturity of two to ten years.

Money market: the market for short-term debt instruments such as commercial paper, negotiable certificates of deposits, banker's acceptances, Treasury bills and discount notes of federal agencies.

Money market fund: an open-ended mutual fund that invests in short-term debt instruments and pays money market rates of interest.

Municipal bond: a debt obligation of a state or local government entity.

Mutual fund: a fund operated by an investment company that raises money from shareholders and invests it in stocks, bonds, options, commodities or money market securities.

Nasdaq: The National Association of Securities Dealers Automated Quotation system, owned and operated by the National Association of Securities Dealers.

New issue: a stock or bond being offered to the public for the first time, the distribution of which is covered by Securities and Exchange Commission rules.

New York Stock Exchange: the oldest (1792) and largest stock exchange in the United States, located at 11 Wall Street in New York City.

Nikkei Index: an index of 225 leading stocks traded on the Tokyo Stock Exchange.

No-load fund: a mutual fund offered by an open-end investment company that imposes no sales charge (load) on its shareholders.

Noncallable: preferred stock or a bond that cannot be redeemed at the option of the issuer.

Odd lot: a securities trade made for less than the normal trading unit, or round lot. For stocks, any purchase or sale of less than 100 shares.

Option: a transaction agreement tied to stocks, commodities, or stock indexes. A call option gives its buyer the right to buy 100 shares of the underlying security at a fixed price before a specified date in the future. A put option gives its buyer the right to sell.

Outstanding stock: stock held by shareholders and shown on corporate balance sheets under the heading of capital stock issued and outstanding.

Over the counter (OTC):   a market in which securities transactions are conducted through a telephone and computer network connecting dealers in stocks and bonds, rather than on the floor of an exchange.

Overvalued: description of a stock whose current price is not justified by its price/earnings ratio or the earnings outlook for the company.

Paper profit or loss: unrealized capital gain or loss in an investment or portfolio. Such a gain or loss becomes realized only when the security is sold.

Par: the nominal or face value of a security.

Passive investing: investing in a mutual fund that replicates a market index, such as the S&P 500 Index, thus assuring investment performance equivalent to the market as a whole.

Payment date: the date on which a declared stock dividend or a bond interest payment is scheduled to be paid.

Payout ratio: the percentage of a firm's profits that is paid out to shareholders in the form of dividends.

Penny stock: a stock that typically sells for less than $1 per share, although it may rise to as much as $10 per share after the initial public offering due to heavy promotion.

Portfolio: a combined holding of more than one stock, bond, commodity, cash equivalent or other asset by an individual or institutional investor.

Preferred stock: a normally nonvoting class of capital stock that pays dividends at a specified rate and that has preference over common stock in the payment of dividends and the liquidation of assets.

Preliminary prospectus: the first document released by an underwriter of a new issue to prospective investors, often called a red herring.

Premium bond: a bond selling at a price above its face or redemption value.

Price-earnings ratio: the price of a stock divided by its earnings per share over a 12-month period. As used in this book, earnings are usually based on reported company earnings for the past 6 months and estimated earnings for the next 6 months.

Principal amount: the face value of a bond that must be repaid at maturity, as distinguished from the interest.

Program trading: computer-driven buying or selling of baskets of 15 or more stocks by index arbitrage specialists or institutional traders.

Prospectus: a formal written offer to sell securities that sets forth the plan for a proposed business enterprise or mutual fund, or the facts about an existing one that an investor needs to make an informed decision.

Public offering price: the price at which a new issue of securities is offered to the public by underwriters.

Realized profit (or loss):   the profit or loss resulting from the sale or other disposal of a security.

Record date: the date on which a shareholder must officially own shares to be entitled to the dividend.

Registered representative: an employee of a stock exchange member broker/dealer who acts as an account executive for customers.

Retained earnings: net profits kept to accumulate in a business after dividends are paid.

Return: profit on a securities investment, usually expressed as an annual percentage rate.

Round lot: the generally accepted unit of trading on a securities exchange, usually 100 shares for stock.

SEC: the Securities and Exchange Commission.

Settlement date: the date by which an executed order must be settled, either by a buyer paying for the securities with cash or by a seller delivering the securities and receiving the proceeds from them.

Share: unit of equity ownership in a corporation.

Short sale: the sale of a security that is not owned (but is borrowed) in the hope that the price will go down so that it can be repurchased at a profit.

Specialist: a member of a stock exchange who maintains a fair and orderly market in one or more securities.

Special situation: an undervalued stock that should soon rise in value because of an imminent favorable turn of events.

Speculation: the assumption of risk in anticipation of gain but recognizing a higher than average possibility of loss.

Split: an increase in a corporation's number of shares of stock outstanding without any change in the shareholders' equity or the aggregate market value at the time of the split.

Stock: the ownership of a corporation represented by shares that are a claim on the corporation's earnings and assets.

Stock dividend: the payment of a corporate dividend in the form of stock rather than cash.

Stockholder of record: a common or preferred stockholder whose name is registered on the books of a corporation as owning shares as of a particular date.

Stock indexes and averages: indicators used to measure and report value changes in representative stock groupings.

Stock symbol: letters used to identify listed companies on the securities exchanges on which they trade.

Tax basis: the price at which a security was purchased plus brokerage commissions.

Tax-exempt money market fund: a money market fund invested in short-term municipal securities and distributes tax-free income to shareholders.

Tax-exempt security: an obligation, often called a municipal bond, whose interest is exempt from federal, state and/or local taxation.

Technical analysis: research into the demand and supply for securities and commodities based on trading volume and price studies.

Technical rally: a short rise in securities prices within a general declining trend.

Tick: upward or downward price movement in a security's trades.

Ticker tape: a device that relays the stock symbol and the latest price and volume on securities as they are traded to investors around the world.

Total return: the annual return on an investment including price change and income from dividends or interest.

Trade date: the day on which a security trade actually takes place.

Undervalued: a security selling below its liquidation value or the market value analysts believe it deserves.

Unrealized profit (or loss): a profit or loss that has not become actual because the security has not been sold.

Unsecured debt: an obligation not backed by the pledge of specific collateral.

Volatile: used to describe a security characterized by rapid and extreme fluctuations in price.

Volume: the total number of bonds or stock shares traded in a particular period.

Warrant: a type of security that entitles the holder to buy a proportionate amount of common stock at a specified price for a period of years or in perpetuity.

Withdrawal plan: an arrangement provided by many mutual funds by which an investor can receive periodic payments in a designated amount that may be more or less than the actual investment income.

Yield: the percentage rate of return paid on a security, calculated by dividing its annual dividend or interest income by its cost to the investor.

Yield to maturity: the rate of return on a debt security held to maturity. Both interest payments and capital gain or loss are taken into account.

Index

$ $